Behind the Lines

Of the Enemy

The Dream

Elma Garlock

Behind the Lines of the Enemy: The Dream- A Prophetic Glimpse into the Spiritual Realms Activities, Demonic Forces, Forbidden Realms, The Three Heavens – Portals - Gates.

Includes references and appendix
Copyright © 2018 by Elma Garlock. All rights reserved.
Headshot by Picture People
Cover design by Dylan Designs

Library of Congress Cataloging-in-Publication Data:
An application to register this book for cataloging has been submitted to
the Library of Congress.
International Standard Book Number:
ISBN-10-1947778870
ISBN-13-9781947778870

While the author has made every effort to provide accurate Internet
addresses, information, quotations and testimonies at the time of
publication, neither the publisher nor the author assumes any
responsibility for errors, omissions and or changes that occur after
publication. No liability is assumed for damages that may result from the
use of information contained within.

First edition
Printed in the United States of America

www.ElmaGarlock.com

Dedication

To my loving husband, sisters, children and grandchildren. Thank you for your prayers, love, encouragement and moral support.

I also dedicate this labor of love to the body of Christ. May all who read it be informed, enriched, blessed, inspired and encouraged.

First and foremost I would love to thank God, in the name of Jesus, for the tremendous love that has been shed abroad in Elma's heart to have such boldness to tackle such a subject as is contained in this book to bring freedom to every captive who is willing to apply it. This is a powerful insight into the very real, spiritual warfare that we, as believers, face daily. Not one scripture in this book has been compromised, but rather elaborated, and rightly-divided through the tremendous power of the Holy Spirit operating through our sister, and she is not afraid to unveil the truth.

In a true battle to effectively pursue your enemy one must first know his schemes and strategies to fight effectively. This book does just that, it unveils the hidden strategies of the enemy and gives us the wisdom needed to assist in teaching our hands to war, and my fingers to fight by using a believer's weapon of choice, God's Word. This book is intended to equip believers to be overcomers in everyday life against all demonic confederacies, and breaking down every curse and snare of witch-craft that has entered our paths. This book should be in the home of every believer to use right along-side the Word of God.

Charles Sivley, Jr.
Pastor/Founder Prevailing Word Publishing & Evangelistic
Association River of Life Training Center

I am delighted to be able to share with you the love I have for the author, Elma Garlock. She is not only an inspiration to many…but she is also able to encourage, exhort and to teach God's word through her ability to take God's heart beat for His people and put it in a simplified way whereby the hearer is able to feel God's love.

It is evident that God put it on her heart to write this powerful book. It is an anointed book packed with an anointed message. I highly recommend Elma Garlock's book *Behind the Lines of the Enemy* and know you will thoroughly enjoy it.

Susan Brown
Pastor, Hope Rope Church

Table of Content

Forward

I am pleased to recommend this book to you for it will inform you, motivate you to dig deeper into the ideas presented and challenge your spiritual understanding of the Scriptures and spiritual things. It is evident that the author, Elma Garlock, has invested much time in researching her subject and presents it thoroughly with clarity.

Equipping believers with sound doctrine and applicable truth is an important and unending task of the Church from generation to generation. I appreciate the author for making a contribution to this task for our generation.

It may be that many believers' have never heard of such a thing as *'spiritual warfare'* and to their ears it may sound rather unusual and strange. Then again, there are other believers who have heard of or are somewhat familiar with the idea of spiritual warfare but their knowledge is incomplete.

For those who are interested and make the effort to read this book *Behind the Lines of the Enemy* it will add to their arsenal of knowledge in Scriptural truth, thus arming and equipping themselves to live in freedom, power and authority through Jesus Christ.

God is raising up an army of believers *who know their God, who shall be strong and carry out great exploits* (Daniel 11:32). In these days, it is no longer sufficient to merely *stand our ground*, we must also take ground back from the enemy. This is what the Lord Jesus Christ has always intended for the Church, and He has abundantly provided all that is necessary for the Church to be successful in it's mission through his work of redemption, his powerful Word and the Holy Spirit.

Elma Garlock has written a book that is worth *reading* and worth *heeding*.

Apostle Jason Guerrero

Regency Christian Center International

Behind the Lines of the Enemy

Elma Garlock

Introduction

The book you are about to read *Behind the Lines of the Enemy*, was conceived and birthed from a prophetic dream the Lord gave me in 2013. As I prayed and sought the Lord the words that continued to echo in my heart were that I was to write a book based on this dream. I soon began to realize that the book would not be just another spiritual warfare book, but a revelation of the demoniac forces we face, the wars, warfare, the battles we will fight and the victory's we would win.

This book is to help you to better understand that revelation is given to us by God to not only reveal His will, plan and purpose for His people, but to communicate unto us His divine truths... and take that truth and expose the false and the forces of darkness... to open our spiritual eyes to the strategies, tactics and plans of the enemy in our life, family, church, community and the world...to emphasize the importance of our spiritual armor and the offensive and defensive weapons we possess and have access to.

It will help you to know the ways that God warns us through dreams, visions...how He trains us, equips us, tests us, builds our character and challenges our courage. It is also a book to help you to apply the power of God's Word in your life...How to fight with the weapons of righteousness with your right hand and the left... identify an attack from the enemy... how to overcome obstacles and the giants in the land...understand the widespread occults and the forbidden realms... the heavens, portals, invisible boundary's and the gates we build in the spirit that strengthens and protect our lives.

This book is a result of over three and a half years of research into various translations of scripture, world religions, archeology, occults, mythology and a wide variety of teachings, books and related articles.

If you are a believer, then you have the potential of becoming a soldier that has "The Heart of a Warrior."

Elma Garlock

Behind the Lines of the Enemy
The Dream

The dream begins with me standing on top of a mountain peak looking down at my feet. "Where am I, and what am I doing here?" I thought. To my amazement I not only saw myself standing on the mountain top, but I could also see myself standing from a distance away. I gazed at a panoramic view of my surroundings. Wearing what looked like a faded gray long sleeve shirt and pants, I was standing barefoot on top of the mountain.

Noticing my surroundings, I was shocked by mountain after mountain of black volcanic rocks peaking high into the sky and seemingly going on forever. Everything around me was dark, foreboding, dry and lifeless, and I knew that nothing had, nor ever would, live in that place. It reminded me of *Matthew 12:43* (*The Hebrew-Greek Key Study Bible*):

"Now when the unclean spirit goes out of man, it passes through waterless places, seeking rest, and does not find it."

Focusing my eyes upward I saw what the bible describes as gross darkness; the sky was thickly blanketed with the blackest clouds that I have ever seen.

"For behold, the darkness shall cover the earth, and gross darkness the people." Isaiah 60:2a (*Dake's Reference Bible*)

This darkness was everywhere, and all around me. I knew it was capable of overtaking me at any time. However, something or someone was holding the darkness back.

The clouds began to change into different hues of black that faded into dark charcoal and gradually lightened into grays that paled into a dirty white. I was reminded of *Job 10:22* (*The Voice*)

"The land of deep, unending night of blackness and shadowy chaos where the only illumination is more darkness."

This scripture describes exactly what I was seeing and experiencing.

Off to the right side of the sky I could see a small glimmer of light trying to penetrate the heavy darkness. Suddenly, the light broke through and shot a clear beam of light onto my feet. I realized I was standing on an elongated plateau that once peaked tall above all other mountains in this dark, dark place. I knew I needed to stand still and not move from my position.

Moments later, the mountain under my feet began to shake. I sensed something terrible was about to happen. Deep rumbling sounds were coming from within the center of the mountain. The sound grew louder into a high pitch as the pressure and shaking accelerated.

Within seconds there was an explosion that sounded like an atomic blast. I quickly lifted my head to see that part of the mountain top about ten feet in front of me exploded. It looked like a volcanic eruption had just occurred. The power and force behind the blast split the mountain top I was standing on and sliced the rock into thin sheets of black slate.

The effect of the blast created an enormously large portal (or hole) that allowed smoke, fire, and molten hot rock to leap high into the air, lighting the whole sky.

Fearless, I walked towards the explosion. The closer I got the larger the hole became. Reaching the edge, I looked down and could clearly see into the center of an enormous volcanic crater.

Glowing flames and smoke poured out at every angle, continuing to leap high into the dark sky. Hordes of demonic creatures of all shapes and sizes were being released at an alarming speed from deep within the bowels of the earth. Immediately, I knew they were released by Satan to head toward the four corners of the world in order to loose catastrophe and devastation upon the earth and man.

The Lord allowed me to see details of some of these demonic spirits while others were mere shadows. One of the demonic spirits was tall, thin, and clothed in a long black hooded cloaked garment that appeared to be worn and frayed from millenniums of wear. Cloaks covered the demons completely so I could not see any definite form. I only knew that they had a head and a body and that their true self had been concealed from my eyes.

They flew out of the portal with lightning speed as if they had been waiting a lifetime to be released. I knew they had a mission to accomplish, a strategy to use against man, and that their purpose was to destroy man.

More demons were crawling out of the pit at the same time, moving very slowly and methodically. Off to my right, I noticed one in particular creeping toward me.

I saw the face of devouring darkness, emanating absolute hatred, capable of performing unspeakable acts. It was the face of a demon-filled with intense hostility, anger, hatred and extreme abomination.

This demonic spirit was longer than a large monkey, grey in color, and shiny with no hair. He had a long tail like the end of a scorpion's tail that was sharp; his tail was to be used as a deadly weapon upon man. Large pointy catlike ears topped his head. His eyes were oversized pointing up at the ends. His face was elongated and unnatural. His glare was utterly evil and demonic. The Lord allowed me to have eye contact with this demon. He continued moving towards me a few steps at a time and then suddenly stopped and did not move.

As I stood staring into its eyes, I suddenly knew who he was and that his name was:

Deceiver, the one who devours, and that he was full of lies, trickery, deceit, evil, wickedness, full of ungodly schemes and perversion, and is one who hides in the darkness, masking himself as truth to mislead the world and the body of Christ.

This demonic spirit was the last image I remember seeing before I awoke sitting up in my bed.

Chapter 1
The Dream Revealed

The Lord gave me this prophetic dream for a reason and a purpose. I prayed to ask the Lord for the meaning of my dream, and almost immediately He began to unfold the revelation and the scriptures I would need for confirmation and reference. He let me know that what I witnessed was not only symbolic of the spiritual realm, it also was a glimpse of the demonic forces that believers face every day.

One of the scriptures the Lord gave me is *Revelations 9:2-3 (Hebrew-Greek Key Study Bible)* which says:

"And he opened the bottomless pit; and smoke went up out of the pit, like the smoke of a great furnace; and the sun and the air were darkened by the smoke of the pit. And out of the smoke came forth the locusts upon the earth, and power was given them as the scorpions of the earth have power."

The scorpions in this scripture represent *destructive enemies.* Merriam-Webster Dictionary defines the word destructive as: *to cause ruin, designed to hurt, or destroy.*

My dream was a portrayal of the vivid description of the end times that John wrote of in Revelation.

Scorpions use their tail to strike their prey with paralyzing venom that will kill its victim. They then can devour their prey at leisure, without a fight. Our enemy wants to paralyze us with fear, because once paralysis sets in, we lose the ability to function and move forward.

The demonic spirits I saw coming forth out of the pit were bred for one single purpose: to bring an end to man. These spirits will attempt to consume everything and everyone in their path and will not stop until they have totally devastated and sucked every ounce of life out of us.

As the Holy Spirit began uncovering truths to me about the spiritual realm, he reminded me of the continued conflict between the forces of light and darkness. Everything God made was good, and everything that is evil, Satan wants to perpetuate and call it good.

"Woe unto them that call evil good, and good evil; who put darkness for light, and light for darkness; who put bitter for sweet, and sweet for bitter." Isaiah 5:20 (Amplified Bible)

Satan has declared all-out war against us as individuals, as well as our families, our ministries, the church and the work of the kingdom of God. The warfare we face today compared to the warfare of yesterday has changed.

We are being confronted as Elijah was with the prophets of Baal in *1 Kings 18:20-40.* We are facing end time portals, gateways, doorways, and entrances that are allowing the enemy to gather forces unlike before. We will experience and fight the enemy in a way our forefathers did not have to fight because of the times we live in.

The church will have to discern that portals open right now are not of God. The King James Bible Dictionary defines the word *discern* as: *to see or understand the difference; to make a distinction; as, to discern between good and evil, truth and falsehood.* They are end-time portals, demonic portals, letting us know Jesus is coming, and every weapon, demonic force, and influence that the devil has is about to come upon the earth. We are going to war with dynamics that our parents never knew or understood. The demonic activity has changed. Times have changed. There is an overdriven homosexual agenda, pornography, sex trafficking, pride, and the narcissism of the "selfie" generation, to name a few. Drug and alcohol addictions are at epidemic proportions, as well as civil unrest, and acceleration in nuclear capabilities.

Believers must discern between natural and supernatural, asking: "who and what am I dealing with? Is it a spirit or my sin nature?" The sin nature is the aspect in man that makes him rebellious against God. Given the choice to do God's will or our own, we inherently choose to do our own thing. When I speak of sin nature, I am referring to our natural inclination to sin; immorality, impurity, passion, evil desire and idolatry. *(Colossians 3:5)*

The church today also seems to be fighting more with one another than the enemy. Our lack of discernment, an understanding of who we are battling with, knowledge of God's word, and our failure to arise in spiritual warfare are evident.

Many of us within the body of Christ are in a stupor of complacency, living a very self-centered life. Some of us live in our comfort zone of religious walls; walls that blind, bind and distort our hearing. These walls keep us from responding to truth so we function in the status quo. Some have lost their focus in the heat of the battle. They walk around wounded and have become numb and deaf to the Spirit of God. Still, others walk in fear of the supernatural; they stand in denial thinking they can avoid confronting the enemy and say, "if I leave him alone, he will leave me alone."

Lord, help us to get a revelation of the truth!

Then there are those who do not understand the importance of the word of God which trains us, equips us, strengthens us, and gives us the power and the authority to win. They don't have a working knowledge of their enemy, let alone know how to fight and wage war against him spiritually.

"All scripture is given by inspiration of God, and is profitable for doctrine, for reproof, for correction, for instruction in righteousness: That the man of God may be perfect, thoroughly furnished unto all good works." 2 Timothy 3:16, 17 (New King James Version)

It is of the utmost importance that we recognize the enemy for who he is and that we are aware of his *tactics* and the *strategies* he uses against us. This is all part of being, seeing and fighting behind the lines of the enemy. The only way to defeat the enemy in your life is to attack and fight through the power of the Spirit and the spoken Word of God. There is no other way.

Be alert and aware, because the enemy watches us. He stalks us like a lion just waiting for that opportune time to gain entrance and take advantage of our weaknesses. He monitors us to see how we live and how we will react in trials. He knows how we think and how we feel, because of what we say and do.

"Be sober (well balanced and self-disciplined), be alert and cautious at all times. That enemy of yours, the devil, prowls around like a roaring lion (fiercely hungry), seeking someone to devour. 1 Peter 5:8 (Amplified Bible)

By continuing to depend on the wisdom of man we have turned our hearts to the spirit of the world and not to the Spirit of God. Therefore, we respond to the things of the Spirit and the supernatural with our natural understanding and wisdom.

"The natural man, (who is governed only by his environment, by his natural or animal instincts, by his fallen nature) does not accept the things of the Spirit of God; for they are foolishness to him." 1 Corinthians 2:14a (Hebrew-Greek Key Study Bible)

Many churches have closed their doors to the supernatural, while the occult and the world embrace it. Satan has taken full advantage of our failure and uses it to discredit the true capabilities of God's supernatural power.

From the pit into the world

Satan sends his demonic spirits into the world to invade and destroy the lives of man.

But God sent into the world His word (Jesus) and the power of the Holy Spirit to save us, deliver us, set us free, and warn us of Satan and demonic spirits.

Demonic spirits I want to highlight throughout this book are:

The *spirit of delusion (2 Thessalonians 2:11) a lying spirit (1 Kings 22:1, 2)* and a *spirit of deception (1 Timothy 4:1).*

If you are under the influence of a *spirit of delusion* it will be difficult for you to distinguish between what is real and what only seems to be real.

A *lying spirit* will speak untruths and misrepresent reality, twist facts and will attempt to deceive you through lies.

A *spirit of deception* is a trickster, an illusionist and intentionally distorts and perverts who Jesus Christ is. This spirit is also behind so-called miraculous aberrations, religions, cults, and philosophies that claim that the bible is only a book of myths. It lures, entices, undermines and counterfeits all that is pure and holy.

These spirits work together to twist, distort, mislead, falsify and hide the truth. Their assignment is to spread false belief systems to be formed and propagated through men. They are manifested through false religions, false prophets, false manifestations, false revelations, false visions and false doctrines that are in reality doctrines of demons.

Their powerful influence works to sway, trick, mislead, manipulate, control, deceive and keep men blinded to the truth. Man's sin and rebellion have opened doors and portals for these forces of darkness to gain entrance into our lives and increase in power. If you take a hard look at the world today and the condition of man, you can't help but see their effects and the destruction that they have caused.

Our enemy doesn't care who you are or who you think you are. Nor does he care if you have a title or Ph.D. behind your name. He hates you with a vengeance and his goal is to destroy you, your reputation, your family and your witness if you are a believer.

The Lord clearly warned us in *Matthew 24:4 "Be careful that no one misleads you (deceiving you and leading you into error)."(Amplified Bible)*

Even those who claim to be a Christian can be deceived if their foundation is not built upon *Jesus Christ* and the *Word of God* as revealed in the bible. The only thing that is restraining Satan and his demonic spirits from completely taking over this world and man, is the power of the Holy Spirit and the prayers of the believers.

"For the mystery of lawlessness (rebellion against divine authority and the coming reign of lawlessness) is already at work; (but it is restrained) only until he who now restrains it is taken out of the way." 2 Thessalonians 2:7 (Amplified Bible)

Lawlessness

Lawlessness is opposition to or contempt of the will of God. It is anarchy, chaos, disorder, unrestrained fallen nature of man, unruliness, and lack of control; a free for all, anything goes attitude.

Everything that is against Christ's stability, peace, order, laws, rules and regulations, authority or against moral and spiritual truth and laws, is rooted in the author of rebellion, Satan, and his demonic spirits.

These spirits manifest and work through man to degrade morality, which effects the laws we pass, how we live, who and what we worship, and the sanctity and value of life.

In our world today, lawlessness is rampant. Every day we hear of shootings, terrorist bombings, riots and protests ending in bloodshed, arrests, and death. These acts enforce fear, unrest, mistrust, despair, and hopelessness in the heart of man.

Today, people are in open defiance and resist those who have the legal authority to enforce the laws of the land. Rebellious behavior, a lack of respect and entitlement are entrenched in the culture. Satan and his demonic spirits have infiltrated and corrupted man's thinking, causing both mind and conscience to be seared, leaving them incapable of ethical functioning. Their heart can no longer distinguish or judge right from wrong.

Man's heart can be very deceptive and devise evil on its own. Every imagination or intent of his heart can be wicked. When the enemy gets involved that becomes magnified, distorted and vile in magnitude proportions.

In *1 Timothy 1:8, 9 & 10* scripture very clearly says:

"Now we know (without any doubt) that the Law is good, if one uses it lawfully and appropriately, understanding the fact that law is not enacted for the righteous person (the one in right standing with God), but for lawless and rebellious people, for the ungodly and sinful, for the irreverent and profane, for those who kill their fathers or mothers, for murderers, for sexually immoral persons, for homosexuals, for kidnappers and slave traders, for liars, for perjurers, and for whatever else is contrary to sound doctrine." (Amplified Bible)

The Forces of Darkness are Marching

Time is counting down and the forces of darkness are marching forward to destroy everyone in their path, and darkness is at work to overshadow the light.

There is a scene in the movie *"Lord of the Rings,"* where "good battles against the forces of evil". The battle is called the "Battle of Helm's Deep."

This battle resembles the battle we face against the forces of darkness that are marching against us. The forces of Satan, his rulers of darkness and the spiritual forces in the heavenly places and earthly realm. (See *Ephesians 6:12*)

A Little Background First

In *Lord of the Rings,* the battle sets the forces of Saruman, a wizard sent to Middle-earth in human form by Valar, which are gods or angelic beings to challenge "Sauron," or also known as Necromancer. Necromancer led the absolute satanic rebellion and evil against the people of Middle-earth - man against the Rohirrim and the soldiers of Rohan, under King Théoden, and his people.

Saruman became possessed with power for himself and tries to take over Middle-earth by forces working through demonic dark creatures. He proceeds to raise an army from the pits, and slimes of the earth, known as black orcs and were a cross-breeding of orcs and Goblin-men. They were treacherous and vile and showed no mercy, fear or sympathy. These dark creatures made up a large part of Saruman's army and were under his total command. Sound familiar?

Gearing up for Battle

The Rohirrim soldiers prepare for battle as they clothe themselves in armor; a helmet, a shield in the left hand and a sword in the right. The king declares that war is upon them and every man must wield their sword. There is fear in the eyes of those who have never experienced battle, yet in others lie a quiet confidence and faith that they will win and that help is on the way. The Rohirrim are 1,000 strong, yet are outnumbered by Saruman's army that consisted of at least 10,000, and have been seen marching towards Helm's Deep which is occupied by the soldiers and people of Rohan.

The king asks a question: "Where are the horse and the rider? They have passed; where is the horn that was blowing? They have passed like rain on the mountains; like the wind in the meadow – the days have gone to shadow, how has it come to this?"

This is the question that all men ask as they face their battles and their enemy.

Hornburg Fortress

Saruman had declared all-out war against the people of Middle Earth and his next target was to be the people of Rohan. Once the king of Rohan heard the news of the impending attack, he immediately directed his people to escape to Helms Deep and the protection of the Hornburg Fortress.

The walls of Hornburg Fortress stood tall to protect the army of the Rohirrim, the king, and his people and became the refuge of the army of the Rohirrim. These 20-foot walls consisted of solid rock and were wide enough for four men to stand side by side. The wall was thought to be impenetrable and had never fallen during an assault.

The Battle Begins

Its nighttime and the men stand ready and armed on the battlements of Helms Deep. They watch as the massive army of Saruman arrive in the valley of Helms Deep with lighted torches. It begins to rain and flashes of light begin to rumble through the skies. The Uruk-hai armies (demonic creatures) draw closer to the walls that protect the soldiers and the people of Rohan. Suddenly the captain of the army of Saruman raises his hand and they stop just a few feet below the fortress walls. The soldiers of the Rohirrim stand in their positions on the wall with arrows pointing towards the vast army of their enemy the Uruk-hai; watching and waiting to see who would make the first move.

The Uruk-hai grunt and growl, stamping their spears on the ground in unison and beating their chests hoping to intimidate the soldiers the Rohirrim.

The soldiers of the Rohirrim load their bows and draw them back in readiness waiting for the order to fire. Suddenly an arrow is released by a soldier of the Rohirrim and hits the enemy and the battle between good and evil begins.

Many soldiers die that night and many others lay wounded as the battle rages on; it seems as though the enemy will win and all will be lost. Dawn begins to break and hope rises in their hearts as a white light appears on the top of the hill that overlooks the valley of Helms Deep. All of a sudden, the Uruk-hai stop fighting and look up towards the bright light as it surges forward and into their ranks. This light is so bright that it blinds them and they begin to run away in fear and defeat.

This scene brings to mind the following scriptures.

"But the path of the righteous is like the light of dawn that shines brighter and brighter until the full day. The way of the wicked is like darkness." Proverbs 4:18,19a (Hebrew – Greek key Study Bible)

'The Lord is my light and my salvation; The Lord is the defense of my life; whom shall I dread? When evildoers came upon me to devour my flesh, my adversaries and my enemies, they stumbled and fell. Though a host encamps against me, my heart will not fear; Though war arises against me, In spite of this I shall be confident." Psalms 27:1-3 (Hebrew – Greek key Study Bible)

As the scene from the movie shows, the forces of darkness want to destroy mankind; but good overcame evil and the power of light destroyed the darkness; the scriptures show that we the righteous shine like the light of day and can be confident that any evil adversary that comes against us will stumble and fall.

We are a light. We are the light of Jesus that shines bright in the world and we are called to fight against all that is evil, dark and demonic.

God has an army of light that is marching against the armies of darkness. Our enemy may think he can win, but God says, "WE WIN!"

Mind Blinding Spirit

Another spirit linked to the *spirit of delusion* is a *mind blinding spirit*. This spirit works to distort or destroy your view and perspective of God, Heaven, and hell. They work to veil the eyes so that the gospel of Christ is hidden from those who are perishing. They blind the mind from the truth and hide understanding from the heart. You may be able to see with the natural eyes, but your spiritual eyes lack sight, discernment, and vision into the spiritual realm.

A mind blinding spirit works like a device (or shade) that is pulled down over your spiritual eyes intending to shut out the light. A result is a person groping in darkness unable to see or discern truth from lies.

These spirits also work to conceal Satan's activities and obstruct our understanding and knowledge of his secret purpose and plans. These spirits are behind false Christs (or messiahs), false prophets, false visions, false dreams, false apostles and false teachers. They speak lies to bring confusion, delusion, to mislead, deceive, and counterfeit the truth. (*2 Corinthians 11:1-15*)

A perfect example of this is in *Revelation 2:18-24*. Verse 24 says: "*But I say to you, the rest who are in Thyatira, who do not hold this teaching, who have not known the deep things of Satan, as they call them.*" *(Hebrew-Greek Key Study Bible)*

These were false teachings that developed in the church of Thyatira, the Roman church of the Dark Ages that preceded the Protestant Reformation. They included every kind of worldliness and demon-inspired corruption of the truth as *1 Timothy 4:1&2* warns us:

"*But the Spirit explicitly says that in later times some will fall away from the faith, paying attention to deceitful spirits and doctrines of demons, by means of the hypocrisy of liars seared in their own conscience as with a branding iron.*" *(Hebrew-Greek Key Study Bible)*

These doctrines were called by their supporters "the deep things of God" but the Lord calls them "the deep thing of Satan."

The Antichrist Spirit

Remember the demonic spirit that the Lord showed me in my dream? Part of its manifestation and character is the *antichrist spirit*. There are specific demons that work to assist this powerful spirit: the *spirit of rebellion, deception, blasphemy, perversion,* and *pride.* Satan assigned them to go into the world to bring religious and spiritual error among men in astronomical portions, and to filter into the body of Christ.

Please note: More than one spirit of a certain type such as a *spirit of rebellion* will work with an *antichrist spirit* and a *spirit of witchcraft. (See 1 Samuel 15:23a)*

The operation of the *antichrist spirit* opposes Christ as the son of God, denies His deity and His priestly office and works to dethrone Him as if He were a mere man. Other demon spirits that work alongside this spirit help to support and strengthen its power and its stronghold in a person, generation, culture, or nation.

They are the *spirit of rebellion 1 Samuel 15:23a), spirit of deception (Revelations 12:9), spirit of blasphemy (2 Timothy 3:2), a perverse spirit (Isaiah 19:14),* and *the spirit of pride 1 John 2:16).*

1 John 2:18 "Children, it is the last hour, and just as you heard that antichrist is coming, even now many antichrists have arisen; from this we know that it is the last hour." (Hebrew-Greek Key Study Bible)

There are denominations that are opening their doors to religious perversion disguised under the banner of love, grace, and acceptance of all; regardless of sexual preference or lifestyle.

The *spirit of perversion* doesn't just work to pervert sex and everything associated with it. It also works to distort, misrepresent, misapply, misinterpret, corrupt and twist the truth, reality, goodness, honesty, faithfulness, uprightness, and love in the heart and mind of man.

In *1 John 4:3* we see that God used the apostle John to warn the church:

"And every spirit that does not confess Jesus is not from God; and this is the spirit of the antichrist of which you have heard that is coming, and now it is already in the world." (Hebrew-Greek Key Study Bible)

The *antichrist spirit* came against the 1st-century church with adversity causing great hardship, oppression, imprisonment and even death to Christians and some of the apostles.

The spirit is behind anti-God movements and individuals who work against Christ, the church and the kingdom of God in the world. This spirit continued to gain momentum throughout the centuries and continues to oppose believers with extreme evil and persecution. This spirit shows no mercy and takes no prisoners.

Revelation 13:11-18 gives us reasonable justification for expecting this spirit to culminate and work in and through a single person who will be the *antichrist,* (singular). The *antichrist* will be destroyed by Christ at His Second coming. The spirit working in the *antichrist*, theoretically a person, will claim to be God himself.

The next spirit we will contend with in greater magnification is an *occult spirit.* This spirit empowers all forms of *witchcraft* by seducing and alluring people with its promise of supernatural, magical, and mystical powers. It enables those under the occult spirit to work supernatural phenomena and to have knowledge of hidden, dark, and forbidden practices, use seductive charms, and perform rituals that bring death and destruction. Satan promises power, wealth and recognition, while in truth they spiral into a darkness that will eventually lead them to despair and death.

The *occult spirit* works in the dark and hidden places. It strives to go undetected by the church. The church has experienced its manifestation and effect, yet we as a church have had little understanding of who or what was behind these manifestations. It is not until God brings revelation do we understand and discern.

God gives revelation to His people at the right time and in the right season. God has been preparing us for what is coming by directing many to write and teach on spiritual warfare, demonic spirits, and the supernatural realm.

From generation to generation we are seeing occult practices arise in society with more recognition and acceptance. There is a massive searching for the power of the supernatural realm. Sadly, society is searching for the supernatural in all the wrong places.

While the church is praying and seeking God for a supernatural move of the Holy Spirit and revival, there are those praying to Lucifer (aka Satan). They are praying against God's people and planting their false prophets in the church. The occult is continuously planting witches, warlocks, and sorcerers and divining false gifts into the church with the purpose of destroying pastors and removing them from their call. The occult works to bring a reproach to spiritual leaders, to divide, destroy, disconnect, and to devastate God's people and His church. They are speaking false prophecies in the church today to mislead, confuse, bring curses on, and redirect God's people, their destiny, and the purpose of the Kingdom of God.

False Prophecy in the church

In 1987, I experienced false prophecy for the first time. While sitting in the congregation of the church I attended, praise and worship had just ended and my pastor walked up to the pulpit, bowed his head and remained in an attitude of worship. It was always his practice to allow the Holy Spirit to move in our services in prophecy either through him or members of the church that he trusted and knew moved in the gifts of the Spirit. The congregation became still and the atmosphere was charged with excitement as we waited to hear from the Lord.

Suddenly, a man sitting towards the back of the church began to prophesy. As he began to speak, I discerned that something was not right and that the Holy Spirit was not speaking through him. A *spirit of witchcraft* and *false prophecy* was speaking through him.

I was sitting on the right side of the church and my body was facing the altar. Quickly my spirit turned towards the man, yet my body remained facing forward. A boldness came over me and out of my mouth, I began rebuking the spirit that was speaking through the man. I slipped out of the row I was standing in and walked towards him.

I began binding the *spirit of witchcraft* that was manifesting in and through the man. He attempted to talk over me but I continued to bind the spirit, stand my ground, and take authority over the spirit.

In minutes, the ushers were escorting him out of the church and many of the congregation were caught unprepared, seemingly frozen. I knew that we had witnessed an attack from the enemy that was trying to bring in confusion, fear, and control. Confrontations with the enemy will increase and we must know how to confront and win!

In order for us to be ready we must:

1. Know who we are in Christ. *(Romans 8)*

2. Understand the power of the blood of Jesus, and how and when to apply it. *(Revelation 12:11)*

3. Know the authority we have over unclean spirits. *(Matthew 10:1)*

4. Understand that it is not by our own might, nor by our own power, or strength, but it is by and through God's Spirit that we can fight and win. *(Zechariah 4:6)*

5. Recognize who and what the enemy is. *(Ephesians 6:12)*

6. Resist and stand your ground immovable against the enemy. *(Ephesians 6:13)*

7. Equip ourselves for battle. *(Ephesians 6:14-17)*

8. Pray at all times in the spirit. *(Ephesians 6:18)*

Chapter 2
Dream Interpretation and Prophetic Symbols

"Hear now my words: If there be a prophet among you, I the Lord will make myself known unto him in a vision, and will speak unto him in a dream."
Numbers 12:6

Interpretation

Interpretation is the act or result of interpreting or explaining.

For us to properly interpret the meaning of objects and symbols in a dream we need to understand a biblical principle called the *"law of the first mention."* It states that the first mention of an object, number, color or symbol in the Bible sets a pattern of interpretation that holds true throughout the rest of scripture.

The first mention in scripture not only gives that word it's most complete and accurate meaning, but it also serves as a key in understanding the Biblical concepts and provides a foundation for its fuller development in later parts of the Bible.

Symbols

Symbols are things that stand for, or suggest something else, by reason of relationship, association, resemblance or representation of; especially: a visible sign of something invisible.

Symbols can be objects, actions or creatures that have a deeper religious application or significance and can involve a deeper spiritual meaning.

Examples:

1. The rainbow: a symbol of God's covenant. *(Genesis 9:13)*
2. A rock: a symbol of stability *(Psalms 18:2)*
3. Washing of hands: a symbol of innocence *(Matthew 27:24)*
4. Anointing: a symbol of empowering by God's Spirit *(Luke 4:18)*
5. The serpent: a symbol of Satan *(Genesis 3:1)*

6. A dove: a symbol of the Holy Spirit *(Matthew 3:16)*

Please note that there can be double imagery in *symbols*. Not all *symbols* in the bible have one and only one meaning.

The Dream Interpreted

The Darkness

Job 12:22 "He discloses deepest recesses of darkness, makes utter darkness enter the light." (Christian Standard Bible)

The dark sky in my dream represents the *spiritual darkness* that hovers over the earth and works to overshadow the truth. Its goal is to blind the minds of men so that they grope in darkness unable to see the light of truth and wisdom. This darkness is also representative of the moral, physical and spiritual evil that man is capable of manifesting.

Law of Accumulation

There is a law called the *law of accumulation*. The word accumulate means to increase gradually in quantity or number, to gather or pile up especially little by little.

This is how clouds are formed, and how darkness amasses. In the natural world, dark clouds are formed as they gather water droplets and ice crystals, thus becoming thicker and denser. The thicker they get, the more light they scatter, resulting in less light penetrating through them. An abundance of clouds and their shadows increase the darkness. Demonic spirits accumulate in the same way. As they gather together and increase in number, they increase in power shrouding light and truth in darkness.

2 Corinthians 4:4 & 5 (Dake's Anointed Reference Bible):

"But if our gospel be hid, it is hid to them that are lost: In whom the god of this world hath blinded the minds of them which believe not, lest the light of the glorious gospel of Christ, who is the image of God, should shine unto them."

This darkness also represents confusion, terror, calamity, disorder, and chaos culminating to a fevered pitch within people, religions, countries, and nations. This darkness will grow worse and it will be as *Matthew 24:5-8 (The Voice):*

"For many will come in My name claiming they are the Anointed One, and many poor souls will be taken in. You will hear of wars, and you will hear rumors of wars but you should not panic. It is inevitable, this violent breaking apart of the sinful world, but remember, the wars are not the end. The end is still unfolding. Nations will do battle with nations and kingdoms will fight neighboring kingdoms, and there will be famines and earthquakes. But these are not the end. These are the birth pangs, the beginning. The end is still unfolding."

The dark events in the world are a manifestation of demonic forces working to affect the natural realm. Demonic forces move and exist in darkness, and it is this darkness that works to influence, manipulate and control man.

In certain cultures, darkness spreads uncontrollably and consumes the land and its people because the enemy goes unchecked and the dark deeds of man are not confronted or exposed by those who claim to know Christ and the truth.

In *Ephesians 5:11* Paul tells us *"And do not participate in the unfruitful deed of darkness, but instead even expose them." (Amplified Bible)*

If man continues to entertain the darkness, then man will suffer its consequences and produce its fruit.

Psalms 107:10, 11 "Some dwelt in darkness and in the deep (deathly) darkness, Prisoners (bound) in misery and chains. Because they had rebelled against the words of God, and spurned the counsel of the Most High." (AMPC)

The good news is that there is hope, salvation, and deliverance for man; and His name is Jesus Christ, the light of the world and the only light that can expose darkness and cause it to flee.

John 8:12 "I am the Light of the world; he who follows Me shall not walk in the darkness, but shall have the light of life." (New King James Version)

The Beam of Light

Did you know there are beams of light called "God rays," "fingers of God" and are also descriptive of "Jacob's ladder"?

These rays of sunlight appear to radiate from the point in the sky where the sun is located. The rays or beams of sunlight that stream through gaps in the clouds are columns of sunlit air separating the dark cloud-shadowed regions. The rays are parallel shafts of sunlight that converge at a point from the sky to the ground.

The *beam of light* I saw in my dream represents God's word. His word is the source of light, truth, guidance, understanding, wisdom, and revelation that God reveals to a believer. This light has, is and will forever penetrate the darkness to light your way.

Psalms 119:105 confirms *"Your word is a lamp to my feet, and a light to my path" (Amplified Bible)*

In my dream, the light also represented vision, the ability to perceive the supernatural, and illumination of the natural and spiritual mind. The more we are illuminated by the light of truth, the clearer we can see and quickly identify darkness.

Job 12:22 "He reveals mysteries from the darkness, and brings the deep darkness into light." (Hebrew-Greek Key Study Bible)

God uncovers and reveals the hidden dimensions and mysteries from the darkness, and floods deep shadows with His light.

2 Samuel 22:29 has this to say concerning light

"Suddenly, God, your light floods my path, God drives out the darkness. I smash the bands of marauders, I vault the high fences. What a God! His road stretches straight and smooth. Everyone who runs toward Him makes it." (The Message Bible)

What Do Colors Represent?

The only colors in my dream were black, gray and white except the red in the flames. Dreams that appear black and white, dark or gray and even muted colors reveal the plans of the enemy. This is exactly why my dream consisted of dark colors. Bright and vivid colors were not important in my dream because the Holy Spirit wanted me to remember the message behind the dream.

The Color Black

Black speaks of death, evil, suffering, judgment, disease, famine, fear and chaos- all of which are the results of sin and spiritual darkness.

Black and darkness can also mean that the time is crucial, a warning, and that action or change needs to take place. It symbolizes the midnight hour; it is a time of decision.

Black also lacks brightness and hue, and it does not reflect light. Instead, black only absorbs light. Black hides things while white brings them to light. The bible tells us *"God is light"* in *1 John 1:5*.

It's interesting that prior to Satan's fall from heaven, he was an angel of light, yet when he fell from heaven scripture says that he fell like lightning.

"I watched Satan fall from heaven like (a flash of) lightning. ".." Luke 10:18 (Amplified Bible)

The Color Gray

The color gray in my dream represents the hidden deceptions that can shroud our vision and the half-truths that the enemy promotes. Gray can also represent weakness, sadness, and the grave.

Gray is the color between black and white and can represent compromise, emotional detachment, sadness, depression, loneliness, and isolation.

It may also speak of a heart and mind that is detached, neutral, impartial and indecisive towards the things of God.

The color gray can be symbolic of a lukewarm church or individual. Gray can be what is called living in the "gray area," that is an undefined or undetermined position, decision or state of mind.

"I know your (record of) works and what you are doing; you are neither cold nor hot. Would that you were cold or hot! So because you

are lukewarm and neither cold nor hot, I will spew (vomit) you out of My mouth." Revelations 3:15-16 (Amplified Bible)

The Color White

The white in my dream is emblematic of not only the light of Jesus, but it represents purity, clarity, righteousness, salvation, peace, comfort, hope, and the victory we have over sin and the enemy of our soul.

"Come now, and let us reason together," Says the Lord. "Though your sins are like scarlet, they shall be white as snow; though they are red like crimson, they shall be like wool." Isaiah 1:18 (Hebrew-Greek Key Study Bible.)

The color white connotes openness, growth, and creativity. You cannot hide behind it because it amplifies everything in its path just like Jesus.

Symbolic Meanings

The Mountain

The mountain in my dream represents the obstacles that we will have to overcome, the difficulties we will have to face, the challenges that will test us to our limit, and where we stand against and confront demonic forces.

The mountain also symbolizes strength, stability, victory or accomplishment, and a solid foundation that must be established in Christ. Remember, the enemy will do whatever it takes to shake your foundation, undermine your stability and deplete your power and strength.

Being on the mountain also represents an encounter with God, a call to come up higher with Him. Higher is where He can reveal Himself to us and where we can experience change by and through the power of the Holy Spirit. It is rising to a greater level of spiritual maturity, the balance of character and developing an intimate relationship with the Father and the Holy Spirit.

It also represents having to rise higher to a new level of warfare with the enemy. New levels – new devils.

Remember when Jesus took Peter, James, and John and brought them up onto a high mountain, and Jesus was transfigured before their eyes?

"Six days later Jesus took with Him Peter and James and John his brother, and brought them up to a high mountain. And He was transfigured before them; and His face shone like the sun, and His garments became as white as light." Matthew 17:1 & 2 (Hebrew-Greek Key Study Bible)

Did you know that the change that Jesus went through and what scripture describes as Him being "transfigured" means? In the Greek, transfigured is the word *"metamorphoo,"* and it means a change by supernatural means.

It is the process of what science calls *"metamorphosis,"* which is a complete transformation. This process of progressive transformation is what God desires to do in our lives.

In *Romans 12:2* scripture confirms to us:

"And do not be conformed to this world (any longer with its superficial values and customs), but be transformed and progressively changed (as you mature spiritually) by the renewing of your mind (focusing on godly values and ethical attitudes, so that you may prove (for yourselves) what the will of God is, that which is good and acceptable and perfect (in His plan and purpose for you)." (Amplified Bible)

Mountains can also represent the difficulties that need to be removed from our life by and through faith as *Matthew 17:20b* states: (*New King James Version*)

"If you have faith as a mustard seed, you will say to this mountain, "Move from here to over there," and it will move; and nothing will be impossible for you."

The Plateau

In geology and earth science, a plateau is called a high plain or tableland and consists of relatively flat terrain that is raised significantly above the surrounding area.

For a plateau to be formed at the top of a mountain, violent inner and outward changes must take place. When volcanic magma rises from beneath the earth, the ground swells upward, lifting very large flat areas of rock. These large flat rocks are what the foundation for plateaus become.

The plateau I was standing on in my dream represents a place of balance, level footing, and established groundwork that needs to be laid. If a solid foundation has not been formed in your spiritual and emotional life, when trials come and the ground beneath you begins to shake, you will fall. Those who can be shaken will be shaken and those who can stand will stand.

"So everyone who hears these words of Mine and acts on them will be like a wise man (a far-sighted, practical and sensible man) who built his house on the rock. And the rain fell, and the floods and torrents came, and the winds blew and slammed against that house; yet it did not fall, because it had been founded on the rock. And everyone who hears these words of Mine and does not do them will be like a foolish (stupid) man who built his house on the sand. And the rain fell, and the floods and torrents came, and the winds blew and slammed against that house, and it fell – and great and complete was its fall." Matthew 7:24-27 (Amplified Bible)

Standing Firm

Position, Balance, and Faith

In my dream, I remember knowing in my spirit how important it was for me to not only position myself on the plateau but to stand firm and establish my stance for balance. I knew that my decision to not move at that time was essential because something was about to occur. Later, as the ground was shaking in the dream, I understood why balance determined whether I would be able to stand.

Physically, our ability to maintain balance depends on equilibrium. If our equilibrium is off it is impossible for us to be steady and stand upright. Part of being balanced spiritually involves learning how to maintain our spiritual and emotional equilibrium. When tests and trials come we are then able to stand and oppose the forces and activities of the enemy. The most important component to standing firm and balanced is faith.

When we stand in faith we are alert, equipped, and ready. We are like soldiers, strong, watchful, on guard, courageous, and bold – keeping our eyes open for spiritual danger and ready for battle. (*1 Corinthians 16:13, 14 Expanded Bible*)

Phillips translation of *Ephesians 6:10-17* expressively explains what it means to be equipped so you can stand firm:

"In conclusion be strong – not in yourselves but in the Lord, in the power of his boundless resources. Put on God's complete armor so that you can successfully resist all the devil's methods of attack. For our fight is not against any physical enemy: it is against organizations and powers that are spiritual. We are up against the unseen power that controls this dark world, and spiritual agents from the very headquarters of evil. Therefore you must wear the whole armor of God that you may be able to resist evil in its day of power and that even when you have fought to a standstill you may still stand your ground. Take your stand then with truth as your belt, righteousness your breastplate, the Gospel of peace firmly on your feet, salvation as your helmet and in your hand the sword of the Spirit, the Word of God. Above all be sure you take faith as your shield for it can quench every burning missile the enemy hurls at you. Pray at all times with every kind of spiritual prayer, keeping alert and persistent as you pray for all Christ's men and women."

Gray Clothing

Clothing in a dream represents covering and the gray color of my clothing was intentional. When a soldier is dressed in a gray uniform on the battlefield he can easily blend in with his surroundings, not bringing attention to himself. The intention of the grey clothing in the dream was to take attention off me and keep the focus on the warning to God's people.

Additionally, the gray and faded clothing represented years of being on the battlefield. My natural clothing didn't matter. Moreover, I was to determine how I was clothed spiritually. Was I clothed in the spiritual armor of God? Was I spiritually dressed, equipped and ready to face the enemy and the battles that were ahead?

Bare Feet

Arranging my feet and widening my stance was important symbolically of the authority I was to project as a believer. Projecting boldness and courage at that moment became more important as the dream progressed. Being barefoot, I felt I could grip the ground beneath me and nothing could move me or knock me down. I knew this authority was not contingent on myself. I stood in the power of Jesus, which kept protected and, emboldened me to stand in darkness. We cannot stand against the enemy alone, in our own power.

1 Samuel 2:9 "He will guard the feet of His godly (faithful) ones, but the wicked ones are silenced and perish in darkness; For a man shall not prevail by might." (Amplified Bible)

Being barefoot in the dream revealed my vulnerability as I encountered the enemy. I was exposed, yet did not feel helpless – humbled, yet not timid.

My Back

In the panoramic view of the dream, I saw myself from the behind. This view represents the past and previous events and which are 'behind' us. Our former circumstances, difficult situations, and history of decisions that cannot be undone. These parts of our past we cannot undo or return to. Our tendency is to look back at our past and say "I wish I would have" or "if only I could." However, God does not want us rehearsing the past. Returning to past behaviors, lifestyles and distorted truths lead to spiritual death, and sometimes even death in the natural.

We are to learn from our past, gaining wisdom, knowledge, and maturity. Going back would mean that you are not moving forward, but instead, are living in your past.

Throughout scripture, we are admonished to leave our old life behind and not turn back. We are to reach forward to what is ahead. We are to press on with the present and reach into the future. Only when the past is dealt with, and when we know Christ in the present can we have the confidence and determination to press forward.

Philippians 3:13b, 14 "But one thing I do: forgetting what lies behind and reaching forward to what lies ahead, I press on toward the goal for the prize of the upward call of God in Christ Jesus." (Hebrew-Greek Key Study Bible)

Luke 9:62 "No one who puts his hand to the plow and looks back (to the things left behind) is fit for the kingdom of God." (Amplified Bible)

Moving Forward

Recall the explosion in my dream? My first instinct was to move forward towards the explosion and not away from it. I was unafraid, and a natural boldness came over me. I was being drawn by an unseen hand to study the entities and discern their plans and purposes. I had to walk forward knowing they were the enemy. I couldn't back down or run away.

What is God telling us? We are to move and advance forward in battle, not cower or back down with fear or intimidation. We are to study and understand our enemy knowing who he is and how he works.

The Lord wants us to realize that we can see and know scripturally what is behind the lines of the enemy. The Holy Spirit will reveal the enemy's plans and show you how he strategizes his forces and positions his troops to battle against us. We have every weapon we need, the power to enforce, and the strength to win.

God reveals demonic forces that are behind the enemy lines in *Ephesians 6:12 "We're not waging war against enemies of flesh and blood alone. No, this fight is against tyrants, against authorities, against supernatural powers and demon princes that slither in the darkness of this world, and against wicked spiritual armies that lurk about in heavenly places." (The Voice)*:

Ephesians 6:10-12 in the *Message Bible* reads: *"And that about wraps it up. God is strong, and he wants you strong. So take everything the Master has set out for you, well-made weapons of the best materials. And put them to use so you will be able to stand up to everything the Devil throws your way. This is no afternoon athletic contest that we'll walk away from and forget about in a couple of hours. This is for keeps, a life-or-death fight to the finish against the Devil and his angels."*

Symbolically, as believers, there are two areas we are to apply moving forward. They are: "Moving forward into our future," and "Moving forward in our authority."

Your future is imminent and your prospects are immeasurable. It is destiny that calls you and sets you on the predetermined course of your life. Your future is the agency that possesses an irresistible power that moves you on.

Moving forward also means walking in the authority you have in Christ as a believer. Christ's authority is what enabled me to walk towards the demonic creatures in my dream.

Authority is not something you see with the naked eye but is an inner strength and confidence that you carry. Through the gift of salvation, you automatically have a measure of positional authority. *(Luke 10:19)*

Authority is the byproduct of your relationship with Christ. The deeper your relationship is with Jesus, the greater your authority.

According to scripture, this authority is the force that removes demons and causes evil spirits to flee *(Matthew 10:1)*. It is that same authority with which Jesus spoke to command demons to leave a person, and the authority can command submission *(Luke 4:36)*.

Fire

In scripture fire can represent destruction *(Numbers 16)*, judgment *(Leviticus 10)*, tribulation *(Zechariah 13:9)*, wrath *(Psalms 89:46)*, anger *(Deuteronomy 32:22)*, a plague *(Ezekiel 29:18)*, and the tongue used to represent fire *(James 3:6)*.

On the positive side, fire stands for cleansing *(2 Peter 3:7)*, God purifying His people *(Malachi 3:2-3)*, and an emblem of a spiritual healing process *(Isaiah 4:5-6)*. Fire also represents an offering to God *(Exodus 29:18)*, is used as a guide *(Exodus 13:21, 22)*, is symbolic for ministers *(Psalms 104:4)*, cloven tongues of fire *(Acts 2:3)*, holy spirit *(Matthew 3:11)*, an unquenchable fire *(Luke 3:17)*, a symbol of the Lord's presence and the instrument of His power *(Exodus 14:19, 24; 3:2)*. Scripture references that God has eyes like fire *(Revelations 1:14)*, that man's work is revealed by fire *(1 Corinthians 3:13)*, and a trial of fire *(I Peter 1:7)*. Lastly, fire is illustrative of the church overcoming her enemies *(Obadiah 1:18)* and represents the Word of God *(Jeremiah 5:14)*.

The fire in my dream speaks to us in two emblematic ways:

Deuteronomy 9:3 "Know then this day, that Jehovah thy God is he that goes over before thee, a consuming fire; he will destroy them, and he will cast them down before thee, and thou shalt dispossess them and cause them to perish quickly, as Jehovah hath said unto thee." (Darby Translation)

Look at the enemy from God's view and see them as totally and utterly defeated. God promises that He will go before you like a wildfire sweeping across and consuming dry land. As we encounter the enemy and speak God's Word, he cannot stand against us. God's Word is an all-consuming fire.

"For our God is a consuming fire." Hebrews 12:29 (Hebrew-Greek Key Study Bible)

Fire also represents the trials and testing we will have to endure.

I Peter 1:6-7 "Wherein ye greatly rejoice, though now for a season, if need be, ye are in heaviness (grieved with many kinds of trials) through manifold temptations: (trials, attacks, put to proof) That the trial of your faith, being much more precious than gold that perishes, though it be tried with fire, might be found unto praise and honor and glory at the appearing of Jesus Christ." (Dake's Reference Bible)

When gold is refined, impurities are removed by a fiery process. The heat of the fire separates foreign and impure materials from the gold and causes the dross to rise to the top. The hotter the flame, the purer the gold.

As believers, we must go through a purifying process. We must go through what is considered the refiner's fire. Our refiner is God, and His process (or fire) tests our faith and builds endurance, patience, character, righteousness, and maturity. Fire brings forth the fruits of the spirit.

"Behold, I send My messenger, and he shall prepare the way before Me. And the Lord, (the Messiah) whom you seek, will suddenly come to His temple; the Messenger or Angel of the covenant, whom you desire, behold, He shall come, says the Lord of hosts. "But who can endure the day of His coming? And who can stand when He appears? For He is like a refiner's fire and like fullers soap; "He will sit as a refiner and a purifier of silver, and He will purify the priests, the sons of Levi, and refine them like gold and silver, that they may offer to the Lord an offering in righteousness." Malachi 3:1-3 (Amplified Bible)

Smoke

The smoke in my dream represents smoke screens that the enemy uses prevent our ability to see the truth. A smokescreen obscures their movement, actions, blocks vision, clarity and hides their destructive behavior. The enemy veils our eyes hoping to conceal and confuse our understanding of the will and purposes of God.

Demonic spirits are the masters of camouflage, disguising themselves to cover up who they are to appear as something they're not. They will also use anything, or anyone, to distract and take focus off themselves and their evil plans.

"The thief comes only in order to steal and kill and destroy. I (Jesus) came that they may have and enjoy life, and have it in abundance." (To the full, till it overflows) John 10:10 (Amplified Bible)

Chapter 3
Ways God Warns Us

"I do not write these things to shame you, but as my beloved children I warn you."

1 Corinthians 4:14

Through Revelation

In the Old Testament God used prophets to bring revelation to His people. Prophets were called by God and anointed to stand in the office of a prophet such as Samuel, Elijah, and Jeremiah. God's Spirit would come upon them, and they would prophesy God's will, plan, and purpose to the people. Prophets would also bring direction, correction, and warning. At times, they would manifest some of the nine gifts of the spirit unknowingly as they brought forth God's words.

Please note: A prophet is a man or woman whom Christ has given the ascension gift of a *"prophet."* A prophet is one of the fivefold ascension gift ministers who are an extension of Christ's ministry to the Church. They have been anointed and called by God to stand in that office. *(Ephesians 4:11; 1 Corinthians 12:28)*

The revelation of the nine gifts of the Spirit was not revealed unto the prophets of the Old Testament and would not come into their fullness and understanding until Pentecost. *(Acts 2)*

The nine gifts of the Spirit are broken down into three groups and they are: *(1 Corinthians 12)*

1. The Revelation gifts: word of wisdom, word of knowledge, discerning of spirits
2. The Power gifts: faith, the gift of healings, working of miracles
3. The Vocal gifts: tongues, interpretation, prophecy

A great example of an Old Testament Prophet God spoke through was Elisha. God used Elisha to warn the king of Israel concerning plans the king of Aram (Ben-hadad), which were spoken in secret. We know from scripture that Israel was almost always at war with hostile kings trying to invade their borders, plunder their goods, enslave them, and take their lands.

In *2 Kings 6:8-23* is the story of one such king, the king of Aram (Syria):

> *"Now the king of Aram was warring against Israel; and he counseled with his servants saying, in such and such a place shall be my camp. And the man of God sent word to the king of Israel saying, "Beware that you do not pass this place, for the Aramean's are coming down there. And the king of Israel sent to the place about which the man of God had told him; thus he warned him, so that he guarded himself there, more than once or twice. Now the heart of the king of Aram was enraged over this thing; and he called his servants and said to them, "Will you tell me which of us is for the king of Israel? And one of his servants said, "No, my lord, O king; but Elisha, the prophet who is in Israel, tells the king of Israel the words that you speak in your bedroom. So he said, "Go and see where he is, that I may send and take him." And I was told him, saying, "Behold, he is in Dothan. And he sent horses and chariots and a great army there, and they came by night and surrounded the city." (Hebrew-Greek Key Study Bible)*

Each time the king of Aram tried to send marauding bands to the borderlines of Israel, the king of Israel was warned. The king of Israel would know the location of the enemy encampments and would avoid passing through those locations. Elisha not only warned the king of the plans of their enemy, but he was also able to tell the king of Israel even "the words that the king of Elam spoke in his bedroom."

How did Elisha know? Through revelation, a word of knowledge, and wisdom given by God. When the king of Aram found out that Elisha was the one that was warning the king of Israel, he knew that if his plans were to be successful, he would have to do away with Elisha. And so, the king went after Elisha. Once the king of Aram located Elisha, he immediately sent an army to surround the city and capture him with the intention of putting him to death.

This story is just one more example of how the enemy (aka Satan and demonic spirits) will always attack those who expose him. He is constantly looking for opportunities to trap, ensnare, and catch us off guard. But God always reveals to His people the plans of the enemy to protect us and make a way of escape. *(1 Corinthians 10:13)*

What is Revelation?

Revelation is an uncovering or unveiling. A term expressive of the fact that God makes known to men divine truths and realities that men could not discover for themselves. This kind of revelation only comes by and through the power of the Holy Spirit and is the most important aspect of understanding a dream, vision or prophecy.

The Spirit of God would come upon the prophets enabling them to receive a word of knowledge, a word of wisdom, to perform miracles, to see into the realm of the Spirit, and to prophesy.

Elisha stood in the office of a prophet for Israel. He spoke to the people on God's behalf and interpreted God's will. He also acted as a mediator between the people and God.

Today we do not need a mediator to know the will of God, or to receive direction. If you are a believer you have direct access to God. His Spirit lives in you and you can receive direction, a warning of impending danger, revelation, a word of knowledge and a word of wisdom directly from the Holy Spirit.

I'm not saying that we don't need prophets today to warn us, nor that God will not use them to warn a people, a church, or a nation. The Holy Spirit has and will continue to use, prophets to confirm what the Holy Spirit has shown or spoken directly to a person.

2 Kings 6:15-17 "Now when the attendant of the man of God had risen early and gone out, behold, an army with horses and chariots was circling the city. And his servant said to him, "Alas, my master! What shall we do?" So he answered, "Do not fear, for those who are with us are more than those who are with them." Then Elisha prayed and said, "O Lord, I pray, open his eyes that he may see." And the Lord opened the servant's eyes, and he saw; and behold, the mountain was full of horses and chariots of fire all around Elisha." (Hebrew-Greek Key Study Bible)

Once Elisha's attendant stepped out of the door his first reaction was fear. All he could see were the enemy's soldiers and chariots quickly surrounding the city. It sounds like Elisha's servant panicked and became blinded by his fear, and why? Because he was seeing with the eyes of the natural man, and to him, their situation probably looked hopeless.

Our natural eyes cannot see what's going on in the Spirit realm unless God gives us supernatural insight. This insight is considered discerning of spirits. Elisha prayed for his servant's eyes to be opened so he could see what Elisha saw supernaturally. With his eyes opened spiritually the servant could see the army of the Lord with their chariots of fire that were stationed all around them.

As Christians, we can react as the servant did if we are not spiritually prepared for our day. We can easily forget that there are unseen spiritual forces working for us and against us. The Holy Spirit must reveal these unseen forces to us.

We need to remember that Satan and his demonic forces are always scheming for ways they can use people, circumstances, and situations to attack or discourage us. Believers must be spiritually equipped, prepared and ready for the daily battle. Be aware that there are more for us than those who are against us.

We know that God exposed the plans of the enemy to Elisha, and he, in turn, warned the king of Israel of an impending attack. The scripture doesn't tell us if God warned Elisha while he was in prayer, if God gave him a dream, or if God spoke through a vision. However, we know that God gave Elisha revelation concerning the plans of the enemy.

God Warns Through Watchman

In *Ezekiel 3:17* God spoke to Ezekiel and He said: *"Son of man, I have appointed you a watchman to the house of Israel; whenever you hear a word from My mouth, warn them from me."* (Hebrew-Greek Key Study Bible)

The Hebrew word for watchman is *"tsaphah"* which means to lean forward, to peer into the distance; by implication means to observe, behold, spy out, wait for, and keep watch. (*Strong's Exhaustive Concordance*)

Watch means to keep guard, to be attentive and protect, vigilant (carefully noticing problems or signs of danger and being alertly watchful).

The word warn in *Ezekiel 3:17* is the Hebrew word *"Zahar"* which means to enlighten, to teach, to admonish, and give warning to. (*Strong's Exhaustive Concordance*)

In the Old Testament, God appointed prophets like Ezekiel to be a watchman for His people. Ezekiel was instructed by God to warn the people of judgments to come due to their sins of idolatry, and rebellion in order to call them to repentance. He would prophesy God's will, and plan. He would prophesy future events that were yet to unfold in the destiny of His chosen people. He also was known as a seer or one who sees.

Ezekiel 33:1-5 tells us that the word of the Lord came to Ezekiel. God told Ezekiel to speak to the people and tell them to take one man from among them and make him their watchman, and if the watchman sees the sword coming upon the land he was to blow the trumpet and warn the people. But if the people do not take the warning and the enemy comes and takes them away, the watchman is not responsible for their lives.

A watchman in the ancient world could either be stationed on a wall that surrounded the city or in a watchtower built within the walls. These walls were built high above the city giving the watchman a clear and unobstructed view of the borders of the city.

Watchman were assigned to watch day and night from the top of the walls; to keep an eye out for any signs of enemy activity, and if he spotted armed soldiers marching towards the borders of the land, he would either blow a trumpet to warn the people or warn them by word of mouth that the enemy was at hand.

"And when you go to war in your land against the adversary who attacks you, then you shall sound an alarm with the trumpets, that you may be remembered before the Lord your God and be saved from your enemies." Numbers 10:9 (Hebrew-Greek Key Study Bible)

Another example of an Old Testament prophet God called to be a watchman for His people was Moses. God called Moses to help deliver His people out of the bondage of Egypt and to intercede on their behalf.

Numbers 21:7 "So the people came to Moses and said, we have sinned, because we have spoken against the Lord and you; "intercede" with the Lord, that He may remove the serpents from us. And Moses interceded for the people." (Hebrew-Greek Key Study Bible)

The word for intercede in Hebrew is *"Palal"* which means to act as a mediator; to pray (to God), to intervene and to make supplication for. (*Strong's Exhaustive Concordance*)

Focusing on the Old Testament prophets helps us to understand the full meaning of the symbolism of a watchman and how important it is that we intercede on behalf of others.

In the New Testament Paul teaches us how the Holy Spirit will work with us to intercede for the saints. In *Romans 8:26 & 27* Paul tells us:

"And the same way the Spirit also helps our weaknesses; for we do not know how to pray as we should, but the Spirit Himself intercedes for us with groaning's too deep for words."

"And He who searches the hearts knows what the mind of the Spirit is because He intercedes for the saints according to the will of God." (Hebrew-Greek Key Study Bible)

The Greek word for *intercede* is *"huperentugchano"* and comes from two words *"huper"* meaning: over, above and beyond for the sake of. And *"entugechano"* which means: *encounter, I call (upon), make a petition, supplication. (Strong's Concordance)*

Jesus is at the right hand of God, interceding for us according to *Romans 8:34.*

In the same way, we are instructed to keep watch (*Mark 14:32-38*) as a watchman does and we are to pray and intercede like Jesus, who is our example.

As you pray and intercede in the Spirit scripture teaches us that: *"With all prayer and petition pray at all times in the Spirit, and with this in view, be on the alert with all perseverance and petition for all the saints." Ephesians 6:18 (Hebrew-Greek Key Study Bible)*

Picture yourself as a soldier in the Army. You've been trained, equipped and are now prepared to face the enemy in battle. Instead of fighting a battle in the physical world for others, we are fighting in the Army of the Lord with the help of the Holy Spirit. You are fighting a battle in the spiritual realm.

As we pray and intercede for others in the Spirit, we know that the Spirit is praying with us and through us the will of God on behalf of others.

"And we know (perceive and understand) that God causes all things to work together for good to those who love God, and those who are called according to His purpose." Romans 8:28 (Hebrew-Greek Key Study Bible)

You are partnering with the Holy Spirit and working together to bring about God's plan, purpose, and destiny for others. We are fighting together side by side like soldiers.

Boundary lines are lines drawn in the spiritual realm through prayer, that limit how far a trespasser can go. Satan and his army are the biggest trespassers of them all.

The boundary lines you build spiritually against the enemy will function as defensive hedges, walls that protect and will act as signposts to Satan saying: "this far and no more." These boundaries can only be established through prayer and intercession. When we are interceding for others we are going beyond a simple prayer, we are petitioning God in an earnest and urgent manner. We are taking an offensive and defensive posture in the spirit and are inviting the work of the Holy Spirit to bring about the will of God.

We are uncovering, canceling, nullifying, uprooting and tearing down Satan's accesses points, assignments and effects. We are rendering Satan and every demonic spirit powerless, and releasing the power of the kingdom of God.

He Warns Through Visions

While praying one morning I had a vision of a young Spanish man that looked like he was in his twenties. He was wearing a blue and white bandana around the top of his head representing the Spanish gang he belonged to. The Holy Spirit explained that this young man was in prison and was about to be attacked with a knife by a rival gang member inside the prison. This rival gang wanted him dead. The vision then shifted to a woman on her knees praying for her son's salvation and protection. I knew that the young man I saw in the vision in prison was her son.

The Holy Spirit let me know that she was praying for him at that very moment asking God to please lay it on the heart of other believers to pray for her son. Her prayer was being answered as I began praying and agreeing with her concerning her son.

In the natural we were miles apart; in the spirit we were standing together shoulder to shoulder, shield to shield, wielding our swords against the demonic forces threatening his life.

"And it shall come to pass in the last days, says God, that I will pour out of My Spirit upon all mankind, and your sons and your daughters shall prophesy (telling for the divine counsels) and your young men shall see visions (divinely granted appearances), and your old men shall dream (divinely suggested) dreams. Yes, and on My menservants also and on My maidservants in those days I will pour out of My Spirit, and they shall prophesy (telling forth the divine counsels and predicting future events pertaining especially to God's kingdom." Acts 17, 18 (Amplified Bible)

He Warns Through Dreams

The Holy Spirit warns us through dreams. To help explain what I mean, allow me to share with you a warning dream the Lord gave me concerning one of my family members.

Weeks before having this dream I found myself praying more for this individual in the Spirit. I felt like the prayers I was praying in my natural tongue and in my own limited understanding were not hitting the mark. I knew in my spirit that something was very wrong and asked the Holy

Spirit to show me what I was sensing. Weeks later the answer came in the form of a vivid and troubling warning.

As I awoke from the dream the reality and shock set in and immediately my heart became burdened. I witnessed the condition they were in and the horrible consequences about to take place in their life if a change didn't come. The Holy Spirit had warned me ahead of time so I could pray and intercede on their behalf.

1 Timothy 2:1 "First of all, then, I admonish and urge that petitions, prayers, intercession, and thanksgiving, be offered on behalf of all men." (Amplified Bible)

God knows the heart's cry of those who need salvation, intervention, and transformation.

When the promptings of the Spirit comes and we yield ourselves to the Holy Spirit, we release God's hands to work on their behalf.

Supernatural dreams are a means by which God brings to us a divine message and that message comes by way of pictures and can be in color or just black and white.

If you are a believer then God has given you spiritual gifts and attributes to operate in both the physical and spiritual world simultaneously.

It is one of the ways He brings confirmation to us and communicates His will, plan, purpose, and destiny. Dreams can convict us of sin; give us answers to questions, show and confirm our future, warn us of impending danger, lead us, guide us, instruct us, and bring revelation, wisdom, and understanding. God can also give us ideas and inventions in a dream, and council us in the night.

Psalms 16:7 declares "I will bless the Lord, who has given me counsel; yes, my heart instructs me in the night seasons." (Amplified Bible)

The Importance of Dreams in the Old Testament

One of the key ways God would communicate a message to men in the Old Testament was through *dreams.*

Some of the examples in scripture tell us:

"I the Lord…speak with him (man) in a dream." Numbers 12:6

"For God speaks in one way, and in two…in a dream…that he may turn man aside from his deed and cut off pride from man; he keeps back his soul from the Pit, his life from perishing by the sword." Job 33:14-18

God came to Abimelech in a dream of the night and said to him behold. *(Genesis 20:3)*

The angel of God spoke to Jacob in a dream. *(Genesis 31:10, 11)*

God gave Laban the Aramean a warning and it came in the form of a dream. *(Genesis 31:24)*

In Gibeon, the Lord appeared to Solomon in a dream. *(1 Kings 3:5)*

God also used dreams as a prophetic foretelling of future events:

Joseph's dream concerning his future. *(Genesis 37)*

The Egyptian baker's and butler's dream and the interpretation by Joseph. *(Genesis 40:5-22)*

Pharaoh's dream. *(Genesis 41:1-32)*

Gideon's encouragement in the Midianite camp from hearing a Midianite relate his dream of Gideon's forthcoming victory. *(Judges 7:13-15)*

King Nebuchadnezzar's dream of world empires. *(Daniel 2:1-45)*

Daniel's dream of the four winds, the great sea, and the four great beasts. *(Daniel 7:1-28)*

The Importance of Dreams in the New Testament

The New Testament tells us that an angel spoke to Joseph in a dream concerning Mary's conception of the Christ child by the Holy Ghost. *(Matthew 1:20-23)*

The wise men who were warned by God in a dream not to return to King Herod, but to depart back to their country another way. *(Matthew 2:12)*

Joseph being warned in a dream to flee to Egypt with the child and Mary. *(Matthew 2:13)*

Pilate's wife who had a dream concerning the innocents of Jesus. *(Matthew 27:19)*

Scriptural references confirm the importance of dreams.

All through the Old and New Testament we clearly see that God used dreams, visions, and prophets to warn God's people. We also learned that God warns us of impending dangers and attacks that the enemy has planned.

Scriptures clearly illustrate how God used revelation to reveal and confirm, and watchmen to pray and intercede for the lives of man.

Chapter 4
The Training of a Soldier

"Take your share of hardships and suffering (which you are called to endure) as a good (first-class) soldier of Christ Jesus."
2 Timothy 2:3

Tests Challenge Our Skills

The training of a soldier in the natural is done in phases. During training soldiers learn the skills needed to accomplish their military jobs. Their drill instructor will do everything possible to push them to their physical and mental limits. After each phase of training is a complete-time of testing which challenges their skills. As believers, our training as a soldier can only be accomplished through times of testing.

Through each test, we will be challenged to see how we respond during trials, trauma, temptations, and crises. And yes, we will be pushed to see where our physical, mental and spiritual limits begin and end.

What exactly is a test? A test is an examination that gauges your knowledge, ability, and experience. It can be a difficult situation that will expose hidden information about yourself or someone else. A test subjects us to challenging difficulties and can be a painful experience that tests our ability to endure. Important areas of testing for us will be in our endurance, our character and in our faith.

Esther is an example of one who was greatly tested. As the story unfolds we understand why God chose her, what her purpose was, areas she was tested in and how she responded.

Tests for Purpose

The scripture tells us that Esther had neither father nor mother, and Mordecai took her in as his own daughter never imagining the significant purpose God had planned for her.

As Esther grew and matured in the house of Mordecai, scripture tells us that she was beautiful in form and face.

God had a specific purpose for Esther and that for her to become queen. As a Jewish woman, Gods purpose for her was to exceed beyond what she, Mordecai or her people could ever imagine. Once she was placed into position as queen her purpose started to be revealed.

In *Esther* chapter 3 our story begins.

Our main characters are: Queen Esther, a Jew whose Hebrew name being Hadassah (meaning Myrtle), Mordecai (Esther's cousin who adopted her), King Ahasuerus (also known as Xerxes I) king of the Persian Empire, and Haman the Agagite, a very vengeful and egotistical man and enemy of the Jews. Haman was known to be a descendant of an Amalekite king who was an enemy of Israel during the time of King Saul. The King promoted Haman to be prime minister over all the princes of the kingdom.

Everyone would bow down and pay homage to Haman the prime minister as he would parade around the king's gate, all except Mordecai the Jew. Once Haman found out that Mordecai refused to bow down and pay homage to him, he became furious and determined to destroy all the Jews.

Purpose-driven people are tenacious and persistent. We see this in Esther as she set her purpose in motion.

Purpose has an intention and a determination to act in a certain way. That way can either be a negative purpose or a positive purpose. The enemy certainly had a negative purpose planned for the Jewish people, and Haman was to be the one to execute that purpose.

But God also had a purpose for the Jewish people and Esther was chosen to fulfill that purpose and set a course of the future and destiny of the Jewish nation.

"Many plans are in a man's mind, but it is the Lord's purpose for him that will stand." Proverbs 19:21 (Amplified Bible)

What areas did God test Esther in?

God Tested Esther's Faith

As we read through Esther, we see that she was a woman of faith. She put her faith in God to action, and the consequences of that faith delivered her people from impending death and destruction.

What does faith do? Faith enables us to believe in what God has spoken to us through His word. Even when we can't see a way out of circumstances, a way through, or light in the midst of darkness, be assured that the Holy Spirit will empower you, support you and enable you to pass the test.

James 1:2 "Consider it all joy, my brethren, when you encounter various trials." (Hebrew-Greek Key Study Bible)

Encounter in this scripture means to engage in conflict. So, what is this scripture telling us? We will encounter the enemy and we will have to fight.

But be encouraged, remember the trials the Lord has brought you through. Recount the many battles you have won. Know that the test will not last forever; that it has a beginning and an end, and once it has passed, you can look back with joy, because once again, God brought you through.

James 1:3 "Knowing that the testing of your faith produces endurance."

God isn't just testing us or our faith, but He is producing endurance in us.

When God is producing His character in us; He is forming, shaping and birthing the Fruit of the Spirit in us that will enable us to endure the tests.

James 1:4 "And let endurance have its perfect result, that you may be perfect and complete, lacking in nothing." (Hebrew-Greek Key Study Bible)

The word perfect in this scripture comes from two Greek words:

1. *Teleo*: to complete
2. *Telos*: a goal or purpose

The word "complete" in verse 4 means: that which retains all that was allotted to it at the first, needing nothing for its completeness, bodily, mentally and moral entireness. "Complete" expresses the perfection of man before the fall.

Now let's break down the word "endurance" in this scripture. Endurance is derived from two Greek words:

1. *Hupe*: under
2. *Memo*: to abide

Endurance is patience, the ability to abide under and have the power to bear prolonged hardship, pain, and suffering; persistence and survival despite the ravages of time.

Endurance is also associated with hope and refers to the quality that does not surrender to circumstances or yield to, or cease to offer resistance when under pressure.

Going back to our scripture, what are these perfect results? They are the attainment, the realization that these works cannot be accomplished by a single act, but by accumulated labor and continued work.

Endurance doesn't have perfect results simply because you go through one or two tests in life. Endurance must be built up like a muscle. With every test, you pass, and crisis you endure, your endurance increases. Your faith becomes stronger, and the fruit of the Spirit begins to produce in you until you become mature and whole in your body, mind, soul, and spirit.

Trust

Trust was revealed when God put Esther through the biggest test of her life. God called Esther and placed within her a purpose. He trusted her with the destiny of the Jewish people. God placed Esther in a position of great responsibility. He knew Esther's heart and that she would accept, embrace, and complete the challenge. Esther trusted God and God trusted Esther.

Trust is assured reliance on the character, ability, strength, or truth of someone or something.

When you trust a person, you depend and rely on them. You have faith and hope in them and are confident they will not let you down. God trusts us in the same way.

Here are questions we should ask ourselves:

Can God trust me when tests come?

What qualities, good or bad, will be revealed?

Will I stand in the heat of the battle to accomplish God's destiny and purpose in my life?

Am I trustworthy?

"It is required (as essential and demanded) of stewards that one be found faithful and trustworthy." 1 Corinthians 4:2 (Amplified Bible)

Esther's Courage Was Tested

Courage is having the mental ability or moral strength to venture and perseveres danger, fear or difficulty; the willingness to confront fear, pain, danger, uncertainty or intimidation. Courage is acting in accordance to one's convictions, beliefs, especially in spite of criticism. (Merriam-Webster Dictionary)

As we continue in the book of *Esther 3:8* Haman presents his diabolical plan unto King Ahasuerus and begins to build his case against the Jews.

Then Haman said to King Ahasuerus, "There is a certain people scattered (abroad) and dispersed among the peoples in all the provinces of your kingdom; their laws are different from those of all other people, and they do not observe the king's laws. Therefore it is not in the king's interest to (tolerate them and) let them stay here. If it pleases the king, let it be decreed that they be destroyed."

Haman overwhelmingly won the approval of the king through deception and so the plans of the enemy were set in motion as a decree was written. In summary, here is what transpired between the king and Haman in *Esther 3:12-15.*

King Ahasuerus summons his scribes to write the decree as Haman proceeds to give instruction to all the king's chief rulers, governors, and officials of every person, and province to annihilate Jews. The decree included young, old, women and children. Included in the decree the Jews belongings were to be plundered and seized. The decree was issued hurriedly by couriers to every province and read publicly, in order that it be carried out on the thirteenth day of the twelfth month of Adar. During the same time, as Haman and the king sat down to drink wine, the city was thrown into chaos and confusion.

Whenever there is confusion, there you will find the enemy. Confusion is exactly what the enemy wanted to bestow upon the Jewish people. Confusion causes disorder affects the way you think and the way you react under pressure.

In chapter 4 of Esther, Mordecai learns of Haman's plot against the Jewish people. He proceeds to tear his clothes in mourning, putting on sackcloth and ashes. Mordecai went into the center of the city and cried out loudly and bitterly. Once each province heard the decree, there was great mourning among the Jews with fasting, weeping and wailing. Many others put on sackcloth and ashes like Mordecai.

Soon word reaches the palace and Esther is informed of the mournful condition of Mordecai as he stood at the king's gate. Queen Esther writhed in great anguish over the news of Mordecai.

The phrase "writhed in great anguish" in the Lexical Aids to the Old Testament is described as to writhe in pain as though you were in labor (of childbirth), to be afraid, to tremble, to shake and to be terrified.

These are powerful words that describe the agony and suffering Esther experienced. Esther being a Jew knew that Mordecai's act of tearing his clothes and putting ashes on his head was a sign of mourning, yet she didn't know why he was mourning. Esther sent Hathach, her personal eunuch out to Mordecai to learn why. Hathach returns to Esther with a copy of the decree ordering the destruction of the Jews. Esther now understands Mordecai's behavior.

Along with the decree, Mordecai sent back a request through Hathach, commanding Esther to go into the king to implore his favor and to plead with him for her people. Esther gives specific instructions to Hathach to go back to Mordecai and say to him that if she approached the king without being summoned she could be put to death.

Mordecai responds back to Esther with a powerful message. *"Do not imagine that you in the king's palace can escape any more than all the Jews." For if you remain silent at this, relief and deliverance will arise for the Jews from another place and you and your father's house will perish. And who knows whether you have not attained royalty for such a time as this?" Esther 4:13, 14 (Hebrew-Greek Key Study Bible)*

Mordecai confronted Esther with the truth forcing her to make a difficult decision. Would she allow her fear to rule her and remain silent? Could she find the courage to oppose the enemy? Could she face the difficult days that lie ahead knowing that her decision might bring sudden death?

Esther's courage was being tested.

God is calling his people to rise, be bold, brave, and fearless. We must face our enemy head-on with courage despite our fears.

"Be strong, courageous and firm: fear not nor be in terror before them, for it is the Lord your God who goes with you. He will not fail or forsake you." Deuteronomy 31:6 (Hebrew-Greek Key Study Bible)

Esther Was Called to Unite Her People

God gave Esther a strategy, found in *Esther 4:16* that would unite her people. Esther sends instructions to Mordecai saying: "In preparation for my audience with the king, do this: gather together (in agreement) all the Jews in Susa, and fast and pray for me. Intercede for me for three days and nights, abstain from all food and drink. My maids and I will join you at this time. And after the three days, I will go into the king and plead my people's case, even though it means breaking the law. And if I die, then I die."

This was the groundwork Esther and her people laid as she made plans to approach the king for direction, favor, and for God to move on behalf of her and her people.

As believers, there are no accidents or coincidences. God's timing is providential, and a heavenly response may be what is needed for an earthly situation.

Fasting and praying open the portal for spiritual growth, humbling us and causing us to focus on the answer and not the problem.

There was significance to the number of days Esther and her people fasted. God instructs us to fast for various reasons and time periods. In this case, three has biblical meaning that represents resurrection, perfection, and divine completeness.

Whenever a people or movement unite, there is power. When God's people unite in agreement with God and His Kingdom purposes, He moves.

"Again I say to you, that if two believers on earth agree (that is, are of one mind, in harmony) about anything that they ask (within the will of God), it will be done for them by My Father in heaven." Matthew 18:19 (Amplified Bible)

This is why it was so important for the Jewish people to agree and unite to fast and pray. Agreement is the act or fact of agreeing; having total consent in a situation in which everyone accepts the same terms, and has the same opinion.

Following the fast, Esther put on her royal robes while courageously explaining to King Ahasuerus, Haman's plot against her people. The Jewish people were saved. Haman was hanged on the same gallows that had been prepared for Mordecai. Esther received Haman's estate. *(Esther 7, 8)*

God used Esther to expose who and what was behind the plans of the enemy of the Jewish people. Instead of the enemies of the Jews gaining and executing power over them, the Jews gained mastery over their enemy. Thus, *the Jews struck all their enemies with the sword and destroyed them. And no enemy could stand against them. (Esther 9)*

"God is to us a God of deliverance and salvation, and to God, the Lord belongs escapes from death." (Setting us free) Psalms 68:20 (Amplified Bible)

Chapter 5
Warriors Be Ready

"Be Strong and courageous; do not tremble or be dismayed, for the Lord your God is with you wherever you go."
Joshua 1:9

Crossing Jordan

According to scripture, Joshua is considered one of the greatest military leaders to lead Israel into victory. His name means "Jehovah saves" and fittingly describes the character of Joshua's military career. He had the heart of a warrior and was filled with the spirit of wisdom *(Deuteronomy 34:9)*, yet he was capable of experiencing fear and defeat.

In *Joshua 1:2* God says to Joshua to arise (to take his place) which is an instruction to get ready to fulfill a command, somewhat like the military command attention.

A command can be a directive, an order, a demand, an instruction or a decree also.

When God commands your attention, He is commanding you to rise, take your place and move. No one can rise for you. No one can take your place, and accomplish what God has called you to do.

Let's go to *Deuteronomy 3*. God instructs Moses and the 40,000 valiant warriors of Israel not to fear the king of Bashan nor its people. God told Israel, for I have delivered him (the king of Bashan) and all his people and his land into your hand. This land they had fought for was to be divided between these valiant warriors, but their family and livestock were to remain in the land God had given them.

These valiant men could not rest in their land until they completed a commandment God gave them. That commandment was for them to go before their countrymen, the remainder of Israel, to protect them so they could possess the land the Lord their God had promised them beyond the Jordan River.

These valiant warriors were the same 40,000 men that crossed over Jordan before Israel. Equipped for the battle they marched into the desert plains of Jericho in *Joshua 4.*

In verse 22 of *Deuteronomy 3,* God speaks through Moses to encourage Joshua with these words *"Do not fear them, (the enemy he and Israel would have to face and conquer) for the Lord your God is the one fighting for you."*

As the time draws near for Joshua and Israel to cross the Jordan, once again God encourages Joshua and He confirms to Joshua and says: *"I will be with you; I will not fail you or forsake you."* then He commands Joshua *"to be strong, courageous, do not tremble (be fearful) or be dismayed for the Lord your God is with you wherever you go." Joshua 1:5, 9 (Amplified Bible)*

In order for Israel to be able to reach the land of promise they first had to overcome, triumph over and conquer many obstacles.

Overcoming Obstacles

Obstacles are anything that would hinder you from accomplishing a set goal or from reaching a direct destination; it can also be a complication that would make things very difficult; anything that would cause an obstruction to get in your way such as a barrier, blockage or wall.

The first obstacle Israel had to overcome was fear. For Joshua, giving into fear was not an option. If Joshua or Israel would have given in to fear, God's will, promise, plan, and future for Israel would not have been fulfilled and their rightful inheritance never claimed.

Crossing over the Jordan River is figurative to connote decision. Joshua and Israel were faced with life-changing decisions that had to be made. These decisions would not only affect Israel at that moment in time but for generations to come.

We as believers will have many fears to face and overcome, and life-changing decision that we will have to make. Our enemy would like for us to cower and give in to our fears because fear invokes failure and failure for us as believers is not an option!

The second obstacle that Israel had to overcome was the raging waters of the Jordan River. The rising water not only represented an obstacle but adversity that they would have to face.

Another faith-driven decision had to be made. And that decision was to be willing to trust God and step into waters that looked insurmountable to cross.

The first to step into the water were the priests who were to carry the Ark of the Covenant. Scripture says that the waters rose up in one heap and the priests were then able to stand in the midst of the Jordan on dry ground while the Israelites crossed over the Jordan into Canaan. *(Joshua 3)*

To cross over is to go beyond, to go forward and lead through. The principle meaning of this verb is the movement of something in relation to a stationary object.

The third obstacle they faced was that they had to be willing to cross a boundary line that would lead them directly into the enemy's territory. For Israel, this boundary line represented limits and a barrier that stood between them and their promise.

According to Unger's Bible Dictionary, the importance of the Jordan in scripture arises from it being a boundary line and a military frontier. To this day the Jordan River is the boundary line between the State of Jordan and the Israeli-occupied West Bank.

Battle Array

Joshua 4:11-13 "And it came about when all the people had finished crossing that the ark of the Lord and the priests crossed before the people. And the sons of Reuben and the sons of Gad and the half-tribe of Manasseh crossed over in battle array before the sons of Israel, just as Moses had spoken to them; About 40,000, equipped for war, crossed for battle before the Lord to the desert plains of Jericho." (Hebrew-Greek Key Study Bible)

Within these verses we find keywords and insight to help us understand the importance of being battle-ready.

It says that the sons Reuben, Gad, and Manasseh crossed over in battle array before Israel equipped for war and ready for battle.

If you are a believer then you are a son or daughter of God and are called to step into the waters of adversity, spiritually equipped and ready to cross over into territory that you will have to fight for like Israel. It means stepping over a boundary line that has been set and protected by the enemy. It will be unfamiliar territory, but it's the only way you can reach the other side.

Being spiritually equipped means arming ourselves with the sword of the spirit which is the Word of God that we use as an offensive and defensive weapon; standing in the authority and power of the name of Jesus and dressed in the whole armor of God for our protection. All are part of being equipped for war.

The conflict begins once you cross over into the enemy's territory. At this point, you must be committed and willing to lay down your life (your wants, your will) like a commissioned soldier.

Once you make a stand against the enemy he will be relentless in his attacks. But always remember *1 John 4:4 "Little Children, you are of God (you belong to Him) and have (already) defeated and overcome them (the enemy, anti-Christ), because He Who lives in you is greater (mightier) than he who is in the world. (Amplified Bible)*

Joshua 4:13 goes on to say that *40,000 men equipped for war, crossed over before the Lord to the desert plains of Jericho.*

These 40,000 men had experienced many wars during their journey across the desert. They were well trained and knew how to fight their enemy; armed with mighty weapons for battle, dressed in battle array and known as valiant warriors. They were the warriors chosen by the Lord to go before the sons of Israel to defeat and destroy the enemy.

They had no fear! They were men of destiny and filled with purpose.

Israel Tested

Throughout Exodus, Leviticus, Numbers, Deuteronomy and Joshua the scriptures tell how God tested Israel's faith as they wandered through the desert places of trials, hardship and faced death.

Even though God provided their every need for 40 years, still they continued to complain, disobey and walk in unbelief and test God. The number 40 in the scriptures represents trials, probations, and testings.

It is interesting that God led the people by the way of the wilderness out of Egypt *(Exodus 13: 18)*. Figuratively desert or wilderness symbolizes temptation, solitude, and persecution. Think about that!

Unger's Bible dictionary says; the deserts (waterless places) were supposed to be inhabited by evil spirits or occasionally visited by them.

Matthew 12:43 "Now when the unclean spirit goes out of a man, it passes through waterless places, seeking rest, and does not find it." (Hebrew-Greek Key Study Bible)

A waterless place is a home, residence, habitation or abode that is dry, parched, arid and dehydrated.

This was the condition of Israel. Spiritually they were dry and parched due to their rebellion, unbelief, and hardness of heart.

Unknowingly the people of Israel gave demonic spirits an open door that caused them to rise up against God. As long as they continued in defiance and judgment towards Moses they were spiritually vulnerable to the enemy.

1 Samuel 15:23a "For rebellion is as the sin of witchcraft, and insubordination is as iniquity and idolatry." (Hebrew-Greek Key Study Bible)

This is exactly why they continued to wander in the desert for 40 years circling the same mountains year after year. Time and time again God would prove Himself faithful to Israel performing miracle after miracle. Yet the generation that had left Egypt with Moses continued to complain, rebel, and walk in unbelief never to see their promised land.

They may have left the bondage of Egypt, however, ended up in greater bondage because of their sins against themselves and God.

Out of Egypt into the Promise Land

There is now a generation that the church and even the world sees as lost and incorrigible.

They are our children, grandchildren, the gang members, the drug addict, homosexuals, lesbians and the prostitute we see on the streets. They are the rejected, the lonely and the abused. They are the children that practice magic and hide in the dark places. They feel entitled, and respond with little or no respect for authority. They are a product of the moral and the spiritual deterioration of a fallen world. They express themselves in their dress and the scarring of their bodies which shouts rebellion, anger, and rage against authority, society, and God.

Isaiah 42:16 "And I will bring the blind by a way they do not know; in paths, they do not know I will guide them. I will make darkness into light before them and rugged places into plains. These things will I do, and I will not leave them undone."

Many in this generation are blind, groping in darkness and merely stumbling through life.

God knows their hearts and has placed a longing deep within their soul. They are searching and seeking for the truth yet don't know where to look or where to go; they are the blind leading the blind.

Too long has the enemy covered up and concealed the truth with distorted lies and blinded their minds. Too long the enemy has kept them in perpetual trauma, and acting out the dysfunctions in their lives.

But praise God, He is getting ready to break through the clouds of darkness and despair, and shine His light of truth so that they can finally see. He will take them by a way they have not known and gently guide them by His Spirit. He will take them from the dark places they have known and guide them into His light to protect them, sustain them and lead them gently on.

Their very character and personality will be changed, their hearts will be transformed, and the nature of Christ will show forth. God will heal them and mark them, protect them and surround them in His love, grace, forgiveness, and peace. He will not leave them undone or unprepared. He will train them for the battle to accomplish the purposes He spoke before the very foundation of the world.

God in His sovereign plan is going to raise them up out of the pits of hell itself and begin to build an army that will go in and possess the land.

Body of Christ, you as a believer, have been automatically enlisted in the Army of the Lord. This is not an option, it is a must for survival for you, your children, your grandchildren, and family members.

You accepting this command is the difference between a victorious life filled with power, purpose, and destiny versus living a life of defeat, destruction, and failure for you, you're family, and the generations to come.

In *Deuteronomy 11:31* Moses told Israel *"For you are about to cross the Jordan to go in to possess the land which the Lord your God is giving you, and you shall possess it and live in it." (Hebrew-Greek Key Study Bible)*

The Hebrew meaning for the word Jordan is to descend as to go downward or the watering-place, and carries in it the idea of passing from the old into the new. This is exactly where the Holy Spirit wants to take us, into a new season of revelation, a new direction and understanding of the enemy we will face.

This will mean moving out of the comfort and familiarity of Egypt and be willing to step into the waters of adversity where Leviathans are challenged. Looking at circumstances through the eyes of the Spirit.

The Holy Spirit wants to move us into a new level of warfare. Before that can happen, we must know who we are in Christ and what we have in Christ and accept the process of change.

A New Season of Change

Many of us are in a season of change and God wants to take us into a new direction that will ultimately bring us into new spiritual territory where we have not been before. Before these changes can take place, we must be willing to descend, go through and cross over our own Jordan.

- No longer can we stand still on the bank of the Jordan where it's safe and familiar.
- No longer can we be a spectator watching the battle from the sidelines.
- No longer can we stand in denial and think disobedience won't affect us.

We must be willing to step into the waters of adversity to go in and possess what is rightfully ours. Once that first step is taken then the battle officially begins. Not only will we have battles with the enemy, but we will also have to fight against our own flesh.

Every time God wants to move us into a new level of anointing, responsibility or position of ministry there will be a Jordan to cross, challenges to face, and giants to fight and defeat.

Giants to Fight and Defeat

A good example of this truth is the story of David and Goliath we find in *1 Samuel 17*. The Philistines, enemies of Israel, had ventured upon another inroad into the country and had taken up a firm position on the slope of a mountain, E`phes-dam 'min, between Shochoh and A-zek`ah, in western Judah.

Israel encamped over against them on the slope of a second mountain at a place called the valley of the Terebinth, and between the two camps laid a deep, narrow valley, which seemed destined as a field on which the warriors of either side might exercise their valor.

From the Philistine camp advanced a champion, Goliath of Gath who was 9'6" tall with a bronze helmet clothed in a Coat of mail weighing 5,000 shekels, (57 kg; 126lbs) and the iron blade of his speak weighed 6.8kg; 15lbs.

For forty days Goliath terrified Israel's army by challenging them, morning and evening to single combat with any of Israel's warriors. David had been sent into Israel's camp with provisions for his brothers who were warriors. David hearing the challenge of Goliath inquired the meaning of the giant's challenges. Upon being told, David offered to become Israel's champion and went forward armed with a sling and five smooth stones.

And David answered the scornful taunt of the giant saying:

"You come to me with a sword, a spear, and a javelin, but I come to you in the name of the Lord of hosts, the God of the armies of Israel, whom you have taunted. This day the Lord will deliver you up into my hands and I will strike you down and remove your head from you. And I will give the dead bodies of the army of the Philistines this day to the

birds of the sky and the wild beasts of the earth, that all the earth may know that there is a God in Israel and that all this assembly may know that the lord does not deliver by sword or by spear; for the battle is the Lord's and he will give you into my hands." 1 Samuel 17:45, 46 & 47 (Hebrew-Greek Key Study Bible)

David then struck Goliath in the forehead, slaying the fallen champion and cut off his head. When the Philistines saw that their champion was dead, they fled and were pursued by the Israelites, who slaughtered them.

When David stood face to face with the enemy, what was the first weapon he used? Truth.

David spoke truth to the enemy and declared the enemy's defeat. This is exactly what we are to do! We are to decree and declare the powerful truth of God's word.

Once truth is released it affects circumstances in the natural and spiritual realm. *Isaiah 55:11 "So shall My word be that goes forth out of My mouth; it shall not return to Me void (without producing any effect, useless), but it shall accomplish that which I please and purpose, and it shall prosper in the thing for which I sent it." (Amplified Bible)*

The word of God is like that single stone David held in his hand, appearing to the enemy to be of no great threat or significance. But in the hands of an almighty God that small single stone became a weapon of death for Goliath and sent the enemy running in fear for their lives.

The generations that we thought were lost will cross their Jordan, go into and possess their land. The Lord will bring them out of the slavery and the bondage of drugs, alcohol, sexual perversion, prostitution, gangs and witchcraft, and they will decree and proclaim *John 8:36 "Therefore if the Son makes you free, you shall be free indeed." (New King James Version)*

Chapter 6
Preparing for the Battle

"For Thou hast girded me with strength for battle."
Psalms 18:39

How Do We Prepare?

By putting on the whole armor of God that we find in *Ephesians 6:11-18 (Amplified Bible)*:

"Put on Gods whole armor (the armor of a heavy-armed soldier which God supplies) that you may be able successfully to stand up against (all) the strategies and the deceits of the devil."

Why do we need to put on God's complete armor? *Ephesians 6:13* answers that question: *"So we can resist the devil and stand our ground on the evil day (of danger) and having done all (the crisis demands), to stand." (firmly in our place)*

Let's break down the word resist to better understand what it means and how we can apply it.

Resist comes from two Greek words:

1. *Anti*: meaning opposite or against

2. *Histemi*: meaning to stand

When you put these two words together we find that we are to take an offensive and defensive stand against the enemy, and establish our position and refuse to be moved, pushed back, stand down, give up ground or territory gained or won in battle. It also is a military term that commands a soldier to strongly fight back all opponents.

As we resist the devil we are waging war against him and demonic spirits in the spiritual realm. When we battle in the spiritual realm we counteract the forces of darkness and deflect every fiery dart that the enemy sends. Spiritual warfare is declaring war against the devil. It is battling the unseen, the invisible supernatural enemy that you cannot see naturally.

The enemy schemes and plots precise attacks. He knows our weaknesses and the vulnerability of our flesh. His goal is to deceive, discourage, defeat, and destroy our testimony and ultimately take our life.

In the natural when soldiers are called into battle to defend and take back the land, what do they do first?

1. They call in strategic airstrikes to drop bombs on known locations that have been invaded by their enemy.
2. They send in ground troops with weapons designed to defeat and destroy the enemy.
3. They then take back and reclaim the land that the enemy has stolen.

We prepare by:

1. Applying the Keys of the Kingdom in warfare which are binding and loosing.

Matthew 16:19 "I will give you the keys to the Kingdom of heaven and whatever you shall bind on earth shall be bound in heaven and whatever you shall loose on earth shall be loosed in heaven." (Hebrew-Greek Key Study Bible)

2. By and through the Authority of the name of Jesus.

Matthew 28:18 "All authority has been given to Me (Jesus) in heaven and on earth." (Hebrew-Greek Key Study Bible)

3. By understanding and appropriating the power of the blood of Jesus.

Revelation 12:11a "And they overcame him because of the blood of the Lamb and because of the word of their testimony." (Hebrew-Greek Key Study Bible)

4. By relying on the Holy Spirit for power, direction and the gifts of the Spirit.

Acts 1:8 "But you shall receive power, after that the Holy Spirit is come upon you: and ye shall be witnesses unto me both in Jerusalem, and in all Judaea, and in Samaria, and unto the uttermost part of the earth." (King James Version)

5. By being established in the truth and immovable in our position.

2 Peter 1:12 "Therefore, I shall always be ready to remind you of these things, even though you already know them, and have been established in the truth which is present with you." (Hebrew-Greek Key Study Bible)

If we are established it means that we are firmly based, settled, secure and have established control over our enemy. When we are immovable we are fixed, permanently set and unyielding in attitude and purpose standing in our position of authority and power.

Luke 10:19 (AMP) "Listen carefully: I have given you authority (that you now possess) to tread on serpents and scorpions, and (the ability to exercise authority) over all the power that the enemy (Satan); and nothing will (in any way) harm you." (Amplified Bible)

God, Himself is the power, the source that is behind our authority, and that authority gives us access to His power.

Tactics and Strategy

Part of the training for warfare is to be able to recognize the tactics and strategy of your enemy.

What Are Tactics?

Tactics are skills of effectively organizing and using soldiers, weapons and equipment in battle. They are carefully worked-out steps taken to achieve a purpose and to help a fighting force achieve the best advantage during combat.

The tactics of the enemy are designed to intimidate you, confuse you, lie to you and exert force and pressure from without and from within. He works from an unseen realm, yet we feel the effects. They are there and they are real and are behind all that brings darkness. They are always maneuvering, watching, waiting and plotting for your surrender and your defeat. Our enemy shows no mercy and he has only one purpose and that is to destroy you in battle.

A great example of tactics used for the battle is found in the Old Testament in *Joshua 8*. God gave the task of taking Israel into the promised land to Joshua once Moses had died.

One of the cities Israel was to possess was Ai, a city filled with Canaanites. The Lord told Joshua, do not fear or be dismayed and to take all the people of war, which was Israel, and go up to fight with the King of Ai and its people.

So, Joshua chose 30,000 men, valiant warriors, and sent them out at night and commanded them saying, *'See, you are going to ambush the city from behind it and to be ready.'*

Joshua also took 5,000 men and set them in ambush between Bethel and Ai that was on the west side of the city. He then stationed people on the north side also and a rearguard on the west side of the city. Then Joshua said to them, *'then I and all the people who are with me will approach the city, they will come out to meet us and we will flee before them.'*

This was the tactic the Lord gave to Joshua because the Lord knew this would give Israel the advantage over the enemy.

Joshua knew that King Ai and his people would come out after them once they saw Israel fleeing from them. Little did King Ai realize that Joshua's intention all along was to draw them away from the city so Israel's valiant warriors could ambush them and take possession of the city.

The Lord told Joshua that He would deliver the enemy into their hands and that once they had seized the city to set it on fire. And all who fell that day by the hands of Israel were 12,000 along with their king and they raised a great heap of stones over the ruins of the city. God gave Joshua tactics and a strategy to defeat and destroy their enemy.

Like Joshua, God has provided us as believers everything we need to win the battle over our enemy. *(Ephesians 6)*

What Is A Strategy?

A Strategy is a carefully devised plan of action to move forces to the field of battle. A strategist specializes in developing and executing strategy.

As a soldier for the Army of the Lord, it is vital that we become strategists because our enemy is a fierce opponent who respects no one and has had thousands of years to perfect his strategy.

It is time that we rise up, and move into action against the forces of hell because the word tells us that *"The gates of hell shall not overpower or prevail against us, His church."* *Matthew 16:18*

The Apostle Paul was a great strategist. A prime example of his ability to execute a strategy against the forces of darkness was his missionary trip to Athens found in *Acts 17:16-34.*

His plan was to bring light to a city that was full of idol worship, pagan temples and every form of debauchery known to man. It was said that there were more statues of gods in Athens than in all of Greece put together and that in Athens it was easier to meet a god than a man (William Barclay; the daily study bible series).

Paul's first attack against the enemy was to maneuver himself into the synagogue of the Jews and then the marketplace where the philosophers would gather to converse, challenge and listen to the latest idea.

Paul then began to engage them as he boldly proclaimed the good news of Jesus and the resurrection. This strange new teaching Paul brought them sparked their curiosity so they took Paul to the Areopagus (Mars Hill) where their exclusive court was held.

God in His sovereignty made a way for Paul to be personally escorted into the camp of the enemy and it was there that Paul delivered his deadly blow. Paul knew who and what he was up against and never backed down.

Paul executed his strategy by speaking the truth, and it was that truth that moved the forces of heaven to stand against the forces of darkness. That action resulted in men and women believing.

"Some men joined him and believed, among whom also were Dionysius the Areopagite and a woman named Damaris and others with them." Acts 17:34 (Hebrew-Greek Key Study Bible)

Understand that we will be challenged by man and the forces of darkness, and within those challenges, God gives us the tactical maneuver needed and specific strategies that will ensure maximum support as you battle for yourself, family and the souls and lives of man.

If God did it for Paul, God will do it for you!

Chapter 7
Battles and the Areas of Conflict

"Who will prepare for battle"?

1 Corinthians 14:8b

A battlefield is a place, area or a frontline location where battles are fought, won and lost. Nearly everything we deal with in life has a spiritual aspect to it and influence behind it. In our battles and conflicts against forces of evil and darkness, there is a constant struggle of a life of faith.

Scripture locates the origins of spiritual warfare in the rebellion of Satan and his angels. It also affirms the hope of God's final victory over the forces of darkness through Jesus Christ's death, burial, and resurrection.

Spiritual warfare began in *Genesis 3:1*

"Now the serpent was more subtle and crafty than any living creature of the field which the Lord God had made. And he (Satan) said to the woman, can it really be that God has said, you shall not eat from every tree of the garden?" (Amplified Bible)

Satan came to Eve in the form of a serpent. This is interesting, because serpent, *"Nahash"* in Hebrew comes from the root word that means to hiss, a whisper of magic and spells. And isn't this what Satan does? He whispers lies of deception and discouragement to defeat you, manipulate you and bring you under his spell?

Satan's dialogue with Eve was a direct attack skillfully implemented by the tempter and the father of lies. Satan's strategy was then, now and always will be to twist what God has spoken and brought doubt concerning the truth.

Eve innocently engaged the serpent not understanding who he really was. Naively she listened to the lies of her enemy and the seeds of temptation, pride, rebellion and the lust of the eyes were forever planted in the mind of man.

Ephesians 4:27 tells us *"Leave no (such) room or foothold for the devil (give no opportunity to him)." (Amplified Bible)*

We must be watchful, fully engaged, actively looking for any impending danger or attack from the enemy.

Attacks

An attack is a direct attempt to overpower one by suddenness or violence of onslaught and to completely bombard the one being attacked. It also threatens with immediate capture and works forcefully against its victim. Attack is a verb and the enemy takes action to break down your resistance with repeated blows.

An attack from the enemy can be a series of problems in your family, your home, finances, your health and all kinds of coordinated efforts coming against you all at the same time.

These attacks are deliberate and executed precisely to pressure you, discourage you and persuade you to give up hope, to cripple you spiritually, emotionally and ultimately lose your faith and trust in God.

Don't give the devil an opportunity to get a foothold in any area of your life. Let me give you an example of what I mean by foothold.

Picture two teams playing against each other on a football field. Team A is the attackers (demonic spirits) and Team "B" is the believer who has the ball and he is running towards the goal. The attackers begin charging towards the believer with the intent of stopping him from advancing forward to execute the play and reach the goal line. The demonic spirits proceed to advance forward towards the believer's feet to trip him, causing him to fall and drop the ball.

The enemy positions himself to get a strong foothold in your life so you, the runner, cannot advance, move forward and reach your goal. If you feel spiritually attacked you must fight back, keep running and do not drop the ball. It is of the utmost importance that we see with spiritual eyes, understand with spiritual minds, and spiritually discern who and what is behind an attack.

Remember to stop, think, pray and listen. Are the attacks you are experiencing the results of your own decisions, or are they the result of an all-out attack against you?

Only God knows what is lurking behind the lines of the enemy, what his plans are when he will attack and what he will use to accomplish his destructive plans.

Within a battlefield, there are different areas or battles of conflict a soldier has to fight for and defend, and one of those areas we will forever be fighting for is our mind. Some of the greatest spiritual battles we will ever have to fight will be fought in the mind. The mind is the first area that the enemy attacks with his lies that bring confusion and where he works to deceive.

Oppression and Discouragement

One of the attacks the enemy uses is oppression.

Merriam-Webster Dictionary defines oppression as unjust or cruel exercise of authority or power; it is a sense of being weighed down in body or mind that can lead to depression.

The enemy uses oppression to hold you down, hold you back, and keep you from moving forward. Whenever you try to move forward in God, the enemy uses oppression as a weapon against you.

He will attack you with oppression to try and overwhelm you, pull you down with seemingly insurmountable issues, problems, and circumstances so that you break under the pressure.

Another oppressive tactic the enemy uses is discouragement.

When we become discouraged we lack the courage and the mental strength to persevere and withstand the attacks of the enemy. The enemy's goal is to break your spirit and for you to lose hope, heart and your faith.

We must remember that oppression begins with a thought but is rooted in a demonic spirit and he will use whatever and whoever he has to, to bring you down.

The enemy's goal is to hit you hard and try and remove you from the fight forever. Don't be counted as one who has either lost their way or given up the fight. *1 Timothy 1:19 says, "All those prayers are coming together now so you will do this well, fearless in your struggle, keeping a firm grip on your faith and on yourself. After all, this is a fight we're in." (The Message)*

Attacks of oppression and discouragement are designed to come against your unique weaknesses. The enemy will take full advantage of character flaws and turn them to work against you. The enemy watches you and waits for an opportunity to strike once a doorway of sin or disobedience has been opened.

Merriam Webster Dictionary defines a doorway as a means of access. A doorway is a way, an opening allowing the enemy access into the mind so he can plant oppressive and discouraging lies.

Once the enemy enters, there is a battle for your mind and you will have to fight against negative, destructive and evil thoughts. It is up to us to stop him and shut any doors that we have opened that are enabling him and giving him legal right to keep harassing us and infiltrating our thoughts.

2 Corinthians 10:5 instructs us on what we must do and that is to:

"Cast down imaginations, and every high thing that exalts itself against the knowledge of God, and bringing into captivity every thought to the obedience of Christ." (King James Version)

We take every thought prisoner just like you would a trespasser or a thief and lead it into captivity (confinement where it can't actively work) to obey Christ. In other words, we capture vain, evil, destructive, discouraging, oppressive thought of all kinds that are contrary to thoughts that are virtuous, pure, righteous, encouraging and of a good report.

Oppression will come against you from within your mind and thoughts, it will also come from the outside. How? By using people such as family member, loved ones, friends, and even strangers to come against you, accuse you, or attempt to discredit you and your ministry.

The enemy will attack you verbally with threats, attack you emotionally to discourage and intimidate you and attack physically to harm you and even try to kill you to stop the work of the kingdom.

Scripture gives us some great examples:

Acts 4:1-3

"And while Peter and John were talking to the people, the priests and the captain (who was in charge of the temple area and) of the temple guard and the Sadducees came up to them, being extremely disturbed and thoroughly annoyed because they were teaching the people and proclaiming in (the case of) Jesus the resurrection of the dead. So they arrested them and put them in jail until the next day because it was evening. (Amplified Bible)

Here Satan used religious people to attack Peter and John. Peter and John were full of the Spirit and moved in the power of God. These religious leaders were so angry that they went so far as to put them in jail to try and discourage them from proclaiming the truth and working miracles.

Another great example is found in *Acts 6.* Stephen was a man full of faith and of the Spirit of wisdom that went about performing great wonders and signs among the people.

Acts 6:8-12 scripture tells us that: Stephen was full of grace and power and was performing great wonders and signs among the people. But some men rose up and argued with Stephen and were unable to cope with the wisdom and the Spirit with which he was speaking. So they secretly induced men to wrongly accuse Stephen of speaking blasphemous words against Moses and against God and they dragged him away and brought him before the Council.

Stephen then begins to deliver the truth to the Council and High Priest and they were cut to the quick and began gnashing their teeth at him. These same men began to cover their ears and cried out with a loud voice and drove Stephen out of the city and began stoning him to death.

Satanic attacks are most frequent when you are battling from a frontline position. On the front lines, Satan hits hard and often, trying to drive back those brave fighters who are storming the gates of hell.

If you are a prayer warrior then you are storming the gates of hell and our enemy will do everything he can to interfere, delay and block your prayer life and you will be attacked.

Always remember that battles are fought and won through prayer.

If you are in any type of ministry, then you are on the front lines and will be attacked.

If you are a believer and stand up for the truth and stand true to the testimony of the Lord, then you will be attacked.

The Word and history verify the inescapable fact that attacks, persecution, and oppression come to believers. However, there is a special working of God's power for you.

That is why *I Peter 4:14* says *"If you are reproached for the name of Christ, blessed are you, for the Spirit of glory and of God rests upon you. On their part, He is blasphemed, but on your part, He is glorified." (New King James Version)*

God's glory and power always come to rest on those who are being persecuted, oppressed or attacked.

Nehemiah's Battle

Nehemiah's story begins in the service of Artaxerxes who was king of the Persian Empire in the year 446 BC. Nehemiah served as the king's cupbearer. This position could only be held by one who the king could trust. This position gave Nehemiah direct access to the king on a personal level.

In summary Nehemiah 1:1-3 tells us that Hanani, one of Nehemiah brothers, along with other men had just arrived from Judah. They came with information concerning the Jews who had escaped and survived the captivity and also gave him information about the condition of Jerusalem. They told Nehemiah that the remnant there in the province who had survived were in great disgrace and were suffering reproach and that the walls of Jerusalem were broken down and its gates had been burned with fire.

Once walls are broken down and gates have been destroyed they are no longer capable of protecting and keeping the enemy from coming in and causing destruction.

Many of us, if we are honest with ourselves and God, can see areas in our life where walls have been broken down and we are no longer able to resist the destructive attacks of the enemy. So, we find ourselves in the condition of *Proverbs 25:28 "Like a city that is broken down and without walls (leaving it unprotected) is a man who has no self-control over his spirit (and sets himself up for trouble)." (Amplified Bible)*

According to the Lexical Aids to the Old Testament, the word "control" in this scripture means to rule or restraint. It originates from the Hebrew word *"atsar"* which is a primary root word that means to enclose, self-close and hold back.

The Lexical of the Old Testament says that our spirit is the rational mind, as the seat of senses, affections, and emotions of various kinds. Examples would be "anger, bitterness, un-forgiveness, and lying.

When we allow sin to rule over an area of our life and we set no boundaries on our thinking, actions or carnal nature, we are allowing the enemy to breach our walls and tear down our gates. Walls that are meant to protect and gates that are designed to keep the enemy out.

Nehemiah 1:4 When Nehemiah heard these words, (the bad report) scripture tells us he wept, mourned, fasted and prayed before the God of heaven.

Nehemiah's prayer is a prayer of deep repentance for Israel and himself. He acknowledges their sin, wickedness and their lack of obedience in obeying God's commands. This prayer is a prayer all should pray and confess.

Nehemiah 1:5b-6a "O Lord God of heaven, the great and awesome God, who preserves the covenant and lovingkindness for those who love Him and keep His commandments, let your ear be attentive and your eyes open to hear the prayer your servant is praying before you day and night for your servants, the people of Israel."

Nehemiah 1:6b-7 "I confess the sins of the sons of Israel, including myself and my father's house, have committed against you. We have acted very wickedly toward you. We have not obeyed the commands, decrees, and laws you gave your servant Moses."

Nehemiah 1:10-11a "We are your servants and your people whom you redeemed by your great power and by your strong hand. O Lord, let your ear be attentive to the prayer of this your servant and to the prayer of your servants who delight in revering your name. Give your servant success today by granting him (Nehemiah) favor in the presence of this man." (King Artaxerxes). (Hebrew-Greek Key Study Bible)

Nehemiah goes before the king, presents his concerns for the state of Jerusalem and what he felt he needed to do. *(Nehemiah 2:1-4)* God answered Nehemiah's prayer and the king granted him permission to return to Jerusalem and repair the ruined walls. That isn't where the favor and the blessings ended.

God opened a door for Nehemiah that no man could. He found great favor with the King and was given great provision for the journey. These provisions included letters to all governors and leaders of all the provinces, and for the keeper of the king's forest to provide the timber and supplies needed to rebuild the walls and the gates.

Nehemiah was a man that was called by God to implement and carry out three vital tasks that would affect Jerusalem and God's people Israel. These tasks were: to rebuild the walls and the gates, to battle the enemy, and restore the people back to God.

When Nehemiah reached his destination, with a full military escort, he brought with him the full authority and the backing of the throne of Persia. News traveled fast to those who would oppose God's plan and God's man.

Always remember: If you determine to bring change in certain areas of your life, fulfill destiny and your purpose, witness to others, pray or minister you have the full authority of the Kingdom of God. You can proceed with full confidence knowing that the power of God is backing you up.

1 Corinthians 4:20 "For the kingdom of God does not consist in words, but in power." (King James Version)

Nehemiah 2: 9-10 explains what Nehemiah did with the letters that were given to him by the king:

"Then I came to the governors of the Provence beyond the river and gave them the king's letters. And when Sanballat the Horonite and Tobiah and Ammonite officials heard about it, it was very displeasing to them that someone had come to seek the welfare of the sons of Israel." (Hebrew-Greek Key Study Bible)

This is interesting to note that the name "Sanballat" means bramble bush or enemy in secret, and my, did he live up to his name. Many times, Israel had to go to battle against the Ammonites, Amalekites, Hittites, Jebusites and the Perizzites to either claim land what was promised to them by God or to reclaim it from their enemies.

These alien tribes represented the enemies that Israel had to fight against physically and spiritually. They were satanic agents sent to kill, steal and destroy God's chosen people, their land and to try to reclaim territory lost. This is always how the enemy works.

When we rise up to resist our enemies, Satan and his demonic spirits will also arise and oppose us. The enemy will use whoever and whatever he can to make life as difficult as he can for us. Again, I reinforce that you have God backing you up and you have His authority and the power to not only oppose the enemy but to destroy him.

Nehemiah 2:11-13, Nehemiah and the captain of the army that King Artaxerxes had sent to escort Nehemiah, finally reached Jerusalem. And on the third night, God woke Nehemiah up and spoke to his heart and gave him a plan on what to do for Jerusalem. So Nehemiah rose up and inspected all of the walls and gates that were broken down.

In *Nehemiah 2:17*, Nehemiah speaks to all who would take part in the rebuilding of the walls and gates and he tries to encourage the people by saying *"Let us rebuild the walls of Jerusalem that we may no longer be a reproach."*

The Lexical Aids to the Old Testament state the Hebrew extended meaning for the word "reproach" as shame; to be scorned. It is someone that is despised, discredited, or disgraced.

One of Satan's tactics is to raise up enemies that will stand up against you and stop the progress of rebuilding the walls of your heart and soul; the soul consists of the mind, will, and emotions. If the enemy can intimidate you and get you to back down, then he has won the battle.

This is exactly how the enemy used Sanballat, Tobiah, and Geshem the Arab. Satan used these men to mock, discourage and falsely accuse Nehemiah of rebelling against the king, but we see in verse 20 of chapter two how Nehemiah answers their accusations when he says: *"The God of heaven will give us success; therefore we His servants will arise and build, but you have no portion, right or memorial in Jerusalem."*

These men had no right to stand against God's covenant or His people. One of the accusers was a pagan, Sanballat the Horonite; one was a renegade son of Lot, an enemy though also a relative of Israel; and one was a total foreigner, a descendant of Ishmael. All three had no claim to the land or the promises of God to inherit the land.

What did Nehemiah encourage God's people to do? To rise up, assuming their upright and rightful position, rising from their complacency, rising from the ashes of destruction and despair. He encouraged them to take up arms and fight for what was rightfully theirs and rebuild.

Nehemiah had the heart of a warrior, determined to stand against all who would oppose him and the work that he and God's people had to do.

Nehemiah was a man of great faith and humility. He was a remarkable spiritual leader. God was the force, the power, and the strength behind this man.

Remember what Paul tells us in *Romans 8:31b "If God be for us, who can be against us"*

As we move to Nehemiah 4, we see how Satan used Sanballat as a verbal weapon to mock and ridicule the plans to rebuild. He was relentless in his quest to turn his brethren and the men of Samaria against Nehemiah and the Jewish people. However, despite the negativity, the discouraging words didn't stop them. They continued building the walls regardless of opposition. The walls advanced in height, strength and all the breaches began to be closed.

Nehemiah 4:7-8 "Now it happened, when Sanballat, Tobiah, the Arab, the Ammonite, and the Ashdodite heard that the walls of Jerusalem were being restored and the gaps were beginning to be closed, that they became very angry, and all of them conspired together to come and fight against Jerusalem and to cause confusion." (New King James Version)

Once more Nehemiah and God's people prayed and as a result, Nehemiah stationed the people behind the walls with their swords, spears, and bows. Even though they were in places that were exposed to the enemy they were willing to fight for what was rightfully theirs despite being filled with fear.

So once Nehemiah saw their fear, he rose up and encouraged the people: "*Do not be afraid of them; remember the Lord who is great and awesome, and fight for your brothers, your sons, your daughters, your wives, and your houses." Nehemiah 4:14*

All along God had been fighting for them. God frustrated the plans of their enemy and the people were able to return to the work of rebuilding the walls. (*Nehemiah 4:15*)

There are two weapons that the enemy will use to intimidate us within warfare. They are the weapons of fear and discouragement. It is vital to our ability to survive spiritually that we learn to conquer our fears and fight discouragement.

Fear and discouragement are emotional responses that we just can't give into or allow to control us.

It is our responsibility to stand, to station ourselves to defend and protect ourselves, our family and possessions. To guard and watch over the walls of our heart and soul.

We are to respond to fear with fearlessness, courage, boldness, and confidence, and attack any discouragement with encouragement and reassurance in knowing that God is fighting for us and with us.

Isaiah 42:13 "The Lord will go forth like a warrior, He will arouse His zeal like a man of war, He will utter a shout, yes, He will raise a war cry. He will prevail against His enemies."(Hebrew-Greek Key Study Bible)

Our enemies are also God's enemies, and God promises that: *No weapon that is formed against us (from the enemy) shall prosper and that we are more than conquers through Christ Jesus and remember that He has given us power over all the power of the enemy. Isaiah 54:17, Romans 8:37, Luke 10:19*

He also encourages us in *Isaiah 41:10 "Do not fear, for I am with you; do not anxiously look about you, for I am your God. I will strengthen you, surely I will help you, surely I will uphold you with My righteous right hand."(Hebrew-Greek Key Study Bible)*

Nehemiah 4:17-23 tells us that the people were then able to carry on the rebuilding of the walls and that they took their load with one hand doing the work and the other holding a weapon, and if they heard the sound of the trumpet, they were to rally together.

Nehemiah once again encourages the people when he says, *"Our God will fight for us."* So, they all remained vigilant and alert as they carried on the work by day and others guarded the work by night.

Even so, the attacks of the enemy did not stop, because in chapter 6 when Sanballat, Tobiah and the rest of their enemies found out that the walls of Jerusalem had been rebuilt and that no breach remained, they were furious. The only thing that remained to be done was to build the doors of the gates.

The enemy plotted once more to spread discouragement, and fear amongst the people, to lie against Nehemiah and accuse him of rebelling against the king. Despite who the enemy tried to use against Nehemiah and the people, God would intervene and protect them.

Nehemiah did more than rebuild walls and set up the doors of the gates. He restored the people and brought them from ruin and despair into a new walk with their God. He restored them into a condition of peace, security, and order.

Jerusalem was to be the place where God would dwell among His people which is symbolic of how God desires to dwell in the human heart and spirit.

Jerusalem, its walls and gates lying in ruin are a picture of a life that has lost its defenses and lies open to the lies and attacks of the enemy. It is a picture of the heart and soul that becomes vulnerable to being hurt, discouraged, fearful and hopeless.

The story of Nehemiah, Jerusalem, and the people are symbolic of the recovery that is available through Jesus Christ.

Only Jesus can take you from breakdown to breakthrough and from ruin to restoration.

Spiritual Walls

Just like the ancient cities that needed protection from enemies, we as individuals need protection from daily temptations of the world, and also the attacks of our enemy Satan and his demonic spirits.

Spiritual walls are built to function as fortifications to protect the treasures that are on the inside of us. These treasures are our heart and our soul.

We must continually build and strengthen our spiritual walls because the enemy will use his entire arsenal to penetrate and tear down our walls of defense.

Be aware that the enemy will test the strength of your walls to see if your gates are closed and protected. He is a relentless enemy who is forever searching and seeking to find you're weakest and the vulnerable places to attack.

The Purpose of Walls

Many cultures would build walls around their cities, castles, and temples for protection. They were intended to separate the outside influences from inside the walls, establishing boundaries.

Built within these walls were towers providing vantage points for those standing guard, to warn the city of danger in time of war.

These walls also had gates that allowed guards to monitor and control those who came in and went out. Still, if an enemy ever breached their walls or gates imminent destruction, pillage, most likely captivity or even death would occur.

Even though physical walls served to protect the cities from human enemies, they can also be illustrative of the boundary between God's people and the world, Satan, and his demonic spirits.

Building Blocks Needed For Spiritual Walls

Building walls in ancient times consisted of laying one brick or stone at a time, creating layer upon layer until the required height, width and strength were accomplished. Before the building could begin, it was vital to the strength, balance, and durability of the walls that they first lay a firm foundation on which to build.

Figuratively speaking, it is the same for us as we build our spiritual walls. Laying a foundation will guarantee you strong, resilient, and sturdy walls that will stand against the attacks of the enemy.

Your foundation must be built on God's word, as it tells us in *Luke 6:47-49.*

"For everyone who comes to Me and listens to My Words (in order to heed their teaching) and does them, I will show you what he is like. He is like a man building a house, who dug and went down deep and laid a foundation upon the rock; and when a flood arose, the torrent broke against that house and could not shake or move it, because it had been securely built or founded on a rock. But he who merely hears and does not practice doing My words is like a man who built a house (walls) on the ground without a foundation, against which the torrent burst and immediately it collapsed and fell, and the breaking and ruin of that house was great." (AMPC)

God's word will not only be the strength of your foundation, but it will also act to set clear walls and boundaries for you and for the enemy. God's word will supply every weapon to fight with and every building brick or stone needed to build. His word will keep and protect you.

As we begin to understand the importance of conforming to the Word of God and as we yield to the transforming power of the Holy Spirit, we will see that they work together simultaneously to bring deep inner changes.

God's Word can dig deep into our soul to transform and renew our mind, will, and emotions.

Romans 12:2 "Do not allow this world to mold you in its own image, be transformed from the inside out by renewing your mind. As a result, you will be able to discern what God wills and whatever God finds good, pleasing, and complete." (The Voice)

Healing begins in the mind, which changes our thinking and enables us to process our thoughts through the truth of God's Word. Your thinking becomes clear. The changing power of God's Word begins the building process. Our self-will adheres to God's will, thus, a spiritual wall is built that will protect you.

Our emotions and reactions become stabilized, healed and whole and another spiritual wall is built.

Another component you will need to build your spiritual walls is prayer.

Ephesians 6:18a. "Pray at all times (on every occasion, in every season) in the Spirit, with all (manner of) prayer and entreaty." (Amplified Bible)

The manner in which you pray is the method and type of prayer that you use.

1 Corinthians 14:4a tells us that *"One who speaks in a tongue (in the spirit) edifies himself." (Hebrew-Greek Key Study Bible)*

The Greek word for edify is *"oikodomeo"* and it is a combination of the Greek word *"oikos"* which means a house and the word *"domeo"* which means to build. (Lexical Aids to the New Testament)

So when we pray in the Spirit, we are building our walls and our house in a spiritual sense. We are edifying ourselves for spiritual profit and advancement. We are doing what *Jude 1:20* instructs us to do and that is to *"Build yourselves upon (the foundation of) your most holy faith (continually progress, rise like an edifice higher and higher), pray in the Holy Spirit." (Amplified Bible)*

1 Corinthians 14:14 reads *"For if I pray in a tongue, my spirit prays, but my mind is unfruitful." (Hebrew-Greek Key Study Bible)*

This is not only praying in the spirit but also praying to God in your normal voice as if you were talking to a friend. It's being fruitful in your understanding of what you are praying.

There are also prayers of appeal, pleas, petitions, requests, supplications, healing, deliverance, and prayers that decree and declare God's word; to use as a weapon against the enemy; to stand on, build on, intercede with, and to increase your faith.

Prayer is the mortar that holds together and supports our spiritual walls.

Ephesians 6:13-18 "Be prepared. You're up against far more than you can handle on your own. Take all the help you can get, every weapon God has issued, so that when it's all over but the shouting you'll be on your feet. Truth, righteousness, peace, faith, and salvation are more than words. Learn how to apply them. You'll need them throughout your life. God's Word is an indispensable weapon. In the same way, prayer is essential in this ongoing warfare. Pray hard and long. Pray for your brothers and sisters. Keep your eyes open. Keep each other's spirits up so that no one falls behind or drops out." (The Message Bible)

Fighting in the Trenches

In the natural world, there are specific military tactics used for warfare that have been proven to be successful throughout the centuries. One of these warfare tactics used during the First World War is called Trench Warfare.

The Encyclopedia Britannica states that Trench Warfare is warfare in which opposing armed forces attack, counterattack, and defend from relatively permanent systems of trenches dug into the ground. The opposing systems of trenches are usually close to one another. Trench warfare is resorted to when the superior firepower of the defense compels the opposing forces to "dig in."

The soldiers who fought in the trenches during the First World War were on the front lines. They were the first line of defense. They were to some degree protected from the enemy's small arms fire yet vulnerable to everyday enemy shell fire. There also was an everyday threat that the enemy could break through their protective barriers resulting in great injury even death. It was not uncommon for soldiers to be in the front line trenches fighting for weeks on end with little rest or replacements. Being in the front-line was extremely dangerous.

Trench warfare is a grueling form of warfare in which you dig in to avoid losing any ground. As believers, we are to dig in for the long haul because we are fighting on the front lines and must take an opposing position against the enemy. The front line is where the bullets, bombs and the flaming missiles are sent by the enemy. *Ephesians 6:16 "Take up the shield of faith with which you will be able to extinguish all the flaming missiles of the evil one." (Hebrew-Greek Key Study Bible)*

In World War I the use of barbed wire was a decisive tactic used by the German military forces. Their goal was to disrupt, delay and slow down infantry who were fighting on the battlefield. Slowed down by wire obstacles, soldiers were much more likely to be hit by the enemy's concentrated fire or possibly deliberately maneuvered into a trap known as the killing zone.

The Killing Zone

This killing zone on the battlefield is covered entirely by defensive fire and initiated by the defensive unit leader who would order the most devastating weapon to be engaged. Who does that sound like to you? Satan will attack you from every angle he can and attempt to maneuver you into his killing zone.

If you become trapped in the killing zone, your spiritual life will cease to move forward and you will become an easy target for the enemy to hit. He will hold you captive to discouragement and bind you to despair. His purpose is to destroy your effectiveness and your ability to fight your way through. The enemy's killing zone is the dark night of the soul. What does the dark night of the soul mean? That the enemy has destined for your destruction.

Barbs

Beyond the front lines of the battle lies barbed wire fences the enemy uses for fortification and are constructed as obstacles for any opposing force.

When a soldier in the natural world is wounded in battle either by weapons or barbed wire fences they must be cared for immediately. These wounds must be cleaned, disinfected, all bullets and shrapnel removed, and bandaged. If these wounds are not cared for properly they will become infected and impact the soldier's strength and his ability to fight, even threatening his life.

As we battle forward on the front lines, we will have to confront the barbed wire fences.

Barbed wire fences represent words that cut deeply into the heart. The enemy will use whoever and whomever he can to speak words to hurt, discourage, wound and tear you down. He then uses those wounds as access points to infiltrate, construct and fortify a defensive position in your heart and soul.

Wounds of the heart and soul affect the way you think, how you filter and process words, and how you will respond. If wounds of the heart and soul are not addressed and dealt with, they will distort, alter and influence the way you feel about yourself emotionally and spiritually. They affect the way you respond to situations, circumstances, tests, and trials. Wounds affect how you think and relate with people. They determine how you relate to God and those in authority, and the way you fight in the spiritual realm.

"Words kill, words give life; they're either poison or fruitful, you choose." Proverbs 18:21 (The Message)

The strategy for fighting in the trenches is to defend your position by aggressively opposing the enemy. We do that by and through the Word of God on our lips. It is how we take back territory that we formerly occupied. We are to offensively pursue the enemy until he is completely defeated and removed from every area he has occupied, dominated and controlled until the victory is won.

Bleeding the Army White

In war, there is a known strategy that is called bleed the army white. Through constant bombardment opposing forces cause their enemy many casualties, rendering them unable to fight back.

This is a great analogy of what our enemy tries to do to us as we battle him in the spiritual realm. He is out for blood and his sole purpose is to repeatedly attack us until we are weak, vulnerable and ineffective. He wants you to *bleed out,* which is a medical term they use for soldiers that are severely wounded in battle and die from blood loss.

Leviticus 17:11 "For the life of the flesh (soul) is in the blood." (Hebrew-Greek Key Study Bible)

The Hebrew word translated here as life (*nephesh*) means soul. It literally reads *"the soul of the flesh is in the blood."*

100

When a soldier is severely wounded and loses too much blood, he will need a blood transfusion in order to live. A blood transfusion involves taking blood from one person (the donor) and giving it to someone else.

Just as blood transfusions save the lives of dying soldiers in the natural, the blood of Jesus gives us a spiritual transfusion that saves our soul and infuses our spirit with resurrection life and fills us with the supernatural power of the Holy Spirit.

Your body will not function properly without enough healthy blood. Your heart pumps blood through blood vessels that reach every organ and tissue in the body. It is the blood flowing through our body that provides oxygen to every part. We can live without food for weeks and without water for days, but if we are cut off from oxygen, we will die within minutes.

As a rich supply of oxygen is vital to our physical health, so is a rich supply of the Holy Spirit essential for us to have a healthy spiritual life.

The difference between a physical blood transfusion and a spiritual transfusion is that the spirit will live for eternity, but our physical body will eventually die.

Physical DNA

DNA comes from our parents and is the blueprint of inherited genetic molecular material for our unique identities. Our DNA comes from the combination of genes contributed by each of our biological parents and is found in our white blood cells. Genes are made up of molecules, DNA, inside the nucleus of living cells that are strung together in such a way that the series carries information: that information determines what we look like on the outside, how we work on the inside, our inherited characteristics, and traits. Physically we are the product of our parents, ancestors, and ultimately Adam.

In Genesis 1:26a, 27 "Then God said Let Us (Father, Son, Holy Spirit) make man in Our image, according to Our likeness. And God created man in His image, in the image of God He created them; male and female He created them." (Hebrew-Greek Key Study Bible)

Adam and Eve's DNA was both physically and spiritually pure at the time of their creation.

God created within them not only the ability to reproduce themselves. He also gave them free will (the ability to make choices) and instructed them to rule over, to cultivate and keep all that He had made. He then placed them in the Garden of Eden. *(Genesis 2)*

But once Adam and Eve allowed sin to enter their hearts, their DNA was changed, polluted and cursed.

Their physical bodies took on death due to sin, *(Romans 5:12; 6:23)* the deeds and lusts of the flesh and mind all of which refer to the fallen nature found in man *(Ephesians 2:3; Galatians 5:19)*. Sin became a natural inclination and was downloaded in our *DNA* as a result of Adam and Eve's sin.

An example of our inherent and instinctive sin nature that we all must deal with is expressed by Paul in *Romans 7:19, 20 & 23. "For I fail to practice the good deeds I desire to do, but the evil deeds that I do not desire to do are what I am (ever) doing. Now if I do what I do not desire to do, it is no longer I doing it (it is not myself that acts), but the sin (principle) which dwells within me (fixed and operating in my soul). But I discern in my bodily members (in the sensitive appetites and wills of the flesh) a different law (rule of action) at war against the law of my mind (my reason) and making me a prisoner of the law of sin that dwells in my bodily organs (in the sensitive appetites and wills of the flesh."* (Amplified Bible)

Spiritual DNA

Before we can receive spiritual DNA, the seeds of God's word must be planted into the soil of our heart and soul. Before these seeds can grow and multiply they must be watered and fertilized by the Word of God through the power of the Holy Spirit.

Integrated and imprinted within every word of the Bible is Jesus and it is through Him that we receive spiritual DNA. Spiritual DNA is His life, His light and His power that resides in us once we receive Him.

We are not born through blood (natural conception), nor of the will of the flesh (physical impulse), nor of the will of man (that of a natural father), but of God (that is, a divine and supernatural birth – we are born of God – spiritually transformed, renewed, sanctified). *(John 1:13)*

When we received the gift of eternal life through our acceptance of Jesus Christ as our Lord and Savior, God breathed new life into us bringing a spiritual birth. *(John 3:16)*

At that moment we received heavenly DNA into our souls in the form of the Holy Spirit and our spirit man became alive. Now we possess two sets of DNAs. One physical set from our earthly parents and one spiritual from our heavenly parent, God.

With God's DNA inside of us, God's divine nature and life begin to grow, and we begin to resemble our heavenly father as evidenced by our new Christ-like attitudes, motivations, perspectives, desires, goals and our new godly value system.

No Man's Land

There is ground between warring armies referred to as 'no man's land'. It is a land where uncertainty, doubt, and insecurity dwell. It is an area you haven't had the courage or strength to advance in, face, fight for, overcome or control. This land lies unprotected, unclaimed and fully exposed to the assaults of the enemy. It's a place that has become barren, unfruitful and void of life. This 'no man's land' is also known as the land of past failures. If you choose to remain in the land of past failures it will only prove to feed your fears.

Scripture tells us in *1 John 4:18b* that *"Fear has torment,"* and this is why we cannot give in to our fears. If we do, the enemy will use torment as a weapon against us. Torment is torture. With torture comes pain, suffering, sorrow, agony, and anguish of mind.

If we don't fight, advancing beyond our failures, we will be captive to our past. Being a captive only helps the enemy advance further into our land. Once he has taken the ground that he needs he will move in for the kill.

Don't allow the enemy to torture you with fear. Don't allow him to torment you with your past. Don't allow the enemy to take you captive as a casualty of war.

God wants to take your failures and turn them into triumphs. He wants to turn defeats into victories and lead you out of captivity into freedom and breakthrough.

Land Mines

There will be times in 'no man's land' that you run into land mines. Land mines are weapons of mass destruction. They are known for being hidden killers; weapons of mass destruction in slow motion, the perfect soldier which never sleeps or misses.

A land mine is an explosive device with a detonating system designed to explode as weight or when pressure is placed upon it. Land mines are buried just far enough below the surface of the ground to go unnoticed. Unlike other weapons, land mines are designed to maim, mutilate, disfigure, and seriously wound a soldier.

Let us now look at land mines from an emotional and spiritual perspective.

Emotional land mines are the destructive thoughts, actions, and reactions that lie just below the surface of our feelings. These emotional land mines can lie in wait undetected and inactive until one day the pressures of life trigger a destructive response.

Destructive responses will manifest as uncontrolled anger, hate, resentment, bitterness, rejection, un-forgiveness, etc., trapping us and linking us to the pain. Traps are laid by the enemy to catch us off guard, to stop us from advancing forward into forgiveness, keeping us from successfully fighting through 'no man's land'. If we don't remove these destructive land mines, the results will be contamination of the heart and the soul (mind, will and emotions) ultimately affecting our character, personality and behaviors.

Our ability to fight our way through no man's land is dependent on how healthy and mature we are emotionally and spiritually. We cannot allow ourselves to be led by painful feelings or controlled by explosive emotions, because like a land mine, once triggered, our emotions explode propelling shrapnel in every direction leaving you and those closest to you severely wounded, shocked, and traumatized.

Most have experienced traumatic events leaving them holding onto emotional baggage. What if a soldier in the military today marched into battle carrying extra weight or baggage in his backpack? How could he run, fight or maneuver effectively on the battlefield? At first, he possibly could hide the pain of the extra weight. However, slowly the weight would begin to wear him down and he would have to lay the extra baggage aside.

God did not create us to live in 'no man's land' or to constantly dodge land mines. His will is that we are emotionally and spiritually healthy. If we say that the past doesn't have any effect on us, then we are in denial. Some of us rationalize our problems to suppress and bury the pain and memory.

Trauma is a difficult or unpleasant experience that causes someone to have mental or emotional problems. The effects of trauma are the wicked and hurtful things we think, say, and do. *Psalms 139:23, 24 "Search me (thoroughly), O God, and know my heart (the totality of man's inner or immaterial nature), try me and know my thoughts! And see if there is any wicked or hurtful way in me, and lead me in the way everlasting." (Amplified Bible)*

God knows the hidden hurts within you that you are unable to see. When you ask Him to search your heart, you are asking Him to uncover the nature of your heart, your innermost feelings, desires, thoughts, emotions, senses, and will.

He will expose those dark areas of your past and bring them to light at the right time. The Holy Spirit will come alongside you and guide you into all truth, and that truth will set you free. *(John 16:13 & John 8:31, 32)*

What Is The Process of Resolution?

Resolution is the act of finding an answer or solution to a conflict, problem; the process of resolving.

First, you are no longer a product of your past. *2 Corinthians 5:17 "If any person is (engrafted in Christ (the Messiah) he is a new creation (a new creature altogether); the old (previous moral and spiritual condition) has passed away. Behold, the fresh and new has come." (Amplified Bible)*

To be in Christ means we are in union with (consecration to) the same end – one in mind, purpose, and life. It is to be one in spirit with God when joined to Him in consecration as in *1 Corinthians 6:17 "But he that is joined unto the Lord is one spirit."* Our spirit becomes alive, active, and sensitive to His spirit. This means you become a recipient of the work that Christ accomplished on the cross. You can look at your past and what you have experienced through the truth of who you are today, as opposed to who you were.

Second, our soul (the mind, will, and emotions) are delivered from darkness, chaos, our fallen nature, and the control of Satan. The old outward and inward sin no longer have power over us because we've been translated (through salvation) into the kingdom of God *(Colossians 1:13).*

We are dead to sin but alive to God in Christ Jesus. Our sin has passed away, forgotten by God, and must never be resurrected to once again rule and reign in our mortal body. Nor should we be used as an instrument of unrighteousness. Instead, we are as instruments of righteousness to God *(Romans 6:11-13).*

Consider the word instrument. In order for a musical instrument to be played at its highest level and capability, it must first go through fine-tuning.

A violin; which is a bowed stringed instrument that has four strings tuned at intervals. Believe me, if those strings are not fine-tuned precisely, the sound will be squeaky and offensive to the listener's ears. The musician will find it impossible to perform at their highest level of effectiveness.

Spiritually speaking, all of us will go through the process of fine-tuning.

The resolution of our past is a process through the ongoing work of the Holy Spirit. If we are to be used as an instrument of righteousness in the hands of the master, being effective in life and ministry, we must be willing to go through the process of fine-tuning in our heart and soul. This allows our spirit man to progress, and advance to wholeness and maturity.

God created us in His image and gave us feelings and emotions. These are to be brought under submission to God's Word, His will and the power of the Holy Spirit.

Don't be a soldier who is counted among those who are wounded in battle and unable to fight their way through and out of 'no man's land'.

Chapter 8
Wars - Warfare – Battles

"Blessed be the Lord, my rock, who trains my hands for war, and my fingers for battle."

Psalms 144:1

Scripture describes the methods Israel implemented in preparing for war. Although they recognized the importance of preparation, scripture stresses that Israel's trust was in God rather than military might. They were to seek God first before entering battles and they were to employ God's strategies in warfare.

Warfare is military operations between enemies. It is fighting a war with the intentions of weakening or destroying your enemy. Battles are the actual fighting, combat and the encounters we have with the enemy.

In warfare, battles are fought on different fronts, for different reasons, and will deviate in degrees of intensity as the battle progresses. This truth plays out in the world's military battles and also in the spiritual battles we face daily as believers.

As we look around our world today we see our world in conflict and in the midst of *wars and rumors of wars* as *Matthew 24:6* tells us *"And you shall hear of wars and rumors of wars: see that you be not troubled: for all these things must come to pass, but the end is not yet."*

Battles are raging causing bloodshed, death, destruction and displacement of people from their homes and birth land.

Warfare operations are strategized by demonically manipulated and controlled men who slaughter the innocent; all in the name of their gods. In reality, they are blinded by hate, greed, lust for power and the darkness that is within.

The bible is full of stories that tell of the warfare and battles God's people were called to fight and win.

Let's examine one of those battles recorded in *Genesis 14.*

First War Recorded

What was the first war ever recorded in scripture? It was a war between four eastern kings and five southern kings. It is interesting to note that Shinar (Babylon, modern-day Iraq) initiated the first war mentioned in the bible. *Genesis 14:4* tells us that the southern kings were controlled by and served King Chedorlaomer, King of Elam.

In the thirteenth year, the southern kings decided to rebel against the King of Elam which caused a war. This war was a power struggle to control a strategic land bridge between Mesopotamia and Egypt. Whoever controlled the land bridge, controlled who came in or out. In response to the southern king's rebellion, Chedorlaomer, King of Elam and the kings that were with him waged war against the Rephaim, Zuzim's, Emims and Horites tribes.

These four eastern kings were mighty warriors who defeated everyone that opposed them. They seemed incapable of being defeated or conquered and were powerful enough to oppose every military force they fought against. Little did they realize that soon they would battle against not only Abram, (Abraham) who would become the father of a nation, but the Israelites who were destined to be God's chosen people.

Genesis 14:8, 9 & 10 says that the king of Sodom and the king of Gomorrah, along with their allies dug in for an all-out battle in the valley of Siddim, which was full of tar pits. The kings of Sodom and Gomorrah thought that these tar pits would work to their advantage, but the pits ended up being the very thing that helped to defeat them. The eastern kings won the battle and took all the goods that were in Sodom and Gomorrah along with Lot, Abram's nephew, and Lot's possessions.

Once Abram heard that Lot was captured, he took three hundred and eighty of his trained men, born in his house to rescue him. Abram's strategy was to divide his forces, employ a march and surprise the enemy by attacking them at night from various positions. This plan required great faith in God. Comparing the number of men that the four eastern kingdoms had to the 318 men and allies Abram had, his plan looked impossible.

However, what seemed impossible for others, became a possibility to Abram. Abram's greatest weapon was his faith. Faith in a God of immeasurable possibilities. So Abram moved forward in his faith. He and his men defeated their enemy, pursuing them until the victory was complete, rescuing Lot, his family and all of his possessions.

Giants In The Land

Who were these southern kings? Three of them were known as giants; the Rephaim, Zuzim's and the Emims.

Rephaim was a race of aboriginal or early inhabitants who lived east of the Jordan in Ashterothkarnaim *(Genesis 14:5)* and in the valley of Rephaim southwest of Jerusalem according to *Joshua 15:8.* They associated with other giant races, as the Emim and Anakim *(Deuteronomy 2:10, 11)* and also the Zamzummin *(Deuteronomy 2:20).* It is probable that they were all of the same stock, being given different names by the different tribes who came in contact with them.

Deuteronomy 3:11 "For only Og king of Bashan was left of the remnant of the Raphaim. Behold his bedstead was an iron bedstead; it is in Rabbah of the sons of Ammon. Its length was nine cubits and its width four cubits by ordinary cubits. " That's about 13.5 feet long by 6 feet wide (9 cubits x 4 cubits wide).

Dake's Anointed Reference Bible has this to say about the giants in the Old Testament:

The phrase remnant of the giants in Deuteronomy 3:11; Joshua 12:4 and 13:12 should be a remnant of the Rephaim, for there were many nations of giants other than the Rephaims who filled the whole country trying to contest God's claim on the Promised Land. They are listed in scripture as Kenites, Hittites, Perizzites, Canaanites, Jebusites, Hivites, Horims, Avims, Caphtorims, and the Kadmonites all found in the book of Genesis and Joshua.

Dake goes on to say that *all these giant nations came from a union of the sons of God (fallen angels) and daughters of men after the flood. Beings of great statue, some of them even had 6 fingers on each hand and 6 toes on each foot and carried spears weighting from 10 to 25 lbs. (2 Samuel 21:16-22.) Goliath whom David slew wore a coat of amour weighing 196 lbs. and was about 13 feet tall (1 Samuel 17:4-6).*

One of Dake's theories concerning the giants is that they built the pyramids of Egypt, the giant cities of Bashan, and other huge monuments of construction. Yet, this will most likely remain an unsolved mystery.

The revelation we have of giants in scripture gives us a true picture of what Greek mythology tries in vain to give. The bible is an accurate account and divinely inspired book. Mythology is the outgrowth of traditions, memories, and legends telling of the acts of the supernatural fathers and their giant offspring – the perversion and corruption in the transmission of facts concerning these mighty beings. These giants were partly of supernatural origin making it easy for men to regard them as gods.

The historian and Jewish priest, Flavius Josephus who lived between A.D. 37 and died sometime after A.D. 100, wrote this about the giants:

Many angels of God accompanied with women, and begat sons that proved unjust, and despisers of all that was good, on account of their own strength.... These men did what resembled the acts of those whom the Grecians called giants (Antiquity Book I, chapter 3). Again, he says, "There was till then left the race of giants, who had bodies so large, and countenances so entirely different from other men, that they were surprising to the sight, and terrible to the hearing. The bones of these men are still shown to this very day. (Ant. Book V, chapter 2)

Nephilim Giants

Another tribe of giants the bible describes is the Nephilim found in *Genesis 6:4*. They were a race that came to dominate the antediluvian (pre-flood) world, and are referred to in the bible as the heroes of old, men of renown. They reportedly were the children born to the *sons of God* by the *daughters of men*, and are described as giants. Egyptian records of about 2000 B.C. also record their existence. Nephilim means fallen, a tyrant, or a bully.

Within every major culture of the ancient world, the astonishingly consistent story is told of gods who descended from heaven and materialized in bodies of flesh. From Rome to Greece and before that, Egypt, Persia, Assyria, Babylonia, and Sumer. The earliest records of civilization tell of the era when powerful beings are known to the Hebrews as Watchers, and in the book of Genesis as the B'nai ha Elohim (sons of God) mingled themselves with humans, giving birth to part-celestial, part-terrestrial hybrids known as Nephilim.

In the Greek Septuagint, Nephilim was translated as *Gigantes* (gigantic). This translation seems to have been used because the Nephilim later became known as giants to the Hebrews and confirmed by the Israelite spies that were sent into Canaan to spy out the land *(Numbers 13:33)*.

The Reformation study bible says this concerning the Nephilim in *Genesis 4.*

They were giant like mighty men, the offspring of the demonic tyrants (verse 2 note) and they filled the earth with violence (Numbers 13:32). The Hebrew root means: "to fall", and may suggest their fate in (Exodus 32:20-28)

An English theologian by the name of George Hawkins Pember, wrote a book called Earth's Earliest Ages, circa 1876, and discusses the Nephilim:

The influences of the Spirit of God are even now in process of withdrawal, as He prepares for that departure from earth which will leave it open for Nephilim, sevenfold worse than those who formerly dwelt in it, to enter, and for a short season to work their will upon the human race; Then will all the Nephilim, who are yet at liberty, be among men, and will quickly make them feel the meaning of that awful utterance, "Woe to the inhabiters of the earth and of the sea! For the Devil is come down unto you, having great wrath, because he knoweth that he hath but a short time.

He also interprets the prophecy of Jesus Christ that we read in *Matthew 24* that says the end times would be a repeat of the "the days of Noah," and that the final and most fearful sign heralding the Lord's Second Coming would be the return of the Nephilim, the appearance upon the earth of beings from the Principality of the Air, and their unlawful intercourse with humans.

Genesis 6:11-12 & 17 describes how corrupted, the violent and wicked man had become on the earth and says that the Lord was sorry that He had made man.

"Now the earth was corrupt in the sight of God, and the earth was filled with violence. And God looked on the earth and behold, it was corrupt; for all flesh had corrupted their way upon the earth... And behold, I, even I am bringing the flood of water upon the earth, to destroy all flesh in which is the breath of life, from under heaven; everything that is on the earth shall perish."

The Lexical Aids to the Old Testament states the Hebrew word for corrupted as *shachath.* This word is used in scripture to explain moral corruption, to act perversely, to violate and to kill. The words *their way* describes the manner in which they lived, the path they chose, their way of life and most often refers to the actions and behavior of men. If we go back to verse 4 of *Genesis 6,* the Nephilim (giants) were part of the corruption, wickedness, and evil being done upon the earth. They were also one of the reasons God brought judgment to what He had made. *(Genesis 4:5-7)*

Throughout the Old Testament, if you do a study on the giants, you will see that God always condemned them and never showed them any mercy; God's judgment was final!

Anakim Giants

The Anakim also is known as giants lived in the south, near Hebron and were the descendants of a giant named Anak. This Anak was a son or grandson of a giant named Arba, from which the ancient city of Hebron was originally called Kiriath Arba or also known as The City of Arba because Arba was the greatest man among the Anakim tribe.

This tribe was so tall that the weak-kneed spies said: *"We are like grasshoppers to them (Numbers 13:33)."* Joshua drove the three remaining sons of Anak out of Hebron in his first battle, but they eventually reoccupied the city of Hebron while Joshua was waging war against the Canaanite cities in the North. Caleb later retook Hebron and killed the three giants.

The Philistine giant Goliath who was nine feet tall was a descendant of the Anakim along with his brother Lahmi "whose spear had a shaft like a weaver's rod."

In Easton's bible dictionary it says that in the days of Abraham *(Genesis 14:5 & 6)* the Anakim inhabited the region known as Edom and Moab, which was east of Jordan. They were probably a remnant of the original inhabitants of Palestine before the Canaanites, a Cushite tribe from Babel, and the same race as the Phoenicians, and the Egyptian shepherd kings. Their formidable warlike appearance as described by the spies sent to search the land filled the Israelites with terror. They seem to have identified them with the Nephilim, the giants of the Antediluvian age *(Genesis 6:4; Numbers 13:33)*. There were various tribes of Anakim *(Joshua 15:14)*. Joshua finally expelled them from the land, except a remnant that found refuge in the cities of Goza, Gath, and Ashdod *(Joshua 11:22)*.

Emim Giants

The *Emim* were also giants and known as a warrior tribe and were conquered by King Chedorlaomer and his allies. This took place around the time of Abram (Abraham) and they lived east of the Jordan. *Deuteronomy 2:10 & 11* says the Emim lived there (Moab) formerly, a people as great, numerous, and tall as Anakim. Like the Anakim, they are also regarded as Rephaim, but the Moabites call them Emim.

Scripture tells us of another giant whose name was Sihon, king of the Amorites in *Amos 2:9.*

"Yet it was I who destroyed the Amorite before them, though his height was like the height of Cedars and he was strong as the oaks; I even destroyed his fruit above and his root below."

Apocryphal Writings On the "Watchers and the Giants,"

Note Some of what these Apocryphal writings say is true and correct, but at the same time, much of it is false and historically inaccurate. This information is to be treated as interesting but fallible historical documents.

The Book of Enoch

Who was Enoch?

Enoch is first spoken of in *Genesis 5* and it appears that he was important enough to be included in the descendants of Adam.

Enoch lived before the flood when human beings were living hundreds of years longer than we do today. In *Genesis 5:21-24* is a written account of Enoch the man and patriarch. Scriptures tell us that *"Enoch lived 365 years, and that he walked with God, and he was not; for God took him."*

The book of *Jude1:14-15* refers to Enoch as a Prophet and this extract in the New Testament is said to have been a part of an apocryphal book containing various prophecies given by Enoch.

However, it is nowhere mentioned that Enoch either wrote down prophetic utterance or had them recorded. It is more likely that Enoch merely spoke these words, and the Lord preserved them through Jude. *Hebrews 11:5 "That by faith, Enoch was translated directly to Heaven."*

Many of the legends about Enoch were written in ancient times and collected in several long passages, the oldest being *The Book of Enoch.*

Let me be very clear concerning this ancient book. There are conflicting beliefs in the authenticity of the apocryphal Book of Enoch. Some believe in its historical value and others deem it as uninspired and not the authoritative Word of God.

The Book of Enoch was found among the *Dead Sea Scrolls* discoveries and is comprised of over one hundred chapters written in Aramaic. Whoever collected and hid the scrolls considered them to be a vitally important text. Even more fascinating is the fact that texts about Enoch were also discovered at Qumran and one of those texts is called *The Book of Giants.*

Who Were The Watchers?

The first *Book of Enoch* states that the Watchers are angels who were dispatched to Earth to watch over the humans, but 200 of the Watchers acted in disobedience and soon began to lust for human women. Their leader Samyaza instructs the Watchers to procreate with humanity.

The offspring of these unions are the Nephilim, savage giants pillaging the earth and endangering humanity. It goes on the say that *Samyaza* and his associates taught their human charges arts and technologies such as weaponry, cosmetics, mirrors, sorcery, and other techniques that would otherwise be discovered gradually over time by humans, not foisted upon them all at once.

Eventually God allows a great flood to rid the earth of the Nephilim, but first sends Uriel, an angel, to warn Noah so as not to eradicate humanity. The Watchers are bound in the valleys of the Earth until Judgement Day.

In section 1 of the Book of Enoch entitled *Enoch's Journeys Through The Earth And Sheol*, the author states in chapter XIX – *And Uriel said to me, (Enoch) "Here shall stand the angels who have connected themselves with women and their spirits assuming many different forms are defiling mankind and shall lead them astray into sacrificing to demons*

Another account of the Watchers is recorded in a book called *The Book of Jubilees which* says; *The Watchers are the sons of God (Genesis 6) sent from heaven to instruct the children of men; they fell after they descended to Earth and cohabited with the daughter of men – for which act they were condemned (so legend reports) and became fallen angels. But not all Watchers descended: those that remained are the holy Watchers, and they reside in the 5th heaven. The evil Watchers dwell either in the 3rd heaven or in Hell. (A Dictionary of Angels)*

Within the writings of the *Dead Sea Scrolls*, they also found an account of the so-called Watchers, and they wrote "In The Days Of Jared," *Jared being the son of Mahalaleel and the father of Enoch (Genesis 5:15-20) Two hundred Watchers, descended on Ardis, the summit of Mount Hermon – a mythical location equated with the triple peak of Jebel-esh-Sheikh, (9,200 feet) placed in the most northerly region of ancient Palestine.*

The book goes on to say: *In Old Testament times its snowy heights had been revered as sacred by various peoples who inhabited the Holy*

Land; it was also the probable site of the Transfiguration of Christ when the disciples witnessed their Lord transfigured before them.

On this mountain the Watchers swear an oath and bind themselves by mutual imprecations, apparently knowing full well the consequences their actions will have both for themselves and for humanity, and it is a pact commemorated in the name given to the place of their fall, for in Hebrew, the word Hermon or Harem translates curse.

In time, each of the 200 Watchers took an earthly spouse. These unions produced children of extraordinary size, who quickly devoured the world's food. To satisfy their enormous appetites, the angel-children roamed the earth, slaughtering every species of bird, beast, reptile, and fish. Finally, the ravenous creatures turned on one another, stripping flesh from the bones of their fellows and slaking their thirst in rivers of blood. As this wave of destruction washed over the earth, the anguished cries of humankind reached four powerful archangels – Uriel, Raphael, Gabriel, and Michael – who upon orders from God enacted swift retribution.

Uriel descended to earth to warn Noah of a coming deluge, advising him to prepare an ark to carry his family and a menagerie of creatures to safety. Raphael then fell upon the leader of the Watchers, bound him hand and foot, and thrust him into eternal darkness. Next, Gabriel charged with slaying the dissenter's offspring encouraged the monstrous angel-children to fight one another. Finally, Michael trussed up the remaining Watchers, forced then to witness the deaths of their progeny and condemned them to eternal torment.

Only then did the heavens open up and wash away the last traces of the destruction that the fallen angels had wrought, as recounted in the Dead Sea Scrolls.

The Book of Giants

Here is what the *Book of Giants* says concerning Enoch, the Watchers, and the giants:

Chapter 15 1 And He answered and said to me (God speaking to Enoch in a vision), and I heard His voice; "fear not" Enoch, thou righteous 2 man and scribe of righteousness: approach hither and hear

My voice. And go, say to the "Watchers of heaven", who have sent thee to intercede for them: "you should intercede" for men, and not men 3 for you: wherefore have ye left the high, holy, and eternal heaven, and lain with women, and defiled yourself with the daughters of men and taken to yourselves wives, and done like the children 4 of the earth, and begotten giants (as your) sons? And though ye were holy, spiritual, living the eternal life, you have defiled yourself with the blood of flesh, and, as the children of men, have lusted after flesh and blood as those also do who die 5 and perish therefore have I given them wives also that they might impregnate them, and beget 6 children by them, that thus nothing might be wanting to them on earth. But you were formerly 7 spiritual, living the eternal life, and immortal for all generations of the world. And therefore I have not appointed wives for you; for as for the spiritual ones of the heaven, in heaven is their dwelling. 8 And now, the giants, who are produced from the spirits and flesh, shall be called evil spirits upon the earth, and on the earth shall be their dwelling. Evil spirits have proceeded from their bodies; because they are born from men and from the holy watchers is their beginning and primal origin; 10 They shall be evil spirits on earth, and evil spirits shall they be called. (as for the spirits of heaven, in heaven shall be their dwelling, but as for the spirits of the earth which were born upon the earth, on the earth shall be their dwelling) and the spirits of the giants afflict, oppress, destroy, attack, do battle, and work destruction on the earth, and cause trouble; they take no food, but nevertheless hunger and thirst, and cause offenses. And these spirits shall rise up against the children of men and against the women because they have proceeded from them.

Chapter 16 1 From the days of the slaughter and destruction and death of the giants, from the souls of whose flesh the spirits, having gone forth, shall destroy without incurring judgment – thus shall they destroy until the day of the consummation, the great judgment in which the age shall be. 2 Consummated, over the watchers and the godless, yea, shall be wholly consummated, "and now as the watchers who have sent thee to intercede for them, who had been aforetime in heaven, say 3 to them: You have been in heaven, but all the mysteries had not yet been revealed to you, and you knew worthless ones, and these in the hardness of your hearts you have made known to the woman, and through these mysteries women and men work much evil on earth. 4 Say to them, therefore: "You have no peace."

The Book of Jubilees

There is also an ancient text called *The Book of Jubilees* that is said to have been written in the 2nd century B.C.E. and is an account of the Biblical history of the world from creation to Moses. It is believed to have been written in Hebrew and a version of the Pentateuch, and parts of which later became incorporated into the earliest Greek versions of the Jewish Bible, the Septuagint.

This is part of an account of Genesis titled *The Fall of the Angels and their Punishment; The Deluge Foretold* (v. 1-20; cf. Genesis vi. 1-12*).

And it came to pass when the children of men began to multiply on the face of the earth and daughters were born unto them that the angels of God, saw them on a certain year of this jubilee that they were beautiful to look upon; and they took themselves, wives of all whom they chose,, and they bare unto them sons and they were giants.

And lawlessness increased on the earth and all flesh corrupted its way, alike men and cattle, and beasts and birds and everything that walked on the earth, all of them corrupted their ways and their orders, and they began to devour each other, and lawlessness increased on the earth and every imagination of the thoughts of all men (was) thus evil continually.

And against the angels whom He had sent upon the earth, He was exceedingly wroth, and He gave commandment to root them out of all their dominion, and He bade us to bind them in the depths of the earth, and behold they are bound in the midst of them and are (kept) separate.

And their fathers were witnesses (of their destruction), and after this, they were bound in the depths of the earth forever, until the day of the great condemnation when judgment is executed on all those who have corrupted their ways and their works before the Lord.

I repeat: This information is only to be treated as interesting, but fallible historical documents.

Chapter 9
The Assaults of the Enemy

"Behold, I have given you authority to tread upon serpents and scorpions, and over all the power of the enemy, and nothing shall injure you."

Luke 10:19

Assault defined

An assault is a violent physical attack by a military force; a mental, emotional, or a spiritual head-on charge (attack) against you.

The enemy's assaults come against you like a battering ram against a wall, or door causing a breach. They are relentless, persistent in their pursuit. Their goal is to destroy your defenses, break you down, overrun you and take you as spoils.

The main target is your heart. The enemy knows who you are and the power you possess, and he fears you.

In the garden, the enemy came after God's creation, man. Why? Because we were made in God's image and created to carry His love in our hearts. For Satan, that is reason enough to assault a believer.

Fragmented Heart

Many believers are walking around with what I call fragmented hearts. Hearts that have been broken, damaged, and are unable to withstand the stress and strain of the assaults of the enemy. This, in turn, has caused our hearts to become disconnected, lacking coherence.

Coherence is being logically consistent, stable; the ability to think through rationally and form a healthy relationship with God and with people. It takes bringing all the fragmented parts back together to make the heart whole and complete again. It's like the glue we use to mend broken pieces back together so it can function the way it was originally created and designed to do.

An example of fragmentation is a bone that's been broken.

We know that there are different degrees of fractures or breaks that occur in a bone, and the degree of the fracture is determined by the severity of the blow to that bone.

What can happen to us in the natural with the fragmenting of a bone can, and does, happen to our heart. The heart is the seat of our emotions and affects our thoughts, judgment and our ability to cope with the assaults of the enemy.

We have all experienced a broken heart. Sadly, some of us are walking around with hearts that are still broken and bleeding.

The natural heart generally functions for seventy to eighty years without maintenance or replacement. During this time, it beats around one hundred thousand times a day, roughly forty million times a year – almost three billion beats in a lifetime. Now that's a miracle!

The heart pumps two gallons of blood per minute, adding up to more than one hundred gallons per hour, through a vascular system that is long enough to wrap around the earth two times- over sixty thousand miles. The heart is like a nuclear power plant, generating five thousand times more energy than the brain and is why the heart has been called the center of our being. Even more amazing, it has its own nervous system that is called the brain of the heart. This heart brain has more than forty thousand nerve cells. Science reveals that the natural heart is also able to feel, sense, learn and remember. How do we know that?

Scientists have observed that the heart sends emotional and intuitive signals to the brain and body that help to govern our lives. How does it do that? Through a chemical called Atrial Peptide, nicknamed "the balance hormone;" it works by regulating our brain's functions, keeping it balanced, and motivates our behavior.

Psalms 147:3 informs us *"He (Jesus) heals the brokenhearted and binds up their (our) wounds." (Curing their pains and their sorrows) (Amplified Bible)*

And this is a fact, yet we have to do our part in the healing process. What is our part? Reading and meditating on God's word, depositing and hiding God's word in your heart.

There are four areas of the brain that information travels through in order for it to penetrate the frontal lobe of our brains. The frontal lobe is where decision-making takes place, which determines appropriate emotional responses. For healing to take place in our hearts and in our thinking, we must fill our minds with the word of God.

Romans 12:2 "Do not be conformed to this world, (this age), [fashioned after and adapted to its external, superficial customs] but be transformed (changed) by the (entire) renewal of your mind (by its new ideals and its new attitude) so that you may prove what is the good and acceptable and perfect will of God, even the thing which is good and acceptable and perfect [in His sight for you].(Amplified Bible)

The word of God is not just written words on paper, it is powerful, living, active words that are performing spiritual surgery on your brain and your heart; eventually affecting your thoughts, your words and your actions.

When we study, pray and apply God's word to our lives His word penetrates the depths of our heart and our soul, ultimately healing our brokenness and restoring wholeness.

God's word will heal our emotions and the memories that are embedded in our subconscious mind that we don't realize are there. Part of this healing process will also affect those negative and hurtful responses and the emotional trauma that torments us and keeps us stuck in pain and bound to un-forgiveness and anger.

Proverbs 14:30 "A tranquil heart is life to the body, but passion (anger, indignation) is rottenness to the bones."(Amplified Bible)

Proverbs 14:10 "The heart knows its own bitterness."

When our hearts are fractured, and if we are harboring bitterness, resentment, or un-forgiveness we give the enemy an open invitation to come in, rob us of our peace, steal our joy, and kill our relationship with God.

How does the enemy do that? By attacking our emotions to accentuate the hurt and the traumas we have experienced. The enemy works to twist our thinking and distort our view of God, people, life, and circumstances. He attempts to keep the trauma we've experienced alive so we act out of the hurt through the condition of our heart.

Remember the instruction in *Proverbs 4:23* "*Keep and guard your heart with all vigilance and above all that you guard, for out of it flow the springs of life.*" *(Amplified Bible)*

Our heart is the target of the assaults of the enemy and we must learn to protect it, defend it, and shield it against his attacks.

How do we guard our heart?

I Peter 5:8-9 "Be of sober spirit (well balanced, temperate), be on the alert (vigilant and cautious at all times). Your adversary, the devil, prowls about like a roaring lion (in fierce hunger), seeking someone (to seize upon) to devour. But resist him, firm in faith (against his onset-rooted, established, strong, immovable, and determined), knowing that the same experiences of (identical) sufferings are being accomplished by your brethren (the whole body of Christians) who are in the world." *(Hebrew-Greek Key Study Bible)*

If Peter is telling us to 'be on the alert' concerning our 'adversary, the devil,' then we as believers must know how to resist him and learn to stand firm even though we are suffering.

Remember *Ephesians 6:13 "Therefore, take up the full armor of God that you may be able to resist in the evil day, and having done everything, to STAND FIRM."*

How do we stand firm against the enemy? We stand confident, secure, and immovable. We do not walk around vulnerable, unaware, or unprotected. We are to be fixed, ready to counteract on the day of battle.

We must battle for our hearts, our mind, emotions, and our physical body.

As I have said before, the enemy's constant bombardment is aimed directly for your heart, because he knows who you are, he fears you and knows just how fierce you can be.

Binding the Brokenhearted

In *Isaiah 61:1* is a prophecy spoken by Isaiah the Prophet through the direction of the Holy Spirit and this is what it says: "*The Spirit of the Lord God is upon me, because the Lord has anointed me to bring good news to the afflicted; He has sent me to bind up the brokenhearted, to proclaim liberty to captives, and freedom to prisoners."*

Good news in this scripture means: to be fresh, to announce, and to tell glad tidings.

This is exactly what the Lord wants you to take to heart. He wants to bring you a fresh, anointed word that will bind up the wounds that have been afflicted upon you and heal your broken heart.

When we encounter a wound physically we need what is called wound closure and wound care.

The medical approach to healing an open wound, obtaining quick healing, with less risk of infection and scarring is to:

1. Clean the wound.

2. Apply ointment to the wound

3. Bind up the wound with bandages, stopping the bleeding and protecting the wound for proper healing and closure

Thinking of this, what does your spiritual and emotional heart look like?

Do you see traces of past wounds that were never properly treated or healed?

Do you see years of scarring and deformity?

Perhaps you see wounds that are still open, hurting, bleeding and have become infected through time?

Once you assess the damage, you will begin to understand why things seem to affect us emotionally and spiritually. For some, these wounds go very deep, and through time thinking has become distorted and our hearts become hardened, resulting in a disconnection from emotions feelings.

Avoiding More Wounds

The first step in protecting your heart is to do as *James 4:7* instructs us to do. *"So submit to (the authority of) God. Resist the devil (stand firm against him) and he will flee from you."(Amplified Bible)*

What does it mean to *resist* the devil? The word resist is an action word. Resist means we stand firm and exert force in opposition to the enemy. We are to fight back against the devil and his forces and refuse defeat. He will run away if you don't back down.

Remember: The Lord is fighting *with* us. Our position in this is not to step back and expect Him or someone else to fight our battles for us.

We can be a mighty weapon in the hands of God and we can hit the heart of the enemy instead of the enemy hitting and wounding our heart.

We resist the enemy as instructed in *Luke 10:19 "Listen carefully: I have given you authority (that you now possess) to tread on (serpents and scorpions, and (the ability to exercise authority) over all the power of the enemy (Satan); and nothing will (in any way) harm you."(Amplified Bible)*

The word tread means to have absolute mastery over, to step or walk on or over, to beat or press with the feet, to trample.

When we tread on the enemy we are stepping or putting a foot on his neck to render him completely helpless. We are subjecting him to the dunamis power and authority that Jesus has given unto us. We render the enemy powerless with the Word of God, the truth and through the power of the Holy Spirit. See *Psalms 91:13*

When we resist and tread upon the enemy we build impenetrable barriers to protect and shield. He cannot stand against us.

The Blood of Jesus

Another way we resist the enemy is found in *Ephesians 1:7*

"In Him, we have redemption (that is, our deliverance and salvation) through His blood, (which paid the penalty for our sin and resulted in) the forgiveness and complete pardon of our sin, in accordance with the riches of His grace."(Amplified Bible)

We overcome the enemy by and through the blood of Jesus. We apply the blood of Jesus by bringing the blood of Jesus between us and the enemy.

The blood of Jesus is alive and powerful. It guards, protects and shields us as a believer. The blood is our atoning cover and is still as powerful today as it was the moment that it flowed from His veins.

It is up to us to remind the enemy and give testimony of what the blood did and continues to do for us. The blood of Jesus redeems, cleanses, justifies and sanctifies a believer. Through the blood of Jesus, all our sins are forgiven. Through the blood of the Lamb (Jesus), there is, always and forever will be victory, power, and authority to overcome the enemy.

"And they have overcome (conquered) him by means the blood of the Lamb, and by the utterance of their testimony." Revelations 12:11a (Amplified Bible)

Chapter 10
The Enemy Revealed

"You shall have no other gods before me."
Exodus 20:3

Mythology

In this chapter, we will explore some of the ancient mythological beliefs, idol worship and demonic influence that plagued Israel.

Mythology is the study of the myths, old traditional stories, legends and beliefs, especially ones concerning supernatural beings and those relating to a people's gods, heroes and to their origins.

We know that at the root source of every idol, their worship, and rituals that man has conceived, lies the influence of a demonic spirit. Study the mythology of different cultures, and you will see that they include the legends of their history, their religions (which include their gods), the rituals and practices they performed, and their creation stories and heroes.

These mythological gods, idols, and rituals were believed to have great powers and were handed down from generation to generation for thousands of years. As they worshiped their idols they were unknowingly worshiping demons, and behind these demons is an entire hierarchy of Satan's kingdom.

These demonic forces have always worked to deceive man. To blind them from the truth, binding them to the tradition of their ancestors, and masquerading as the one true god. The truth is that they are the same demons following one generation to another, manifesting to man under a different name or god.

What Are Demons?

They are unclean, evil and disembodied spirits that seek to operate through the possession of a human body or animal. They are the masters of deception and influence men to worship idols and other gods.

While searching for information concerning demon worship in the Old Testament and their understanding of how demons affected their lives, I discovered the ancient Jewish myth of a demon spirit that they called Lilith.

Her origin lies in Babylonian demonology and migrated to the world of the ancient Hittites, Egyptians, Israelites and the Greeks. She appears in the Bible, as a wilderness demon shunned by the prophet in *Isaiah 34:14 "And the wild beasts of the desert will meet here with howling creatures (wolves and hyenas) and the (shaggy) wild goat will call to his fellow; the night monster will settle there and find a place of rest." (Amplified Bible)*

The Lexical aid to the Old Testament describes the "hairy goat" as Satan or hairy demon that was worshiped.

The Greek-Hebrew bible states: *And the desert creatures shall meet with the wolves, the hairy goat also shall cry to its kind, yes, the night monster shall settle there and shall find herself a resting place.*

Isaiah's passage lacks specifics in describing Lilith, but it locates her in desolate places and links Lilith directly to the demon of the "Gilgamesh Epic," which is an ancient Sumerian poem found on a tablet at Ur and dated from approximately 2000 B.C.E.

Ur was an ancient city located in southern Babylonia and was the city where Abraham of the bible once lived. The Gilgamesh epic according to Biblical Archeology appears to be the earliest written mention of the name Lilith.

There is also a terracotta plaque called the Buren Relief (named after the founder) in the ruins of Babylon and has been identified as the demoness, Lilith. Here she is identified as the goddess of love and war. She is also known as Inanna to the Sumerians and Ishtar to the Akkadians.

Scholars say that this is the first known pictorial representation of Lilith.- biblicalarchaeology.org

The picture shows a woman wearing a horned crown and has the wings and feet of a bird. She is flanked by owls (associated with Lilith) and stands on the backs of two lions, which are symbols of the gods Inanna and Ishtar. According to Mesopotamian myths, the demoness Lilith, flew at night, seducing men and killing pregnant women and babies. The King James Bible (*Isaiah 34:14*)) describes the Lilith as the screech owl, and notice Lilith's feet resemble owl claws.

Lilith resurfaces in the Dead Sea Scrolls that were found at Qumran. It seems that the highly ritualistic Jewish sect called Essenes, lived at Qumran on the shores of the Dead Sea and were responsible for producing the Dead Sea Scrolls, dated from around 250 B.C, to 68 A.D. The Essenes were engrossed with demonology, and Lilith is mentioned in the *Song for a Sage*, a hymn possibly used in their exorcisms.

The hymn says, "And I, the Sage (a Hebrew title of respect for a wise and highly educated man) sound the majesty of His beauty to terrify and confound all the spirits of destroying angels and the bastard spirits, the demon, Lilith..., and those that strike suddenly, to lead astray the spirit of understanding, and to make desolate their heart."

In the Babylonian Talmud, they also wrote about female demons. The Babylonian Talmud, is a combination of legal discussions, instructions, and tales of great Rabbis and contains meditations on Bible passages passed down through the generations. It also contains the written and oral law, legends, and was compiled between 500A – 600 C.E.

The Babylonian Talmud's Lilith refers to older Babylonian images and describes her as having long hair and wings, and reinforces older impressions of her as a Succubus that is a demon that appears in female form who had sex with men while they were sleeping. This same demonic spirit comes in the form of a male for women and is called Incubus.

There is also an ancient rabbinic myth concerning Lilith. The legend states that Lilith was the first wife of Adam, and was created by God from the filth and sediment, but Adam was created by the dust from the ground. Lilith was a failed mate and refused to submit sexually to him from an inferior position below. Soon she rebelled against her husband unleashed her long hair and shouted the holy ineffable name of God. She supposedly supernaturally sprouted wings and fled from the Garden of Eden.

I think you will find this very interesting. Yet, once again I want to make it very clear that this is mythological teaching and belief. I do not believe this is true.

The more popular version of her legend states that Jehovah then sent three angels to return her to Adam, finding her in the midst of the Red Sea, but she refused to return with them. She chose instead to mate with angels (watchers) and is said to have become the mother of demons. Because she refused to go back with the angels to Adam, they, in turn, cursed her and that every day 100 of her seed would die. God then created Eve to replace Lilith, but once she found out that Eve was to replace her, Lilith resolved that she would visit Eve's children in childbirth and kill those who were not protected.

Most versions of Lilith legends, including the Jewish Kabbalah, which is a branch of Jewish mysticism, thought to have originated in the 13th century and active today still believe in her. The myth goes on to say that Lilith returned to the garden under the title of Serpent as the Serpent of *Genesis 3*. The legend goes on to say that she got her revenge by causing Adam & Eve to fall.

Below you will see one of the famous scene paintings by Michelangelo called "The Temptation and Fall" from the Sistine Chapel Ceiling. This painting depicts Adam, Eve and Lilith as a woman serpent.

The spirit behind Lilith represents everything that is evil, lustful, seductive, immoral, debased, perverted, wicked, corrupt, controlling, rebellious and vile and is a spirit that resurfaces in many disguises and forms, male and female. It is a powerful demonic witchcraft spirit.

It is my belief that this spirit is the demonic spirit that is behind homosexuality, lesbianism, child molestation, rape, adultery, fornication, sodomy, and bestiality. These debased, immoral and perverted practices have been going on since the fall of Adam and Eve. It is the spirit that has seduced man as an individual, controlled and bound generations, hypnotized, dominated and possessed cultures and civilizations, leading them to their demise, and total destruction, such as Sodom and Gomorrah (*Genesis 19*).

I have already spoken of Jewish mythological beliefs in a she-demon call Lilith, today in the 21st century she has been resurrected due to the feminist movement. This new interest in her has led modern writers to invent more stories about her, ignoring the fact that Lilith represents everything that is dark and demonic. Today, the Jewish feminist movement has embraced Lilith because of her independence and self-determined attitude, not realizing that at the heart of this movement lies a spirit of rebellion, witchcraft and demonic control.

There is a Jewish feminist magazine called Lilith and a Lilith fair that is a tour for Jewish female singers-songwriters. The Lilith that was once a source of fear has been recreated into an icon that represents freedom for women across the world.

I am saddened and yet thankful at the same time to have found this information and to be able to share it with you. It is my belief that the more we know and understand our enemy, the clearer we can see and discern what lies behind his power. Mythological beliefs and the lies behind them are a power tool the enemy uses to deceive and mislead man.

Demon Worship

Deuteronomy 31:1-29 is the account of Moses' last counsel, commands and instructions he would give to Israel. God spoke to Moses saying that his time to die had come and to call and present Joshua before the people. God also said to Moses that these people would arise and play the harlot with strange gods of the land, into the midst of which they were going. God then instructed Moses to write a song and to teach it to the sons of Israel.

Genesis 31:30 "Then Moses spoke in the hearing of all the assembly of Israel the words of this song until they were complete."

Deuteronomy 32 is the song that Moses taught the people, but what I want to focus in on is verse 17, because it speaks of the future sacrifices Israel would do unto other gods. *"They sacrificed to demons who were not God, to gods whom they have not known, new gods who came lately, whom your fathers did not dread."*

Let's look at the word *demon* in this verse. The Hebrew word for demon is *shed* and means *evil or wicked demon, an idol, a lord (Baal).*

The Jewish people generally regarded idols to be demons who allowed themselves to be worshipped by men. *See Psalms 106:37.* They also believed that the realm of the dead was the realm of the demonic because *Deuteronomy 18:10-11* says: *"There shall not be found among you anyone who makes his son or his daughter pass through the fire, one who uses divination, one who practices witchcraft, or one who interprets omens or sorcerer, or one who casts a spell or a medium, or a spiritist, or one who calls up the dead."*

The passing of a son or daughter through fire was an initiation into the belief and worship of the deity they worshipped at the time. You will find out later in this chapter more about how Israel also sacrificed their children unto demon gods by fire.

The *Book of Enoch* (a non-canonical apocryphal work) has this to say about sacrificing to demons in section 1, chapter 19:1-3 *Here shall stand the angels who have connected themselves with women, and their spirits assuming many different forms and defiling mankind, and shall lead them astray into sacrificing to demons as gods, (here shall they stand) till the day of the great judgment in which they shall be judged till they are made an end of. 2. And the women also of the angels who went astray become Sirens, (temptresses, a woman who is very attractive, but also dangerous) 3. And I, Enoch, alone saw the vision, the ends of all things: And no man shall see as I have seen.*

She, being a Siren, is also described as one of a group of female creatures in Greek Mythology who's singing attracts sailors and caused them to sail into dangerous waters or towards rocks; a mermaid.

Demons/Evil Spirits

First, let's define the word demon and what it means. The word demon is not found in scripture but means evil spirit or devil. The word devil is used to describe Satan, the prince of demons; *(Matthew 9:34).*

In many other scriptures, the words devil and devils are found, and they refer to evil spirits or demons and are derived from two different Greek words *"diamonion"* and *"diamon."* Demons are the source and agents of all that is evil, unclean, perverted, unnatural and seductive.

In *Mark 16:17* they are called devils, in *Leviticus 20:6* familiar spirits, in *Mark 1:27* unclean spirits, and in *1 Timothy 4:1* seducing spirits.

There are demon spirits that cause sickness either physically or mentally *(Matthew 8:16 & 17:15-18),* and they are behind all doctrinal error, deception and all that is false and counterfeit *(1 Timothy 4:2).* They blind, bind and torment *(Matthew 4:23-24),* and if allowed they will oppress you and depress you *(Acts 10:38).* They work together to bring confusion, delusion, persecution, and to pervert God's word. Their goal is to undermine God's will, plan, and purpose, and wage war on the saints *(Acts 13:6-10; Ephesians 6:10-18).*

Demons are disembodied spirits or unclean spirits that have no bodies and seek a body to inhabit. They are formless and occupy who or what they can possess. Therefore demons can manifest themselves in and through various forms *(Revelations 16:13, 14; Luke 8).* They can also cohabitate in one human body with thousands of other spirits, even legions as *Mark 5:1-13* confirms.

A legion can be from 3,000 – 6,000, but notice that only one demon spoke out to Jesus, and why? Because He was the chief ranked demon and more powerful than the other demons that possessed the maniac of Gadara.

They can go out and come back into men as they will, and as God commands *(1 Samuel 16:23),* unless cast out and rejected. Demons can move and travel from one individual into another (such as an animal) unnoticed and undetected. (*Matthew 12:43-45*)

Demons speak and can use the voice of the one they inhabit *(Acts 8:7; I Kings 22:21-23)*. They can imitate the departed dead *(1 Samuel 28:3-9, I Chronicles 10:13, Isaiah 8:19)*, torment *(Matthew 4:23-24)*, cause bondage *(Romans 8:15)*, oppression *(Acts 10:38)*, grievous vexation *(Matthew 15:22)*, and execute and achieve many evil works when in possession of a person they are permitted to operate through.

These demons must be discerned, resisted and rejected by believers *(1 John 4:1-6; 1 Corinthians 12:10; Ephesians 4:27; 6:10-18; I Peter 5:8-9)*. They must be bound, rebuked, and commanded to come out in order to experience deliverance and release *(Matthew 18:18; 10:1; 17:18)*.

They are made subject to Christ and believers by and through the atonement, the name of Jesus, and the power of the Holy Spirit (*Romans 5:11; Matthew 8:16-17; 12:28; Mark 16:17*).

Disembodied Spirits Myth

There are some who believe that the sons of God (*Genesis 6:4*) were the fallen angels and that the Nephilim were the hybrid offspring of the union between the fallen angels and human women. If that is the case, then what happened to the spirits of the Nephilim after they were killed in the flood?

The theory is that the disembodied spirits are the offspring of the Nephilim who remained on the earth and became what we now refer to as demons. Presumably, as angelic-human hybrids, the spirits of the Nephilim would have been different from the human soul-spirit, having the ability to remain present in this world despite no longer having a physical body. This would possibly explain the desire demons have to possess human beings, thus gaining control over a physical body. To them, this makes sense from the perspective of the fallen angels, who are outnumbered 2-1 by the holy angels, giving them a good reason to seek to increase their ranks.

An explanation given for the origin of demons is the result of a misunderstanding of *I Peter 3:19* concerning who were the *spirits in prison* that Jesus preached to.

Many interpret spirits in prison to be all the fallen angels who rebelled against God. Yet, if all the fallen angels are imprisoned, then there must be an alternate explanation for the existence of demons; hence, the need for the Nephilim explanation.

Idol Worship & Pagan Gods

Our information and knowledge of idol worship and pagan gods of the ancient world comes from religious literature, idols, and other objects discovered by archaeologists. These artifacts confirm the authenticity and accuracy of the Bible, as well as reinforce scripture references of time, people, dates, and locations of the ancient world.

Idol worship during Bible times, especially the false gods of Egypt, Mesopotamia (Assyria and Babylon) and Canaan, played an important part in civilization. Scores of examples and references to idol worship appear in the Old Testament. Idolatry was the greatest temptation Israel would have to face, and time and time again they would slip back into this sin even after receiving the Ten Commandments (*Exodus 20:4-6*).

In *Leviticus 19:4* Moses is instructed by God to speak to the sons of Israel concerning idolatry: *"Do not turn to idols or make for yourself molten gods; I am the Lord your God."*

Joshua 24:2 states that Abraham's father (Terah) served idols. One of the earliest references in the Bible to idols was a Teraphim (small figures), also known as household idols, which Rachel stole from her father Laban when she and Leah fled with Jacob (*Exodus 31:34*).

In the ancient world, these gods were viewed as a powerful force and were a temptation for Israel. Any force of nature that could not be controlled or understood was considered supernatural powers to be worshiped and feared.

Superstitions also played a large part in the worship of idols. Scripture teaches that idol worship is empowered by demons and the demon spirit world would offer magic, threaten retaliation, and provide the manifestations necessary to establish false religious worship. Once established, shame, family tradition, honor, pride, fear of rejection and retaliation from family, neighbors, and government were enough to sustain and support idol worship.

The pagan nations made statues or images to represent the powers they worshiped. Most of these idols were in the form of animals, human beings, or sometimes a combination of both. There were also idols that represented celestial powers such as the sun, moon, and stars. Idols were also represented by forces; forces of nature like sea and rain, or life forces of death and truth. Belief in false gods is steeped in superstition, mythology, and displayed through magic.

Idol worshippers truly believed that their idol was a living and feeling being, and had a separate (though not independent) existence from the statue. They also believed that the spirit of the god lived within the idol and that the god was not confined to a single idol or shape, but dwelt within many idols of varied shapes and could even take human form. And because the gods took the human form they also had human qualities. These gods could be foolish, intelligent, shy, humorous, jealous, angry and demanding.

Those who worshiped idols were convinced that their god perceived and sensed their prayers, ceremonies, and cult offerings were given. Since the god identified fully with its idol, the images to its worshipers were living idols. They offered food to their gods and believed they could draw the energy needed to sustain them and enable them to live and perform their activities.

These same demonic spirits that supposedly inhabited inanimate objects will continue their deception as long as their followers believe and have faith in the god.

Forms of adoration followers showed towards the ancient Hebrew gods were kissing and stroking the idol. This is said to be one of the oldest characteristics of worship (*I Kings 19:18*). Where idols were inaccessible such as the sun, moon, and stars, the person would kiss their hand and throw the kiss towards the idol (*Job 31:27, Deuteronomy 4:19, 2 Kings 17:16, Zephaniah 1:4-5*).

Appearing barefoot in the sanctuary was another way of showing adoration unto the god. The idea being, to avoid polluting the deity residing in the shrine by bringing the dust off the street.

The Old Testament is full of the detestable idols that were worshiped by Israel and Judah. I have listed a small amount of the names, images, rituals and the idolatrous practices they performed that were part of the worship of each idol. My intention is to provide a better understanding of the demonic powers that are behind idol worship, how perverted and evil Israel became, the destructive powers of occult practices and how distorted their worship was. You will see how demons manipulate, tempt, and seduce man through the lusts of the flesh and their sinful fallen nature.

Once Israel made the choice to rebel against God and embrace foreign gods the consequences were devastating. Defilement of the body and debauchery brought great moral and spiritual decay.

There is always a price to pay for our actions and the decisions we make, and Israel was no exception. Ultimately their idolatry forced the hand of God to bring upon them His judgment.

Idols of Israel

Anat

Anat was the patroness of sex and war and supposedly the lover of Aliyan Baal. She was identified with the "queen of heaven" to whom the Jews offered incense in Jeremiah's day *(Jeremiah 44:19)*. Figurines of the nude goddess were dug from Palestinian sites at levels dating from the second and first millennia B.C. It was against the degrading religion of the Canaanites that Moses and Joshua gave such stern warnings to Israel. They realized the effect the Canaanite cults would have upon Israel's morality. They knew too well that Jehovah demanded the complete and heartfelt worship of His people, yet they also sensed the draw and temptation Israel would have to face.

Asherah Worship

Asherah, also known as Ashtoreth, Ashtaroth, Astarte, Anath and Asherat, are various names given to this pagan goddess. This demon presented itself as a female who had power over conception and birth (in some cultures). Others worshiped her as the Lady of the Sea, wife of the god El, or as the sister and chief female deity in Canaan. In south Canaan, she was worshiped as the goddess that stood by the side of Baal.

Asherah was also portrayed as a nude woman bestriding a lion, with a lily in one hand and a serpent in the other. She was called by her worshippers "the holiness," in a perverted moral sense. The lily symbolizes grace and sex appeal and the serpent fertility.

In biblical Gebal, located on the Mediterranean, a center dedicated to this goddess has been excavated. She and her colleagues specialized in sex and war. Her shrines were temples of legalized prostitution and sodomy. The degraded cult and pagan beliefs of Asherah drew Israel into idolatry, standing as a perpetual danger of polluting and sinking them into deeper depths of lust, perversion, evil, and every detestable act the heart could conceive, including murder.

Judges 10:6 "And the children of Israel did evil again in the sight of the Lord, served the Baals and the Ashtaroth, the gods of Aram, the gods of Sidon, the gods of Moab, the gods of the sons Ammon, and the gods of the Philistines; thus they forsook the Lord and did not serve Him." (Hebrew-Greek Key Study Bible)

Baal Worship

Baal means *lord master and possessor.*

Baal was known to be worshiped as the sun god. His altars and sanctuaries were located on high places, even the summits of high mountains, to get the first view of the rising sun, and the last of the setting sun. Baal was believed to be the source and emblem of all life and the generative power of nature. He was also known as the storm god and was portrayed as holding a lightning bolt.

In Canaanite mythology, Baal was believed to be the son of El, and most powerful of all gods. Within the battles of their gods, Baal was the one who defeated Yamm (also Yam, the god of the sea), and Mot (the god of death and the underworld).

In ancient Mesopotamia, Baal was the deity associated with agriculture, the farm god who gave increase to family and field, flocks and herds. He was likewise identified with the Semitic storm god Hadad, whose voice was believed to the thunder, which brought the rain necessary for the success of their crops.

Part of the cult worship included animal sacrifice, ritualistic meals, and licentious dances rooted in sensuality, and ritualistic prostitution in the temples that include males and females. If Baal needed to be appeased, they would sacrifice the firstborn of the one making the sacrifice *(I Kings 14:23 & 24; Jeremiah 19:5)*.

Baal worship became widespread by Ahab king of Israel who erected an altar to him *(I Kings 16:31-33)*. King Ahab married a Phoenician princess named of Jezebel and she brought the cult of Baal from her home in Tyre to Ahab's court in Samaria. Queen Jezebel had 450 prophets of Baal as her court counselors. The priests of Baal would beseech their god with wild behavior that included loud, ecstatic cries and cutting themselves with swords and lances until the blood would gush out of them *(I Kings 18:28)*.

Baal worship was a powerful attraction to the people of Israel and eventually led to their destruction and exile. The Northern Kingdom of Israel was overrun with idolatry and would not repent of their evil, and so the Lord gave them over to Assyria. The Southern Kingdom of Judah also would not repent of their idolatry and the Lord gave them over to Babylon.

Throughout the Old Testament Baal appears in many forms and under many different names and is considered the chief evil spirit by the Jewish people. The Bible often refers to the name Baalim, which is plural for Baal. Baal-ze'bub is a form of the name Baal and in Hebrew means lord of the flies, which was the god of Ekron (*2 Kings 1:2-6*). Other names include Baal-berith, Baal of the covenant, god of Shechem (*Judges 8:33*), and Bel, the god of Babylon *(Isaiah 46:1).*

According to the history of religions, the gods of one nation became the devils of its neighbors and enemies.

Golden Calf Worship

In the ancient world, the bull was a symbol of strength and power. According to Biblical Archeology, it seems every culture was connected to bull worship in some way. History shows that many of the cultures would seek the bull deity for divine blessings, abundant crops, fertile harvest, or victories in battle.

Bull worship was common in Egypt where the Hebrews lived in bondage for four hundred and thirty years (*Exodus 12:40*). They became very familiar with the worship of Apis bull. In fact, they served many gods in Egypt (*Joshua 24:14).* The Oxford Dictionary states that the golden calf was actually the image of the Apis bull that not only represented a god but also strength, fierceness, power, fertility and vital energy.

Cult worshipers rose early, offering sacrifices, then carrying on in the manner befitting fertility rites – feasting, carousing, and performing licentious acts (Jewish bible.org).

Egyptians believed that after the death of Apis bull it became the incarnation of the god Osiris, and was closely linked with the pharaohs of Egypt. They believed that the very breath of Apis bull to be an oracle conferring the gift of prophecy. Mythology says that when an Apis bull died there was a great mourning in the land. Egyptians would embalm them and place them into their very own sarcophagus. This explains why Aaron made a golden calf for Israel to worship.

Additionally, throughout the rule and reign of the kings of Israel bull worship was prevalent and one of those kings that made Israel sin was king Jeroboam *(I Kings 12:28-30).*

Moloch Worship
Moloch worship in ancient Israel is found in legal and historical accounts and prophetic writings of the bible. The word Moloch is the biblical name of a Canaanite god associated with child sacrifice. The name of this deity is also sometimes spelled, Molech, Milcom, or Malcam.

Moloch was also known as the god Chemosh, the god of Moab. *I Kings 11:7-8* tells us that Solomon built a high place for the god Chemosh, in the hill that is before Jerusalem, and that he burnt incense and sacrificed unto this god. God commanded Solomon not to follow other gods. Yet, because his foreign wives brought their strange gods with them, Solomon's heart was turned from the Lord God of Israel, and God judged him for his sin.

Ashtoreth, also known as Asherah, was supposedly his mate. Prostitution was a known form of worship that was practiced as a part of the rituals performed for Molech.

Between the years 1550 BC and 300 BC, Canaan, God's Promised Land for Israel, was occupied by the Phoenicians and Canaanites. They practiced sexual rituals and Molech worship included child sacrifice and "passing children through the fire."

Before the Israelites could enter Canaan, Moses was to speak to the sons of Israel and warn them not to walk in the customs and practices of those who lived in the land. In *Leviticus 18:21* God warns Israel:

"Neither shall you give any of your offspring to offer them to Molech, nor shall you profane the name of your God; I am the Lord."

Israel disregarded God's warnings and soon began to incorporate Molech worship into their own traditions.

Psalms 106:37-38 "Israel sacrificed their sons and their daughters to the demons, and shed innocent blood, the blood of their sons and their daughter, whom they sacrificed to the idols of Canaan, and the land was polluted with the blood."

A 12th century Jewish Rabbinic Commentary I found concerning *Jeremiah 7:31* states that *"Tophet is Molech, which was made of brass; and they heated him from his lower parts; and his hands being stretched out, and made hot, they put the child between his hands and it was burnt; when it vehemently cried out; the priests beat a drum so the father might not hear the voice of his son, and his heart might not be moved."*

The idol was hollow and divided into seven compartments, in one of which they put flour, in the second compartment they put turtle doves, in the third a ewe, in the fourth a ram, in the fifth a calf, in the sixth an ox, and in the seventh a child, which were all burned together by heating the statue inside.

God used the Old Testament prophets to sternly denounce this form of heathen worship in *Jeremiah 7:29-34, Ezekiel 16:20-22, 23:37-39,* and *Amos 5:26.* No form of idolatry was more abhorrent then Moloch worship.

Nehushtan/Brazen Serpent

Nehushtan was the name that Israel applied to the brazen serpent that God had instructed Moses to make and to set it on a pole that we read in *Numbers 21:6-9.*

As the Israelites set out from Mount Hor by the way of the Red Sea, they began to rebel against God and against Moses. Punished by Jehovah with fiery serpents, many of them died. These serpents were called fiery serpents because of the heat, violent inflammation and thirst caused by their bites. At the command of God, Moses made the figure of a serpent and set it on a pole; any of the bitten Israelites looked at it, lived, and recovered from the serpent's bite.

In *2 Kings 18:4* we read of the first acts of King Hezekiah and it says that *"He did what was right in the sight of the Lord. He removed the high places and broke down the sacred pillars and cut down the Asherah. He also broke in pieces the bronze serpent that Moses had made, for until those days the sons of Israel burned incense to it; and it was called Nehushtan."*

Among objects of superstitious reverence and worship was this bronze serpent which, in the course of 900 years, had become invested with a mysterious sanctity that quickly degenerated into idolatry.

Goat God – Pan

Pan was what is called a Seirim devil that literally denotes hairy or shaggy goats, and goat-like deities or demons. These demons were said to dwell in deserts, preside over mountainous regions, and are referred to as demonic creatures that would dance among the ruins of Babylon *(Isaiah 13:21)*.

While Israel was wandering in the wilderness they were powerfully influenced to call on this goat god they had brought from Egypt. The Egyptians and other nations of antiquity worshiped goats as gods. The ceremonies observed in this idolatrous worship were extremely licentious and obscene, and the gross impurity of the rites gives great significance to Moses' words, "they have gone a whoring." There are many accounts of the continuous idolatry worship of Israel (See *Joshua 24:14; Ezekiel 20:7; 2 Chronicles 11:15*)

The ancient cult of Pan involved rites of passage. In the rites of Pan, music, and wine were used to entice spirits to possess the ritual's participants. Possession by Pan resulted in an obsession with sex, lust and a need for immediate gratification and physical satisfaction.

The deities Pan, Silenus, Satyrs, fauns, and the woodland gods among the Greeks and Romans evolved into the goat-like form of the devil that is depicted having a tail, horns and cloven feet that we see even today.

In Caesarea Philippi, in Northern Galilee at the foot of Mt. Hermon, sat the ruins of the city and the niches of Pan's images which can still be seen in the rock's façade. In the Old Testament times it was called Ba'al Hermon *(Judges 3:3)*, because this was one of the locations the god Ba'al was worshipped. In Hellenistic times it was called Paneas because the god Pan and his worship had apparently replaced the ancient Ba'als. Pan was the ancient god of fright who was half man and half goat and is often pictured as playing the flute that would mesmerize little children and lead them away.

Caesarea Philippi's location was especially unique because it stood at the base of a cliff where spring water flowed. At one time, the water ran directly from the mouth of a cave set in the bottom of the cliff.

The pagans of Jesus day commonly believed that their fertility gods lived in the underworld during the winter and returned to earth each spring. They viewed water as a symbol of the underworld and thought that their gods traveled to and from that world through caves. These pagans believed that their city was literally at the gates of the underworld – the gates of hell. In order to entice the return of Pan each year, the people of Philippi engaged in horrible deeds, including prostitution and sexual interaction between humans and goats.

When Jesus brought His disciples to the area of Caesarea Philippi, they had to have heard stories describing the pagan worship and the idols that his city was known for. They would have known of the detestable rituals being done at the base of the rock and wanted to avoid any contact with them. This was a challenge the disciples would face head-on, not avoiding, nor be intimidated by the horrible actions. That day Jesus spoke revelation truth to the disciples and gave them a promise they were not expecting.

In *Matthew 16:13-20* Jesus presents a revelation. He asks a question and then makes a bold prophetic statement to his disciples. And Jesus asked them, *"Who do you say that I am?"* Peter then boldly answers and says, *"You are the Son of the living God."* Jesus then continues, *"You are Peter, and on this rock, I will build my church, and the gates of Hades will not overpower it."*

Jesus knew about the pagan worship and rituals performed at the caves in Philippi. He knew that the people there were literally knocking on the doors of hell and opening themselves to demonic spirits. Jesus didn't want His followers to be fearful or hide from the evil they would have to one-day face. Jesus wanted them to storm the gates of hell and understand that they had the power and the authority to stand against, and prevail over the powers of Satan and any demon they would confront.

Today it is in witchcraft that Pan, the symbol of nature still lives. In Wicca, he is the horned god who is half male and female and is associated with nature, wilderness, sexuality, hunting and the life cycle. Depictions of the deity vary yet are always shown with horns or antlers upon his head, in this way emphasizing the union of the divine. Pan is the demonic pagan god of sexual perversion, pedophilia, and rape.

He is portrayed as roaming through the forests with an erection, drunk and lascivious, frolicking with nymphs, and piping his way through the forests while playing the flute. According to legends, Pan is the tempter of the lower nature of man and this is what draws those to worship Pan, especially those who are in witchcraft and Satanism. Pan is the universal symbol of Satan.

While searching out information on the goat god Pan, I found a very interesting article on bbc.com entitled *Decoding The Symbols on Satan's Statue*. At the beginning of the article, there is a picture of the goat-headed figure Baphomet that was unveiled by the Satanic Temple at a secret ceremony in Detroit where hundreds of Satanists turned out to see it unveiled. This Satanic group describes itself as "Satanists, secularists, and advocates for individual liberty."

The inscription that was put on the back of the statue reads "Then who was the Demon? He who would not let ye live, or he who would have made ye live forever in the joy of power and knowledge?"

Baphomet, another name for Pan, was created and drawn by a French occultist by the name of Eliphas Levi and placed in his book, *Transcendental Magic: Its Doctrine and Ritual.*

This goat god is supposedly a winged hermaphrodite, with breasts and a torch between his horns, and a pentagram on his forehead and his throne. His arms bare the Latin words *solve* (separate), and *coagula* (join together) – the power of "binding and loosing" usurped from God.

If you have ever seen satanic symbols have you noticed that there is the head of a goat in the center of the satanic pentagram?

The original goat pentagram first appeared in a book written by a French occultist Stanislas de Guaita in 1897. This symbol would later become synonymous with Baphomet and be commonly referred to as the Sabbatic Goat.

The Hebrew letters at the five points of the pentagram spell out Leviathan, a creature that is referred to in the Bible. This symbol was later adopted by the Church of Satan in 1969 and officially named the Sigil of Baphomet.

Chapter 11
The Seduction of the Enemy

"But the way of the wicked seduces them"
Proverbs 12:26b

Seduction

Seduction is the act of seducing, especially to entice sexually, and to cause by persuasion someone to act contrary to the principles by which they normally abide by. Seduction lures tempt, bribes, persuades, charms and beguiles its victim. It also leads aside or away from good to evil by seductive persuasion or through temptation, especially by evil forces that work through people.

All of us have experienced and even succumbed to the power, sway and the sting of seduction. And who is behind the seduction? Our enemy, Satan and his demonic forces. Demonic spirits will work through people, and circumstances, to entice and seduce you into compromising the truth, your morals, and to betray the call and will of God for your life.

A prime example of how the enemy will use people or a person to seduce another person is found in the Old Testament in the book of *Judges.* In this case, a demonic spirit used a woman to seduce a man named Samson whose name means sunlight. The enemy used the Philistines, particularly a Philistine woman named Delilah (*Judges 16*). Let us delve into the book of Judges that will give us the background of the apostate condition of Israel, and why God chose to raise up Samson.

"And the children of Israel did evil again in the sight of the Lord; and the Lord delivered them into the hand of the Philistines forty years." *Judges 13:1*

Judges portray a troubled and unstable period in the history of Israel. Once Joshua died there was no one to take his place, *"But that every man did that which was right in his own eyes."* *Judges 17:6*

Doesn't that sound like the attitude and state of mind of our world today?

God raised up judges to deliver Israel from serving Baal, to restore true worship, lead Israel to repentance and victory in war, and deliver them from their enemies.

And the Lord brings forth a son of promise unto Israel that was destined to be born into the tribe of Dan. This son was to begin the deliverance of Israel after 40 years of oppression by their enemy the Philistines. That son of promise was Samson, who was anointed with supernatural strength and the power of the Holy Spirit to fight with his fists and wit. Samson was one of the few in scripture whose birth was divinely pronounced by an angel of the Lord and called by God to accomplish a specific task even before he was conceived (*Judges 13:3*).

Even though Samson had extraordinary strength and heroic faith, he had weaknesses and was vulnerable to his passions and Philistine women. *Judges 16 "And it came to pass afterward, that he loved a woman in the valley of Sorek, whose name was Delilah."*

The Hebrew name Delilah means amorous, delight, languishing, and temptress. Some sources give her name to mean "she who weakened."

Jezebel Spirit

What was behind the seductive and heartless behavior of Delilah? The Spirit of Jezebel (*Revelations 2:20*).

Let me clarify: When I refer to a particular spirit or spirits working through people such as Jezebel, what I am describing are the actions and the ways demonic spirits exhibit their behaviors and personalities in and through people (*I Kings 18*).

Please note: Jezebel can and does manifest through men also. Demonic spirits do not care if you are male or female necessarily. Their objective is to influence, control, possess and work through a human body. The Jezebel spirit uses bewitching powers of seduction to lure its victims into its spell to create soul ties. It will use intimidation, pressure, control, and fear and will bully its victim into submission.

This spirit is the "strongman of the house," *(Matthew 12:29)* and works with other interdependent and related spirits to gain control of its victim and dominate their lives.

Some of the demonic spirits Jezebel works with to gain control and work in your life are a spirit of witchcraft, rebellion, and spirit of divination, Spirit of Python, seduction, lust, harlotry, etc. All sexual perversion, adultery, and fornication are manifestations that work through these demonic spirits.

Delilah was a master of seduction as she lied, sexually enticed, tricked, intimated, deceived and manipulated Samson into her trap.

Samson appeared unaware of the supernatural ability of the enemy to work through natural means or people. Demonic spirits were behind his natural enemy the Philistines. Satan used Delilah to manipulate, control and maneuver Samson into her arms and into the hands of his enemies. This resulted in the deterioration of Samson's spiritual walk with God, his Nazarite vow, and the anointing and power of God in his life.

Soul Ties

One purpose of seduction is to lure its victim and create ties that bind themselves to the soul.

Ties to the soul are a uniting and binding force that can influence, attach and fasten themselves to your mind and affect your thoughts, imagination, memory, will, and emotions to trigger a response. These ties are called soul ties.

"Be ye not unequally yoked together with unbelievers: for what fellowship hath righteousness with unrighteousness? And what communion hath light with darkness?"

"And what concord (harmony, peace, agreement, and unity) hath Christ with Belial? Or what part hath he that believeth with an infidel?" 2 Corinthians 6:14, 15 (Dake's Anointed Reference Bible)

Soul ties are formed when you become one with someone sexually, as Samson did with Delilah. They bind you together physically and emotionally and will continue to draw you back to the one you have bound yourself to. This bonding force (demonic spirits) will influence, attack, and fasten to your thoughts, which trigger an emotional response.

Soul ties can be ungodly ties that affect you spiritually and lead to apostasy, idolatry, doctrinal error, religious perversion, self-deception, delusion, false religions, and idol worship. A person can be soul tied to a person or worldly possessions they are unnaturally attached to.

"But the (Holy) Spirit explicitly and unmistakably declares that in later times some will turn away from the faith, paying attention instead to deceitful and seductive (seducing) spirits and doctrines of demons." 1 Timothy 4:1 (Amplified Bible)

The Greek word for seducing in this scripture is *planos* and it means an imposter, to cause to wander, lead astray, a misleader and a deceiver.

Delilah played the role of an imposter by deceiving Samson and unfortunately played him for a fool. *Proverbs 7:21-23 (Amplified Bible)* clearly warns:

"With her many persuasions she caused him to yield; with her flattering lips, she seduced him. Suddenly he went after her, as an ox goes to the slaughter (not knowing the outcome), or as one in stocks going to the correction (to be given) to a fool. Until an arrow pierced his liver (with a mortal wound); like a bird fluttering straight into the net, he did not know that it would cost him his life."

Samson betrayed himself and his God and paid dearly for his foolishness and sin.

Samson allowed his heart, emotions, passions and the lust of the eye to rule over God's will, purpose, and Nazarite vow. His very soul would have been lost if he had not humbled himself before God and prayed in his final confrontation with his enemy.

Satan used Samson's natural enemies, the Philistines, to get to him, and he worked through Delilah to go in for the kill. You could also put it this way, Satan operated his demonic power through man, so that Samson would reveal his secret and the source of his power.

"The acts of the flesh are obvious: sexual immorality, impurity, and debauchery; idolatry and witchcraft; hatred, discord, jealousy, fits of rage, selfish ambition, dissensions, factions, and envy; drunkenness, orgies, and the like. I warn you, as I did before, that those who live like this will not inherit the kingdom of God." Galatians 5:19-21 (NIV)

Python Spirit

The spirit of Python works with and through seduction.

In the natural world, the python is classified as a constrictor and kills its prey by causing asphyxia. It wraps its body completely around his victim until they suffocate and stop breathing. A python will always ambush its prey and it will camouflage itself to hide and blend easily with its environment.

Who does this sound like? Satan and his demonic spirits.

The Python spirit is a demonic spirit and is not a snake. It seeks to gain legal entry into the church and our lives through the works of divination which are false prophecy, forth-telling, and hidden knowledge that are aided by and through demonic supernatural powers. The Python spirit works to keep God's children from coming into the manifested truth and power of the Holy Spirit. If it can get you to believe what is false over what is true, then it has accomplished its purpose. One of the Python spirit's goals is to keep us from receiving, understanding, and implementing God's authority and power in our lives and ministry.

If you already know and experienced God's power and are walking in His authority, as Paul did in *Acts 16:16*, then the spirit of Python strives to slither into your life by acquiring ground and gradually crushing the life and anointing of God out of you.

"And it came to pass as we were going to prayer that a certain female slave, having a spirit of Python, (spirit of divination) met us, who brought much profit to her masters by prophesying. She, having followed Paul and us, cried saying, these men are bondmen of the Most High God, who announce to you (the) way of salvation." Acts 16:16 & 17 (Darby translation)

In Gills Exposition Commentary has this to say concerning *Acts 16:16* and the *spirit of Python:*

"So it was, that a certain damsel possessed with a spirit of divination, met us; in the Greek text it is, "the spirit of Python"; the Alexandrian copy and the Vulgate Latin version reads, "the spirit Python; the same with Apollo, who was called "Pythius," as was his oracle, from the people coming to him, to inquire and consult with him about difficult matters; or rather from the Hebrew word which signifies a "serpent"; and so Apollo is said to have his name Pythius, from his killing the serpent Typhon or Python; hence the city of Delphos. The feasts and plays instituted to the honor of Apollo were called the Pythian feasts and plays, and the place of the oracle Pythium."

And so, this maid or the spirit in her would not only foretell of things to come but was able to discern through the help of a familiar spirit that knew who Paul and Silas were and why they were there.

What was the purpose behind this spirit and why did it speak the truth? Its purpose was to discredit their effect and the message of the apostles. If the people thought they were in league with the controlling demonic spirits that ruled the city, then the people would conclude that Paul and Silas were performing miracles by and through the same demonic spirit. This would hopefully discount the effect of the gospel in the eyes of the people. But when the demon was cast out of the girl in the name of Jesus, that action proved that their power came from God and not from a demon.

In Greek mythology, there is the story of a Python that lived in the caves of Mount Parnassus. It is said that the Greek god Apollo founded the sacred Oracles of Delphi after he killed the Python.

An *oracle is* a person or agency considered to provide wise counsel, prophetic predictions or precognition of the future that was inspired by the gods of ancient Greece. As such it is a form of divination.

The word *oracle* is derived from the Latin verb *orare*, meaning to beg, pray, beseech and refers to the priest or priestess who utters the predictions.

Ancient oracles were thought to be portals through which the gods spoke directly to people. The most important oracle of Greek antiquity was Pythia, priestess to Apollo at Delphi in Greece. Apollo according to Greek mythology, was the god of revelation and inspiration. It is believed that Apollo used the Pythia as his mouthpiece taking possession of her during oracular sessions. The Pythia would fall into a trance, and the words she spoke were supposedly those of Apollo, delivered in a voice very unlike her normal tones. This Pythia who was appointed to sit on a tripod and prophecy was to be an older woman of blameless life and chosen from among the peasants of the area. Before she could mount the tripod, a goat had to be sacrificed to ensure that the day was propitious.

The origins of the oracles are recounted in a story about a goat herder named Koreta, who pastured his flock on the slope of mount Karnassus. Koreta noticed that when the goats grazed near a certain fissure in the mountainside the goats began to bleat strangely and when Koreta approached the fissure, he was filled with a prophetic spirit.

Mythology says that when Apollo slew Python, a huge serpent fell into the fissure and according to legend fumes arose from its decomposing body. Intoxicated by the vapors, the Sibyl (prophetesses who uttered divine revelations) would fall into a trance allowing Apollo to possess her spirit. Under the influence of the vapors, she would go into a trance, rave in a form of ecstatic speech and behavior, and supposedly prophesy. She acted as a medium, a go-between for those who worshiped Apollo and the Python god.

Who really was speaking through these priestesses? It was a demonic spirit. These priestesses were hosts and vehicles the demons used.

The Python spirit was the stronghold spirits that ruled over Philippi and who possessed the slave girl that was harassing Paul that we just read about in *Acts 16:16-18.*

How Does The Python Spirit Operate?

The Python spirit operates through deception, lies, false revelations, and beguiles you as the serpent beguiled Eve that we read in *2 Corinthians 11:3 "But I am afraid that, even as the serpent beguiled Eve by his cunning, your minds may be corrupted and lead away from the simplicity of (your sincere and) pure devotion of Christ." (Amplified Bible)*

When a person is beguiled they are led by deception. This spirit entices, lures, charms and mesmerizes it captive putting them under its spell. Skilled in its craft it knows how to twist and distort the truth, warp the mind and thinking, and persuades one to believe that there is another way to salvation other than Christ.

Another way Python operates is through lies. *John 8:44* confirms: *"You are of your father the devil, and it is your will to practice the desires (which are characteristic) of your father. He was a murderer from the beginning and does not stand in the truth because there is no truth in him. When he lies, he speaks what is natural to him, for he is a liar and the father of lies and half-truths." (Amplified Bible)*

Satan and especially the Python spirit are identified with serpents. In *Luke 10:19* and *Revelations 12:9* says:

"Behold! I give you authority and power to trample upon serpents and scorpions, and [physical and mental strength and ability] over all the power of the enemy [Possesses]." (Amplified Bible)

"And the huge dragon was cast down and out, that age-old serpent, called the Devil, and Satan, he who is the seducer (deceiver); he was forced out and down to the earth, and his angels were flung out along with him." (Amplified Bible)

God has given to us, as a believer, the power to crush and defeat the enemy, in the spiritual realm, just as if you were fighting physically with him in the natural. We can put the squeeze and pressure on this spirit just like he pressures us. The difference is that it's not by our own strength. It is by the strength, power, and authority of the Spirit of God that is in us.

This serpentine spirit works to crush our vision, dreams, faith, and hope, and to suffocate our prophetic voice and gifts. Python is after the very breath of God in us that gives us life.

There is a Christian song titled "Wrapped up, Tied up, Tangled All Up in God," written by a Nancy Harmon.

This metaphor describes a positive condition and position we can be in, in God. Unfortunately, this also describes a negative state many people are unknowingly in- they are wrapped up, tied up and tangled all up and under the influence of a deceiving spirit.

I have seen this spirit manifest in and through a person as I was assisting them through deliverance. This spirit would use the person's tongue and vocal cords to display the same actions as a snake does in the natural. The spirit would cause the person to stick their tongue in and out at a fast pace just like as a snake does and hiss as if they were going to attack; this was only a tactic to induce fear. I know experientially that this spirit is real and is still at work in the lives of people who have (knowingly or unknowingly) opened up a door for it to enter.

In many of the world's religions, myths, cultures, rituals and beliefs, serpents and snakes are worshipped and historically have played an important role in everyday life.

In ancient Egypt, Apophis was a demon of chaos that appeared in the form of a serpent. Cobras were especially worshiped in ancient Egypt and became one of the protective emblems on the pharaoh's crown.

Tradition states that one of the Jewish Gnostic sects known as the Ophites declared the serpent of paradise to be wisdom itself since wisdom had come to the earth through the knowledge of good and evil, which the serpent had brought. They also believed that they owed their origin to the serpent, the devil, and the demonic Hebdomad, seven spirits that were under the dominion of the serpent.

Snake Handlers

Believe it or not, there are Pentecostal Holiness churches in the United States today that are known as snake handlers. Part of their religious practice is to handle snakes and drink poison in their worship services. These beliefs and practices are based on their interpretation of the biblical passage in *Mark 16:17 & 18*: *"And these signs shall follow them that believe; in my name shall they cast out devils; they shall speak with new tongues; they shall take up serpents; and if they drink any deadly thing, it shall not hurt them; they shall lay hands on the sick, and they shall recover." (Hebrew-Greek Key Study Bible)*

There is a Pentecostal minister that is best known for popularizing the practice of snake handling. This Pentecostal minister's name is George W. Hensley, born in Virginia on May 2, 1881, and was one of 13 children.

While living in Big Stone Gap, Virginia as a young boy in the 1890's, he witnessed an elderly woman handle a snake during a revival service at a coal mining camp. As a young man, this experience would be a catalyst that would cause him to become fixated on the experience and on *Mark 16:17-18.*

"And these signs will accompany those who have believed: in My name they will cast out demons, they will speak with new tongues; they will pick up serpents, and if they drink any deadly poison, it shall not

hurt them; they will lay hands on the sick, and they will recover."
(Hebrew-Greek Key Study Bible)

Hensley became saved in 1910 but soon began to question whether he was living a righteous life. He questioned his salvation.

In 1947 Hensley gave a newspaper interview and stated that he claimed to have seen a snake while walking on a hill and as he knelt in prayer. Hensley stated that he took hold of the snake and brought it to his church and told the congregation to prove their salvation by holding the snake.

This was the beginning of introducing snake handling practices into the 'Church of God Holiness with Signs' following around 1914. His belief was that if believers truly had the Holy Spirit within them, they should be able to handle rattlesnakes and venomous serpents. They should be able to drink poison and suffer no harm whatsoever. He also taught that snake handling was to be a test or demonstration of faith.

This is a prime example of how the spirit of deception can work through a man to sway, manipulate and control people into interpreting and applying scripture incorrectly. One of the scriptures incorrectly used to reinforce this practice is *Acts 28:3-6.*

Paul and his companions had been shipwrecked on the island of Malta where they were greeted by the natives and shown great kindness. It was raining and cold so the natives kindled a fire for them. Paul wants to help with the fire began to gather sticks to lay on the fire. When Paul laid the stick on the fire, there came a viper out of the heat, and fastened itself onto Paul's hand and bit him. Paul shook the snake off into the fire and suffered no harm. The natives were expecting Paul to die and when he didn't, they began to say that he was a god.

Nowhere in scripture does it teach or encourage us to take up serpents to prove that we have faith, nor does scripture give us permission to be so foolish by testing God in this way. Jesus clearly states in *Matthew 4:7 "You shall not put the Lord your God to the test."*

The whole idea of having immunity from snakebites in *Acts 28,* and power over them is in total conflict according to *Luke 10: 19* and *Psalms 91:13*. Handling snakes in public is no more proof that one has faith or that he is a Christian than the snake charmers of India or Burma.

Just because someone proclaims they are a Christian and say they have received great revelation doesn't mean that they necessarily walk in truth. This is the time when you need to test the spirits as *1 John 4:1* tells us:

"Beloved, do not believe every spirit (speaking through a self-proclaimed prophet); instead test the spirit to see whether they are from God because many false prophets and teachers have gone out into the world."(Hebrew-Greek Key Study Bible)

Always question and never assume. Seek and search for the truth in the scriptures, and ask yourself; are they speaking the truth or are they speaking deceptive lies? Are those who claim to be a prophet prophesying falsehoods? Is it lying divination at work and declaring that the Lord sent them? See *Ezekiel 13: 6 & 7.*

There is no question that these are powerful spirits the enemy uses to lead man away from God and the truth. Even so, these spirits can be discerned, cast out and defeated. This is the will of the Father, because in *Act 16:18 Amplified Bible* Paul did this very thing. *"Paul, being greatly annoyed and worn out, turned and said to the spirit (inside her), "I command you in the name of Jesus Christ (as His representative) to come out of her!" And it came out at that very moment."*

Chapter 12
A Glance Into Ignorance

"My people are destroyed for lack of knowledge."
Hosea 4:6

Who and what is behind some major Occults and beliefs today?

Ignorance Is Not Bliss

Whoever penned the saying *ignorance is bliss*, most assuredly was not talking about being ignorant of Satan and demonic spirits. Ignorance for a believer is a death sentence. You would have to be living in total denial or fear to ignore that there are forces that are working against you.

Ignorance is a state of mind that Satan works hard to keep you in. As long as you lack the understanding and knowledge, and are unaware of who and what is behind the growing problem of cults, the occultism, witchcraft, Satanism, Islam, Atheism and the New Age Movement, then you are in an inferior position and vulnerable to deception.

Occultism is on the rise today because our youth are looking for answers to life, purpose, truth and spiritual identity through the supernatural realm. They are seeking knowledge of the unknown and those things that are hidden or secret. The esoteric nature of the occult attracts people who want to know things others don't know. Little do they realize that there are demonic powers underlining, manipulating and drawing unsuspecting and innocent people into the occult world that ultimately results in bondage and death.

These occult powers have a primary goal to alter and distort values, morals, prior belief systems, God and society at large. Occults promote isolation from non-occultists and seek answers from the god-self, creation (mother earth), and "angels" who are demonic spirits that appear as light and truth.

The Darkness We Face

The lies and deception of the enemy have so blinded and darkened the minds of men that life no longer has value in many countries and cultures. Children are kidnapped only to be found later as victims of some bizarre ritualistic crime, while others become child brides and part of the child sex trade. Children are being aborted, killed and sacrificed all in the name of the god of convenience. Consequences and accountability seem to be mere words that hold no regard.

Then there are the children who are manipulated and offered money to strap a bomb onto their body, resulting in the deaths and severe injuries of innocent people they target. All of this is done in the belief that they are doing the will of their god.

If a man allows himself to be deceived and if God is excluded from the life of man, then man degenerates back to his fallen nature and reaps ruin and destruction.

Galatians 6:8 "For the one who sows to his flesh (his sinful capacity, his worldliness, his disgraceful impulses) will reap from the flesh ruin and destruction, but the one who sows to the Spirit will from the Spirit reap eternal life."(Amplified Bible)

Major Beliefs/Definitions/Descriptions

Deuteronomy 18:10-12a "There shall not be found among you anyone who makes his son or daughter pass through the fire (as a sacrifice), one who uses divination and fortune-telling, one who practices witchcraft, or one who interprets omens, or a sorcerer. Or one who casts a charm or spell, or a medium, or a spiritist, or a necromancer (who seeks the dead. For everyone who does these things is utterly repulsive to the Lord." (Amplified Bible)

What Is A Cult?

A cult is a group of people polarized around an individual with a magnetic personality, who deviate from orthodox Christianity. They distort the central message of the Bible by introducing their personal understanding or revelation of biblical doctrines.

Occult: Matters regarded as involving the action or influence of supernatural or supernormal powers or some secret or hidden knowledge and practices such as magic, fortune-telling, etc. Occult practices usually entail learning complex systems such as astrology, magical rituals, and numerology.

Occultism: Occult beliefs or practices.

Witchcraft: It is the use of scripturally forbidden supernatural powers that are obtained from evil spirits and are used to manipulate and control people and events.

Satanism: Is the worship of Satan, innate wickedness and obsession with evil. It promotes a do what you want attitude and is ultimately the worship of oneself. Satanism challenges the biblical teaching that says we are to esteem others better than ourselves. Satanism says to esteem the self over others.

Islam: Islam is a monotheistic religion, meaning they believe in only one god and that god is Allah. They are taught to practice the five pillars of Islam, that Mohammed is Allah's one and only true prophet and that the Quran is the absolute word of God.

Atheism: It is an absence of belief in the existence of gods or God or of any supernatural reality.

New Age Movement: Is an extremely large, loosely structured network of organizations and individuals that are bound together by common values based on Eastern mysticism, which attempt to bypass the mind using the third eye. This gives light and monism. Monism is the belief that all is one, all is God, humanity is God, a change of consciousness, all religions are one and cosmic evolutionary optimism.

Witchcraft

At the root of all pagan occults and beliefs is Satan, the deceiver of man.

Witchcraft is seeking help or guidance from any spiritual source other than God. Witchcraft comes in many forms such as Wicca, horoscopes, astrology, tarot cards, sorcery, magic, séances, psychics, palm reading, Spiritism, fortune-telling, necromancy, divination, new age meditation, channeling, zodiacs, chants, spells, potions, charms, and Ouija boards. These are all Satan's counterfeits to the power and purpose of the Holy Spirit.

Pagan belief states that Witchcraft is more than a pagan religion; it's a spiritual practice, a way of life and a belief system. It is a religion that holds a common set of nature-based fundamental beliefs and practices. These beliefs include a deep desire to live in harmony and balance with one's natural world, a respect for all things, reincarnation and karma. They believe that all things are connected on both a physical and spiritual/soul level through energy and the god, goddess or divine and that this energy can be used to advance the soul toward spiritual enlightenment.

That doesn't sound so bad, does it? This is the deception because there is a very dark side and encounter with the spirit world that is not disclosed. The darkness is hidden yet readily discoverable by those who delve into the many websites, books, and occult stores pertaining to witchcraft.

The truth that hides behind the shrouds of mysticism is unsettling at best and disastrous at their worst.

During my research on witchcraft, I came across the testimony of a young girl that had been a former witch and involved in Wicca, fortune-telling, voodoo and casting spells for over twenty years. I will refer to her as Jane to protect her anonymity. Here is her story:

Jane's Testimony

Jane grew up in a Baptist church but was severely beaten and molested by her step-father. Being so young she couldn't comprehend or understand why God did not help her and because of that, she began to hate God. She said that she felt powerless as a young girl and so once she got older she was able to leave home. One day, Jane got up and decided to go for a walk and felt a force propelling her to go into a store and when she opened the door, greeting her was a woman that said to her, hello sister, I've been waiting for you.

The store was a voodoo shop filled with the paraphernalia needed for the dark craft, and the woman that greeted her gave her a book to begin exploring the religion of Wicca. Jane states that her interest in the earth-based cult merely whetted an appetite for more knowledge and more power.

Jane started out with Wicca thinking she was just worshipping the earth but soon it just wasn't enough and she was compelled to check out books about necromancy and voodoo. Towards the end of twenty years of practicing the occult, she was just about to open herself up to channeling but for some reason, she didn't. She was starting to use her own blood in her rituals and her spells and had started making voodoo dolls and casting bad spells on people. She says that the spells actually occurred.

Jane downward spiraled into ever-deeper negative pagan practices until she had a collision with a truck that nearly took her life. This experience caused her to consider the life she had chosen because when the truck hit her it spun her around 180 degrees, and the first thing she said that popped into her mind was "thank God." At that moment she said it was like God came down and said, you've got to stop, I don't want that for you.

There is a real spirit world connected with occult practice and you cannot experiment with it and not expect negative consequences. To those that see witchcraft as fiction or something to be toyed with, Jane explains the results of twenty years of dancing with witchcraft. The occult honestly brings nothing but disaster into your life. She went on to say, "I had an altar that was six feet long with idols on it and still couldn't control my life."

The Bible says that Satan has come to kill, steal and destroy and I don't think people grasp the gravity of how that is so relatable to witchcraft and Wicca and the summoning of spirits. Jane experienced how these spirits want to keep you as far away from God as they can, and the illusion that yes, you have this power to communicate with us and we (demonic spirits) can do things for you, but there is always a negative effect and a price to pay.

Jane went on to say that she could feel an evil presence with her and that, that presence was trying to drive her insane, and that presence was constantly with her and constantly trying to manipulate her. Before she was done with witchcraft, it got so bad that she was to the point of seeing things, hearing things and unable to sleep well. She was angry all the time and it was eating at her soul. Jane's last comment was to say that by the end they wanted to destroy her soul, and whatever light she had in her.

Witchcraft is part of the work of Satan and the demonic kingdom. Satan always has a counterfeit for what God does in His kingdom. At the core of witchcraft is a desire and need for power, recognition, to feel important, the ability to control your own life and destiny, and to control others.

Whenever anyone or anything actively seeks to control you, the influence of witchcraft is most likely at work. In *Galatians 5:19-21* is a list of the works of the flesh (our sinful nature) and part of those works are idolatry and witchcraft.

In these last decades, witchcraft has become continually more mainstream, aggressive and accepted. Its supernatural element fascinates and stirs up the curiosity of the unknown. Satan entices with the suggestions of power, self-realization, and spiritual enlightenment apart from submission to the Lord God.

Satan comes as an angel of light and disguises, deceives and lies to the innocent and vulnerable people who are hurting, looking for love, acceptance, importance, and power, to feel special, a place to belong and to be unique and different.

If you are not worshiping God or communicating with God's Holy Spirit, then you are worshiping and communing with the devil and demonic spirits, which is idolatry.

Evil is a spirit, just as God is the Holy Spirit. We can only worship God in spirit (*John 4:24*). Our battles in this life are ultimately against evil; not flesh and blood according to *Ephesians 6:12*. These demonic evil spirits work inside the mind to control your thoughts and to sever and pervert your conscious and moral actions so that you will do evil and abominable things.

In the *Galatians 5:20* the word, sorcery is translated from the Greek word *Pharmacia*, from which we get our word pharmacy. Witchcraft and Spiritism often involve the ritualistic use of magic potions and mind-altering drugs. Using illicit drugs opens a door for the invasion of demonic spirits. Engaging in a practice or taking a substance to achieve an altered state of consciousness is a form of witchcraft.

Seeing demons while in an altered drug-induced state is a known fact and many are the stories and testimonial of people who have had this experience.

Satanism

Satanists, devil worshippers, Luciferians and members of the Church of Satan claim to have roots in LaVeyan Satanism that was named after Anton LaVey, known to be the author of the Satanic Bible and founder of the first Church of Satan in 1966.

In 1969 LaVey wrote the Satanic Bible, followed by *The Satanic Witch*. In 1972 he published a book called *The Satanic Rituals* that can be found today in most bookstores.

All forms of Satanism promote self and claim that life exists to consume and that selfishness is a virtue. Some Satanists believe that the only existence they will ever know is here on Earth, so they live for the moment and believe in gluttony and debauchery; gratification of all one's desires; vital existence, not spiritual pipe dreams; indulgence, not abstinence; that man is just another animal, vengeance, not turning the other cheek; kindness to those deserving of it, not love wasted on ingrates.

Part of Satanist theology states that people have created gods in many forms and that Heaven and Hell do not exist. Satan is not closely related to the devil defined in the bible. Instead, Satanists view Satanism as a pre-Christian life principle which represents the carnal, earthly, and mundane aspects of life. Satan is not a being or living entity, he is a force of nature. Satanists believe that Satan represents love, kindness, and respect to those who deserve it.

Satanism pledges its allegiance to Satan, and there are some in the Church of Satan who believes that no God or devil exists and that there is no redeemer for them or anyone else. Each person is fully responsible for the path for his own life. Yet they pray to Satan in rituals, asking for his sovereign hand to be manifested in their lives. This kind of thinking illustrates the depth of deception and reveals the lies they believe. Some of the names they use for Satan are Lucifer, Belial, and Leviathan.

Satanism celebrates man's carnal desires, instincts and promotes pursuing unbridled passions. Their Magic rituals consist of three types. The Lust ritual- sex magic which can include masturbation, the Compassion ritual to achieve healing or happiness, and the Destruction rituals which may include sticking pins in a doll, drawing a picture or writing a description of the victim's death, and performing someone's death as a group. These rituals can include a black candle placed to the left of the altar (representing the powers of darkness) and a white candle placed at the right of the altar, magical language, a bell, silver chalice, and other ritual tools such as a gong, sword, and elixir (usually wine), phallus and parchment.

During rituals, Satanists often dress is in full-length black robes, with or without a hood. Young women generally wear sexually suggestive clothing and older women wear all black with amulets carrying the symbol of the goat god Baphomet, pentagrams, and sometimes the infinity sign with a Roman cross placed at the center with a longer cross piece added.

In 2005 the very first Pagan Pride Day festival was held in New York and those who were part of this festival handed out a pamphlet entitled *What is Satanism?* Here are excerpts from that pamphlet:

The worst thing Satan is said to do in the New Testament is to drive people insane. (Insanity is blamed on alleged "demon possession.") Indeed, if one is careless, one can drive oneself insane through exploring the unknown and seeking to "become as gods," as Satan invites us to do. On the other hand, if one takes reasonable precautions in pursuing one's explorations and ambitions, one can reap great benefits.

Thus, most Satanists do not see themselves as *"worshiping evil."* Rather, most Satanists associate Satan with such values as pride, independence, individuality, knowledge, thinking for oneself and exploring unknown and forbidden realms.

Theistic Satanist believes in and revere Satan as a deity and are polytheistic and regard both Satan and the Christian "God" as just two of the many gods. Some believe that all the gods, including both Satan and the Christian "God", are just very advanced extraterrestrial humanoids.

Religious Satanism

Religious Satanism is believed to have existed in the 1950s in the United States and the United Kingdom., largely unknown to the public. Various groups within this sect of Satanism believe that Satan is either an actual god or a principle and that the Satan they follow is not evil as Christians see and describe Satan to be.

They also believe that he is a pre-Christian Satan stemming from the pagan image of power, sexuality, sensuality, vitality and a force of nature. They believe that their Satan has nothing to do with hell, demons, pitchforks, sadistic torture, demonic possession or any evil. Some believe that Satan is a god, that he is the original creator of the universe and a being of light. They believe that God is the evil one trying to infringe on Satan's right to universal sovereignty.

This religious form of Satanism has a twisted view of biblical passages, which present God and the bible as evil.

Once again Satan attempts to elevate humans to god level and promote selfish endeavors which are essentially what enticed Adam and Eve in the Garden of Eden *(Genesis 3:1-5)*. The devil made the forbidden fruit as attractive as possible, but he did not reveal the poisonous repercussions that would affect them and all of mankind.

What deception Satanists are under. Satan has hardened their hearts and veiled their minds with his darkness and lies.

Satanists appeal to the egocentric, self-ambitious, non-conformist aspect of our fleshly nature, teaching that self is the most important entity in the universe and that an individual is his or her own god. The enticing influence is promoting one to seek after one's own ambitions and one's own pleasures, and even encourages women to use their femininity to get whatever they want. The selfish, self-centered and pleasure-seeking mentality is encouraged. It's all about me, myself, and I, and being accountable to no one. Self is glorified and individuality is the key. They promote an unforgiving lifestyle that is entirely opposite to the teaching of Jesus.

Satanism and its different forms never mention love, purity, or self-denial; and the dark side of the occult is never mentioned or promoted. Any involvement in the occult is spiritually dangerous and is one of the easiest ways to come under demonic influence. The occult is a direct invitation for evil spirits to infiltrate one's life.

The devil is a master of disguise and his true motives are not usually seen until a person is in nearly too deep to get free. At first, involvement in the occult seems harmless (the lie) and even fun and exciting, but the deeper a person gets, the darker it becomes and the more control it has over the person. Soon the person is trapped in darkness and in bondage, and once trapped, he will use and abuse the person and keep them in chains.

Luciferianism

Luciferianism is another form of Satanism and is the worship of Lucifer as a god. "Ism" means belief, practice or doctrine. The name Lucifer means bright star or morning star. It is the name of Satan before he rebelled against God (*Isaiah 14:12*). In essence, Luciferians worship a spirit entity called Satan. They believe that Satan is a spirit of knowledge, light, and magic and that he is not an evil entity.

Their goal is to elevate themselves to godlike status by living a life of goodness, seeking knowledge through magic, and opening themselves to Lucifer's mind to become one with that mind.

Some Luciferians believe that Lucifer is the god of the universe. Some believe him to be one god among many gods. Others believe him to be a principle instead of a god- neither good nor bad and neither male or female. Some Luciferians teach that "nothing comes before self and its progression is a newly manifested self."

It is interesting to note the Freemasons regard Lucifer as a "light-bearer," taken from their book *Morals and Dogma*, page 321.

The Enticing Factors

The promise of power and knowledge is the dominant drawing card Satan uses to lure humanity into Satanism and the occult. This power is sought after on the physical, mental and spiritual levels. While power and knowledge have become an obsession with occultists, drugs and sex have become bait to ensnare unsuspecting youth.

Christian research concerning teens interested in Satanism notes several factors that often accompany teenage involvement in Satanism. These factors include teens that alienate themselves to the extreme, those with a morbid fascination with horror, death, and pain, drug and alcohol use, nonconformity in school, home or job, and those who have an unnatural attraction to the mysterious, occult or magical.

Satanism can be very persuasive in convincing a person that the true God of the bible is either evil or nonexistent and that Satan is a beneficial entity or concept. Anyone without a solid knowledge of the Bible can fall victim and be persuaded as they manipulate bible passages to make their teachings seem right. This is all part of the deception.

Islam and Muhammad

Islam means submission or surrender, and Islam emphasizes submission to Allah. A follower of Islam is called a Muslim, one who submits. A Muslim submits to Allah by obeying Allah's commands in the Qur'an (believed by Muslims to be the literal word of Allah), along with the teachings of Muhammad, Islam's prophet, contained in the Hadith (a collection of stories about Muhammad).

Islam teaches that their god is the origin of good and evil (al-Falaq 113:2). He is the creator of virtue and sin in the universe and in man. The Islamic doctrine of absolute predestination teaches that all good and evil thoughts, words and deeds have been predetermined, decreed, willed, created by, and originate from the god of Islam.

Essential Islamic doctrines are outlined in the Six Articles of Faith, which include belief in Muhammad's teachings concerning: Allah, angels and spirit beings, prophets, scriptures, the Day of Judgment, and predestination.

Islam is a system of beliefs originated by a man that lived in Arabia from the years 570-632 AD named Muhammad. He is considered in this religion to be the last and greatest of all prophets. Born an orphan, he was raised by his uncle and grandfather.

Muslim tradition says that in the month of Ramadan in the year 610AD Muhammad was visited by the angel Gabriel who appeared to him while he was in a cave at Hira, which is situated a few miles from Mecca.

While the primary source of Islamic doctrine is the Qur'an, the Qur'an is not biographical in nature, and it tells us practically nothing about Muhammad. To learn about Muhammad, we can explore the Hadith and Sira literature.

The Hadith are collections of the sayings and deeds of Muhammad. The goal of the writers was to describe what Muslims should do in a given situation, based on the example set by their prophet. These writings were written more than two centuries after Muhammad's death.

The Sira literature was quite different. Sira writings often attempted to write complete accounts of the life of Muhammad, and these writings are similar to biographies. Sira writings were also written more than a century after the life of Muhammad, and Muslims themselves typically reject this source.

There is no detailed historical source written within a century of the prophet of Islam. Additionally, there is a time gap of over 100 years where virtually nothing that was written about him. Thus, we approach the information of the Hadith and Sira with caution and skepticism.

The story begins *One night on which God honored him (Muhammad) with his mission and showed mercy on his servants thereby, Gabriel brought him the command of God.*

Muhammad states: "He came to me," said the apostle of God, "while I was asleep, with a coverlet of brocade whereon was some writing, and said, "read!" I said, "What shall I read?" He pressed me with it so tightly that I thought it was death; then he let me go and said, "Read!" I said, "What shall I read?" He pressed me with it again so that I thought it was death; then he let me go and said: "read!" I said, "What shall I read?" He pressed me with it the third time so that I thought it was death and said: "read!" I said, "What then shall I read?" – and this I said only to deliver myself from him, lest he should do the same to me again.

He said: "Read in the name of thy Lord who created, who created man of blood coagulated. Read! Thy Lord is the most beneficent, Who taught by the pen, Taught that which they knew not unto men." "So I read it, and he departed from me. And I awoke from my sleep, and it was as though these words were written on my heart."

Muhammad was terrified by what happened to him. He believed that he had encountered a demon, and he became suicidal. His wife Khadija and her cousin Waraqah, however, convinced him that he was a prophet of God and that he had met the angel Gabriel in the cave.

Muhammad would periodically revisit this cave outside of Mecca for prayer and meditation and it was there that the archangel Gabriel appeared once again declaring him to be a prophet of God, and revealed the words of Allah that were recorded in a 114-chapter document named the Qur'an.

Muhammad believed that the angel that appeared to him was the angel Gabriel and that the words that he spoke to Muhammad were from the one true God, Elohim. In truth, this angel was none other than a demon of deception that disguised himself as an angel of light.

Approximately 578 years before Islam existed, Christians were warned against pagan gods and false prophets that we read in *Galatians 1:8 "But even if we (or an angel from heaven) should preach a gospel contrary to the one we preached to you, let him be condemned to hell!"*

During Muhammad's early years of preaching his message in Mecca, he was not driven toward violence. At that time, he was tolerant and cooperative even in the face of the Meccan people who opposed him and his new converts. In the year 622 Muhammad and his followers fled Mecca to Medina. In Mecca, he and his followers at that time were a weak and persecuted minority. This changed in Medina where he acquired political power, and his followers grew in number and military strength. A dramatic difference existed between the Qur'an he provided in Mecca and Medina. The former was characterized by conciliation, tolerance, and accommodation, the latter by vengeance, oppression and a self-serving revelation of convenience.

When studying the life and background of Muhammad you will see that his lust for power, wealth, sex and control dominated his life and drove him to stop at nothing less than killing what they considered the infidels (those who would not embrace Islam).

As Muhammad and his Muslim armies raided town after town, they would capture the women with the intention of selling or trading them. Yet, since the Muslim men were a long way from their wives, they needed wisdom from Allah to guide them in their treatment of their female captives and it wasn't long before Muhammad received a revelation allowing the soldiers to sleep with the women as quoted by the Qur'an (4:24), along with other quotes for the Qur'an (23:1-6; 33:50; 70:22-30), granting Muslim men the right to have sex with their female captives and slave girls, even those who were still married or who were going to be sold or traded. In other words, they had permission to rape the women. It seems that Muhammad conveniently received revelation from Allah giving them the ability to satisfy their lusts.

Most disturbing of all is that Muslims could have sex with girls who hadn't even reached puberty. The opening verses of chapter 65 of the Qur'an present Islamic rules for divorce. According to chapter 65:4, if a Muslim male divorces a girl who hasn't yet reached puberty, he must wait three months to make sure she isn't pregnant.

Muhammad posed as an apostle and prophet of God, yet his life was filled with lust, rape, warfare, conquests, and unmerciful butcheries. He had 12 marriages, many concubines and sex with a 9-year-old child whom he married at the age of 7. Her name was Aisha. Although he waited three years to have sex with her, Muslim sources report that Aisha still hadn't reached puberty. Since Muhammad is the moral exemplar in Islam, his actions still affect young girls today.

Was Muhammed Demon-Possessed?

Muhammad himself admitted that he was possessed by a devil; (quoted in Al-Hadis, volume 4 page 367. Attended by Muslim) and this is what it says:

Anas (a well-known companion of Muhammad) reported that Gabriel appeared before the Apostle of Allah (Muhammad), while he was playing with some boys. Gabriel took him, laid him down, pierced his heart, and took out a blot of blood. Then he said, "This is the portion of you possessed of a devil." Next, he washed it in a gold cup with water from the well Zamzam. Thereafter sewed him up and took him back to where he found him...

Research reveals that these next verses were present in the original Qur'an, but were later edited out, admitting that they were inspired by Satan himself:

"We have not sent a messenger or prophet before you but when he recited, the Devil would intrude into his recitation," (Al-Qur'an Sura (chapter) 22 verse 53).

'Muhammad admitted that he had a Jinn (demon) up his nose' (Al-Hadis, literature about the oral traditions, words and deeds of Muhammad. Volume 4, Book 54, No.513.

"Muhammad had his own resident demon, the one-eyed Dajjal" (Al-Hadis. Volume 3, page 803).

Muslims believe that Muhammad was morally perfect and that examination of his life proves that he was a prophet. However, evidence proves Muhammad was far from morally perfect and that there is no substantial reason to believe that he was sent from God.

It is likely that Muhammad was completely deceived by Satan, controlled by demons and used to execute Satan's diabolical scheme of lies and deception to mislead nations.

Muhammad Moral Standards

Muhammad was responsible for the first Islamic massacre in the bloody history of Islam– the massacre of the tribe of Banu Qurayza, the last Jewish tribe in Medina, in 627 AD. All the men of the tribe approximately 800-900 men were beheaded (Bukhari 4.52.280). Its wealth was looted and its women and children were sold into slavery. Muhammad urged Muslims to kill his critics, silencing them. He praised his followers for doing so. On his deathbed, Muhammad instructed them to cleanse the Arabian peninsula of all non-Muslims (Bukhari 4.52.288).

Muhammad taught that women are inferior to men (Al-Nisa' 4:34) and that women inherit half of their brother's inheritance. He also taught that the testimony of a woman in court is equivalent to the testimony of half a man (al-Baqarah 2:282). He considered wife-beating (al-Nisa' 4:34), breastfeeding adults, temporary marriage, polygamy, and sexual abuse of child-girls as acceptable (al-Nisa' 4:3)

Muhammad also condoned:
- Punishments of stoning, limb amputation, and flogging for fornication and theft
- Killing and enslaving non-Muslim children (Muslim 19.4321-4323)
- Killing and subjugating of non-Muslims (al-Tawbah 9:5; Muhammad 47:4)
- Spreading Islam by offensive war (Jihad)
- Lying if a threat is perceived to a Muslin or to Islam to further the cause of Islam
- The fictitious carnal lustful Islamic paradise of sexual promiscuity and gluttony (al-Tur 52: 17-24)
- The killing of apostates, Muslims who renounce Islam
- Immoral values that produced the most violent, greedy and evil aspects of the fallen human nature

Background of the Name Allah

Allah comes from the compound Arabic word, al-ilah. Al is the definite article meaning 'the" and "ilah" is an Arabic word for god, i.e. the god. This is not a proper name but a generic name like the Hebrew El. Allah is not a foreign word (as it would have been if it had been borrowed from the Hebrew Bible) but a purely Arabic one. It would be incorrect to compare Allah with the Hebrew or Greek for God (El and Theos, respectively) because Allah is an Arabic term exclusively referencing an Arabic deity.

The Encyclopedia of Religion reads: *"Allah is a pre-Islamic name ...corresponding to the Babylonian "Bel"."*

I have listed statements from present archaeological findings that are found in the Encyclopedia Britannica that bring to question what Muslims teach concerning their explanation of Allah.

"The name Allah is found ...in Arabic inscriptions prior to Islam" (Encyclopedia Britannica, I: 643).

"The Arabs, before the time of Mohammed, accepted and worshipped, after a fashion, a supreme god called 'Allah'" (Encyclopedia of Islam, eds. Houtsma, Arnold, Basset, Hartman; Leiden: E.J. Brill, 1913, I: 302).

"Allah was known to the pre-Islamic Arabs; he was one of the Meccan deities" (Encyclopedia of Islam, ed. Gibb, I: 406).

Archaeological evidence shows that the dominant religion in Arabia was the cult of the moon-god.

In 1944 an Archeologist by the name of G. Caton Thompson wrote in the book *The Tombs and Moon Temple of Hureidah*, that she had uncovered a temple of the moon-god in southern Arabia. The symbols of the crescent moon and no less than 21 inscriptions with the name Sin were found in this temple along with an idol which is believed to be a representation of the moon-god himself. According to numerous inscriptions, while the name of the moon-god was Sin, his title was Al-Ilah, the deity, meaning that he was the chief or high god among the gods.

Evidence gathered from North and South Arabia demonstrates that moon-god worship was active even in Muhammad's day, and was still the dominant cult.

The moon-god was called Al-Ilah, the god which was shortened to Allah in pre-Islamic times. The pagan Arabs even used Allah in the names that they gave to their children. Muhammad's father's name was Abd-Allah and his uncle's name was Obied-Allah.

The Arabs said that the moon-god was the greatest of all gods. While they worshipped 360 gods at the Kabah in Mecca, the moon-god was the chief deity. Mecca was built as a shrine for the moon-god which made it the most sacred site of Arabian paganism.

The claim that Allah is the God of the Bible and that Islam arose from the religion of the prophets and apostles is refuted by overwhelming archeological evidence. Islam was simply a revival of the ancient moon-god cult. It has taken the symbols, the rites, the ceremonies, and even the name of its god from the ancient pagan religion of the moon-god.

Islam's god Allah is not the same God that Christians worship nor is he the God of the Holy Bible. Let's compare some of the main differences between Allah the god of Islam, and the God of the Holy Bible.

Allah - Love or Lack Thereof

"The concept of love as one of God's essential attributes is conspicuously missing from Islam because in Islamic thought love is a sign of weakness" (M. Youssef, America, Oil, and the Islamic mind, p. 82).

Islam describes a god that seems to have no compassion. Contrary to the Christian position, Muhammad objects to the love covenant of Christ saying in Al-Ma'idah 5:18 *The Jews and the Christians say, "We are God's children and His beloved ones... say: "Why then does He cause you to suffer for your sins? Nay, you are but human beings of His creating. He forgives whom He wills and He causes to suffer whom He wills: for God's is the dominion over the heavens and the earth and all that is between them, and with Him is all journeys end."*

Allah's love is conditional upon a faithful response to his revelations. According to the Qur'an, the Islamic god only loves the righteous (Al-'Imran 3: 159), the godly (Al-'Imran 3:76), the repentant (al-Baqarah 2: 222), the just (al-Ma'idah 5:42), and those who fight for him in Islamic Jihad (al-Saff 61: 4). Allah does not love the wicked, the wasteful, the proud, the infidels or the ungodly (Al-Imran 3:57, al-An'am 6:141, an-Nahl 16:23; al-Qasas 28:77). Love is something he does; it is not his nature. It is a love that condescends, not a love that shares in a relationship or in a personal way. The god of Islam does not satisfy the longing of the human soul for divine love, forgiveness and the assurance of salvation.

Is There Forgiveness in Allah?

The god of Islam has no basis for forgiveness because Allah does not provide atonement for the forgiveness of sins. He is arbitrary in granting forgiveness (al-Ma'idah 5:18). The god of Islam condones, instructs and urges Muslims to pursue massive destruction and murder of human life; they are to fight and slay unbelievers. These instructions are provided in the Qur'an (al-Baqarah 2: 193, 216, 244), many other chapters of the Qur'an, and in the life and example of Muhammad and Islamic history.

A great example and comparison between the loving merciful Biblical God and the vengeful vindictive Islamic god is found in these illustrations taken from the Qur'an and the Holy Bible.

1. *A woman confessed her adultery to Muhammad. She was penitent and asked for purification. Muhammad gave her the chance to give birth to the child, and nurse him. After she weaned him, Muhammad ordered her stoned to death. She was buried in a ditch up to her chest, and they stoned her to death.* (Muslim: 17.4206).

2. This is the story of the woman who was caught in the act of adultery. *Jewish religious leaders brought her to Jesus and they asked him whether they should stone her to death as the Law of Moses required. Jesus stooped down and wrote on the ground with his finger, as though He did not hear. So when they continued asking Him, He raised Himself up and said to them, "He who is without sin among you, let him throw a stone at her first". And again He stooped down and wrote on the ground. Then those who heard it, being convicted by their conscience, went out one by one, beginning with the oldest even to the*

last. And Jesus was left alone, and the woman standing in the midst. When Jesus had raised Himself up and saw no one but the woman, He said to her, "Woman, where are those accusers of yours? Has no one condemned you?" She said, "No one, Lord." And Jesus said to her, "Neither do I condemn you; go and sin no more." (John 8:6-12)

Jesus manifested the exceeding love and mercy of the true living Biblical God, while Muhammad projected the condemnation and vengeance of the Islamic god, which lead to desperation and death.

What is the Qur'an?

After Muhammad's first vision in 630 A.D., and up until his death, Muhammad was said to have prophesied from time to time in a kind of trance. These pronouncements, in the Arabic language, dealt with many subjects such as God's prophets and scriptures, God's mercy and punishment, death, the Last Day, good and evil spirits, laws of marriage, divorce, and warfare.

It is said that Muhammad delivered verses to his scribes and companions for memorization and recording over the next two decades. These verses were written on flat stones, bones, palm leaves and anything else they could find because the paper was scarce at that time.

All these pronouncements were collected and edited in a single book, but there are differences of opinion among Muslims as to whether this editing was completed before or after his death. It is this collection of pronouncements that we know as the Qur'an. Qur'an literally means proclamation or recitation.

Muslims believe that these are the word of God himself, spoken through the lips of His Prophet, but not in any way coming from the mind and experience of Muhammad. They believe that the "mother of the Qur'an" (ummu-l-kitab) is in heaven, written by God Himself on a "guarded tablet" (lawhu-l-mahfuz). They believe that the angel Gabriel brought the tablet down to Muhammad; therefore, the Qur'an today is a copy of the "guarded tablet" in heaven. (cr.Q.81)

The Qur'an is the main scripture base for Muslims and is considered infallible. Believed to be divinely inspired, the Qur'an was allegedly revealed to Mohammad by Gabriel over a period of approximately twenty-three years beginning in 610AD. Muslims also believe that the Qur'an was precisely memorized, recited and written down by Muhammad's companions, the Sahaba which were the disciples and scribes of Muhammad.

Yet, there are disputes among Muhammad's scholars and it is believed that the Qur'an has changed significantly over the years. These scholars say that the evidence shows that entire chapters were lost, large sections became missing, individual verses were forgotten, and phrases have been left out. Muhammad's best teachers and reciters could not even agree on which chapters were supposed to be in the Qur'an. The texts of the Qur'an consisting of 114 chapters of varying lengths, each known as a *sura*. Each sura is formed from several verses, called *ayats,* and marked by a number.

Muslims also use their own commentaries and exegesis that are called *tafsir*, which is a body of commentary and explication to explain the meanings of the Quranic verses.

There is also the *Reasons of Revelation* they used called *asbab al-nuzul* that is a secondary genre of Qur'anic exegesis directed at establishing the context in which specific verses of the Qur'an were revealed.

The different translations of the Qur'an are:

1. Hadith – Traditions of the prophet.

2. Sira – Prophetic biographies of Muhammad.

3. Sunna – Sunna Is the traditional portion of Muhammad's words or acts, accepted (together with the Qur'an) as authoritative by Muslims and followed particularly by Sunni Muslims. They are usually oral traditions found in collections of Hadith and Sira. Muslims do not agree

on the same set of texts or sources and emphasize the different collection of Hadith depending on which Islamic school or branch they belong to.

What is the Kaaba?

The Kaaba is a large cube-shaped building inside the mosque known as al-Masjid al-Haram in Mecca, Saudi Arabia and was built around the original Kaaba. Muslims believe it is a reflection of a heavenly house primarily built by Adam, made of standard blocks, with black and gold cloth around it.

To Muslims, the Kaaba is the holiest place in Islam. All Muslims pray towards this when they perform the five fardh (necessary acts mentioned in the Qur'an) Salaah or prayer.

Muslims say that Adam and Eve first built the Kabba – a flat-roofed stone house, estimated to be 50 feet high, and 35 feet broad by 40 feet deep. Adam and Eve had met at Mecca after being driven from Paradise. Later Muslins believed the shrine was restored by Abraham and Ishmael, and maintained by other prophets. This is the shrine that holds the Black Stones.

What is the Black Stone?

This Black Stone is the eastern cornerstone of the Kaaba and is said to have set intact into the Kaaba's wall by Muhammad himself in 605 A.D. Since then it has been broken into fragments and is now cemented into a silver frame in the side of the Kaaba's wall. Its physical appearance is that of a fragmented dark rock, polished smooth by the hands of pilgrims. Islamic tradition holds that it fell from heaven as a guide for Adam and Eve to build an altar; often been described as a meteorite, the hypothesis is now uncertain.

Muhammad found the Meccans worshipping the stone as an idol and he restored it to the worship of the one god for which it had originally been dedicated. Going around the Kabba (3 times running, four times walking) is one of the most important rites of the Pilgrimage, and each time around, the pilgrim does his best to kiss it, or at least to touch it with his fingers and touch his fingers to his lips. The worshipper feels he obtains divine blessing by doing this.

The Five Pillars of Islam

The primary path to salvation is centered on submission to Allah, submission to the Qur'an, and submission to the *Five Pillars of Islam.*

The 1st pillar is the testimony of faith. Shahada Worshippers are to declare the Allah is the one and only creator god and that Muhammad is his Prophet. This confession must be repeated frequently, especially on conversion to Islam, on hearing the call to prayer, in the prayer itself, and at the point of death.

The name of Allah actually denotes the name of a pagan idol and to declare this testimony of faith is to declare their belief in a pagan idol, thus making way for the influence of the demons that possess and work through Islam.

The 2nd pillar is the ritual prayer Salat, which is prayed five times each day while pointed in the direction of the Kaaba in Mecca. Part of this ritual prayer is the preparation of purifying themselves by washing the face, the hands and arms up to the elbows, the head and the feet up to the ankles, etcetera. All this must be done exactly according to the rule.

3rd pillar Ramadan – This is the month of fasting. During the month of Ramadan Muslims cannot eat, drink, smoke or have sexual relations between dawn and sunset.

4th pillar Zakat – Almsgiving: two and a half percent of the annual savings must be donated to charity.

5th pillar Hajj – Pilgrimage: a Muslim is expected to make a journey to Mecca once in his lifetime.

Jihad

The Dictionary of Islam says that *Jihad* has two meanings: an inner spiritual struggle (the "greater Jihad"), and an outer physical struggle against the enemies of Islam (the *lesser Jihad*), which may take a violent or non-violent form. Jihad is often translated as "Holy War."

In Muslim law, the Holy War is Jihad and considered an obligation imposed by God and his Prophets, and that the religion of Islam must be spread to all the world, by force if need be. To Muslims, idolatry is the greatest evil that exists, so warfare is considered legitimate as a means to rid the world of this evil.

Idolaters may be forced to convert to Islam by pain, death threats, or enslavement. It is considered an act of piety to make converts in this way, and the Muslim who dies fighting "in the way of god" is thought to go straight to Paradise.

Verse 9:29-30 of the Qur'an concerning Jihad:

"Fight against those who: Believe not in Allah, Nor in the Last Day, nor forbid that which has been forbidden by Allah and His Messenger and those who acknowledge not the religion of truth (i.e. Islam) among the people of the Scripture (Jews and Christians), until they pay the Jizyah (taxes that were paid) with willing submission, and feel themselves subdued." (29)

"And the Jews say: 'Uzair (Ezra) is the son of Allah, and the Christians say: Messiah is the son of Allah. That is a saying from their mouths. They imitate the saying of the disbelievers of old. Allah's curse be on them, how they are deluded away from the truth." (30)

Jihad is derived from the Arabic verb *Jahada*, meaning to endeavor, to strive, to struggle. It is sometimes translated as Holy War. The closest Arabic words for war are *harb* or *qital (fighting)* which are found in the Qur'an and its companion commentary-the Hadith. In religious contexts, Jihad means to struggle against one's evil inclinations, to strive for the moral strengthening of society, or to promote the spread of Islam.

From the recorded history of Islam, from the lifetime of Muhammad onward, the word Jihad was used in a primarily military sense. Although some Islamic scholars have different perspectives on the implementation of Jihad, there is a strong consensus amongst them that the concept of Jihad will always include armed struggle against what they see as persecution and oppression.

What are the different Denominations of Islam?

Most Muslims are of one of two denominations- *Sunni's* or *Shi'ites* and within these, there are 73 sects branching out within the Islamic religion.

1. Sunni Muslims include 75% - 90% of all Muslims. Sunni means tradition and Sunnis regard themselves as those who emphasize following the traditions of Muhammad and of the first two generations of the community of Muslims that followed Muhammad.

Movements to reform Islam originated in the 20th century. Some are limited to one country and others have a broader influence. Most are Sunni movements, such as the Wahhabis, the Muslim Brotherhood, and Jama`at-i-islami.

2. Shia Muslims make up about 10% - 20% of all Muslims. Shia's are the "party of `Ali, who believe that Muhammad's son-in-law `Ali was his designated successor (imam) and that the Muslim community should be headed by a designated descendant of Muhammad. Three main subgroups of Shia's are Twelvers, Zaidis, and Ismailis.

3. Sufism is Islam's mystical-ascetic dimension approach to Islam. Sufis's go beyond external requirements of the religion to seek a personal experience of God through forms of meditation and spiritual growth. A number of Sufi orders exist. Most Sufi are also Sunni Muslims, although some are Shi`ite Muslims. Many conservative Sunni Muslims regard Sufism as a corruption of Islam.

The Allure and Deception of Islam

The spirit behind Islam is like a pied piper, enchanting his victims into believing it is a religion for the young and heroic, those that feel a need to fight for something worth dying for. Islam is presented as a romantic cause that accepts people of every color, ethnicity, walk of life, and economic background, and claims to honor women. Promises of paradise (heaven) filled with unlimited drinking and eating, young women, and heavenly concubines. These promises are full of lies and deception.

According to Islam, a person is required to declare their creed openly, to pray (Salat) five times every day, fast during a specific month each year, give alms to the poor, and attempt to visit Mecca once in his lifetime. This ensures that a person is accepted by Allah.

It is interesting that the performance of the five pillars of Islam guarantees salvation from Allah, and that a Muslim can do any dastardly act and yet qualify to go to Paradise.

There are those within the Islamic faith who believe they are not to be held accountable for their actions. They are self-serving and non-repentant. They are void of any guilt if they kill, rape, plunder and destroy people, communities, cities, and nations. These are extreme devotees of Islam and believe they are acting in the will of their god, Allah.

I read an article containing an interview of an American Muslim that gave 5 reasons why young people were converting to Islam. The reasons given were: Islam doctrine is simple and rational, all believers are equal, it is a practical religion, and lacks a priesthood. The article goes on to say that Islam offers a conversion experience and the opportunity to get one's life in order, without needing to confess one's sin and need for salvation. How very convenient.

Another reason people convert to Islam is that it appeals to the animalistic, lustful and perverted desires of men and women, because in their concept of Paradise (heaven), stated in the Al Qur'an Susa 56, verses 15-24 reads *They recline on beds interwoven with gold, supplied with unlimited limpid drink, fruits and flesh of fowl and wide-eyed houris (heavenly concubines), like hidden pearls, as a reward for what they do.*

Muhammad was reported to have said: "There is in Paradise a market, wherein there will be no buying or selling but will consist of men and women. When a man will desire beauty, he will have intercourse with them." Reported by Ali and attested by Tirmizi (Al Hadis, Book 4, chapter 42, no. 34)

By participating in the rituals of obeisance to the pagan idol named Allah, they unknowingly invite demonic manipulation and control into their lives. Blindly they walk into the trap of Satan and are captive as he whispers the lies and deception that are behind Islam and the Qur'an.

Muslims are worshiping their enemy and are blinded to the truth of who their god really is. The god of the Qur'an does not exist, and the god of the Qur'an is not the God of the Bible. If you study the God of the Bible and the god of the Qur'an, you will find two distinctly different personalities.

In looking at the God of the Bible through the work and ministry of Jesus Christ and looking at the god of the Qur'an through the life of the prophet Muhammad. There is a huge difference between Muhammad and the Messiah, Jesus Christ.

Within the Islamic religion, there is what one ex-Muslim call:

1. Cultural Muslims who don't practice Islam and are Muslims in name only because they were born into a family.

2. Moderate Muslims who practice Moderate Islam and do practice their faith and claim to be peace-loving people.

3. Radical Muslims who practice Radical Islam and teach hate and violence against non-believer and their goal is to bring America down, to dominate, and to dictate core values and religious rights.

You are either the one who is deceived or the one who is deceiving others if you are a Muslim.

As a young girl, I remember seeing many churches of all faiths in the town that I grew up in. I also remember knowing that many of them did not believe as I did. Yet, I didn't feel they were a threat to me, my family or to my faith.

Islam was not a word that I was familiar with nor had I ever heard of Muhammad, let alone terrorism. However, in the twentieth century that we live in today, we face an enemy that will stop at nothing to dominate and to spread the radical religion of Islam and the false god known as Allah.

There is an Arabic word *Da'wah* that most Christians or western culture are not familiar with. *Da'wah* is the quiet way that Muslims are attempting to make new converts to Islam especially in the West.

Da'wah is a quiet revolution. It is Islam's method of converting one person at a time always using somewhat convincing arguments as to why we should accept them.

Da'wah, similar to missions, means *to* call or *invitation*, and is the proselytizing (or preaching) of Islam. It is an activity that embraces Muslims going out into the world and inviting non-Muslims to join Islam. Another important word in Arabic is the word *Da'l* meaning missionary. It seems that there are more Da'ls working in the United States and the UK than Christians working as missionaries in Muslim countries.

The World Muslim League located in Mecca strategizes and finances most of the work with the goal of uniting various branches of Islam to establish a *worldwide ummah* (i.e. Nation of Islam).

One of their strategies is to target University students. One group specializes in sending foreign students to schools in the United States to study and to also act as missionaries to their fellow foreign students and recruit others into the Muslim religion.

Have you noticed how many Mosques have been built around you within the last ten years?

Wake up America! We are not only in a physical war with radical Islamic terrorists, but we are also at war with the demonic spiritual forces behind terrorism, and it is a battle that can only be fought and won in the spiritual realm.

We as believers need to come together and take up our spiritual weapons praying, fasting, and fighting against the forces of darkness together as a mighty army. We must stand against the enemy by pulling down the principalities, powers, and the thrones Satan has built up in the minds and hearts of man, binding spirits of deception and breaking the power over those who have been deceived and blinded by the lies of Islam. We must shatter the darkness with the Word of Truth.

Testimony of an Ex-Muslim

Mosab Hassan Yusef is the son of Hamas leader Sheikh Hassan Yousef, one of the founders of the Muslim Brotherhood and Hamas. Mosab was born in Ramallah, Palestinian territories, 6.2 miles north of Jerusalem and is the eldest of five brothers and three sisters. As his father's eldest son, he was his heir and became an important part of the Hamas organization.

As Mosab grew up he wanted to be a fighter, because that was expected of Palestinian children. Being arrested at the age of ten for throwing rocks at Israeli settlers was the first of many arrests he would encounter by Israeli soldiers.

While in prison, Mosab's doubts about Islam and Hamas began forming when he realized Hamas' brutality towards their own people and religion. He hated that Hamas used the lives of suffering Palestinian civilians and children to achieve its goals.

In 1996 Mosab was arrested and held by Israeli agents known as "Shin Bet," and he was shocked by their interrogation methods. To his amazement he found their interrogation methods to be humane compared to how Hamas operatives tortured imprisoned suspected collaborators.

During the year Mosab was in prison, the Shin Bet asked him to become an informant for them. In 1997 he was released from prison and soon became the most reliable source in the Hamas leadership. The intelligence he supplied to Israel led to the exposing of many Hamas cells, preventing dozens of suicide bombings and an assassination attempt on the President of Israel, and the detention of several Palestinian leaders and the lives of many Jews.

In 1999 a British missionary introduced him to Christianity that led him on a seven-year journey to seek the truth. Gradually he embraced Christianity and in 2005 he was secretly baptized in Tel Aviv by a Christian tourist. He soon left the West Bank and moved to the United States in 2007 where he lives in San Diego, California and is part of a fellowship called Barabbas Road church.

Mosab publicly revealed his Christianity in 2008 and renounced Islam and Hamas. This endangered himself and his family in Ramallah subjecting them to persecution by Arab leaders, Hamas, and the Palestinian people. In 2010 he released his autobiography, *Son of Hamas*.

In an interview with Tyndale House Publishers, Mosab says that the scripture that caused him to question the god that he believed in was *Matthew 4:4 "Love your enemies."*

Before Mosab read the bible and began to understand the teaching of Jesus Christ if he did not comprehend loving your enemy. He said that this scripture was something different because everyone says love your neighbor, love your country, love your family, but nobody says to love your enemy. Mosab admits that he thought it was stupid because this is not how he was raised. He was raised to hate his enemy.

He began to question, who is my enemy? Is it my neighbor? Is it the Israelis, the Palestinians or the Americans? He realized that his enemy was not a man, his enemy was the enemy that lived inside of him. He understood that this enemy wants us to destroy each other through hate. When he read the scripture *Love your enemy*, he was genuinely moved.

Mosab struggled with this for many years until he came to believe that the Jesus of the bible was God. To Mosab what revealed that Jesus is God is that He has the highest standards above all other gods, which He lived and taught His followers.

In an interview, Mosab affirmed that miracles are happening in the Middle East and in the darkest places and that God is working. He said that God is working at the root of the problem within the Palestinian and Israeli people; that Jesus is sending His message, clearly declaring that He didn't come to take sides, but to take over.

Mosab's mission is to fight the ideology of Islam and expose the god of Islam. To proclaim the forgiveness, love, grace, healing, and salvation of Christ to Muslims and Israeli's. Thousands of saved Muslims and Israelis are marching in the streets and carrying signs that read "The Messiah came, don't keep waiting for Him, He is already here, and He came over two thousand years ago."

Mosab went on to say that the answer to the Israeli-Palestinian conflict does not lie in security or politics, because at the root it is a war between two gods, two religions. Between the God of the Torah and the God of the Qur'an. Hamas teaches that Palestine is "Waqf land" – a sacred endowment that must not be given up. The Torah teaches Jews that this is their land and must not be given up.

Mosab went on to say "There will be no peace in the Middle East. Israel's problem is not with Hamas or with any other organization, nor with the interpretation, Hamas reads into the Qur'an. It is with the god of the Qur'an.

Mosab states that even a moderate Muslim who reads the Qur'an reads and believes that the Jews are the sons of apes and that infidels must be killed. Mosab declares that the Palestinians must stop blaming Israel, or the West for their problems, and if they want true freedom, they must free themselves from their god.

191

New Atheism

Atheism means without belief in God. Atheism is an absence of belief in the existence of gods or God or any supernatural reality. Many Atheists will say that they have reached this position reluctantly, yet add that intellectual honesty has forced them into this position. They believe that religion is a crutch for weak and gullible people.

Karl Marx said "Religion....is the opium of the people" and "the first requisite for the happiness of the people is the abolition of religion."

Religion in its simplest form is a personal set or institutionalized system of religious attitudes, beliefs, and practices. A system is defined as an organized set of doctrines, ideas, or principles usually intended to explain the arrangement or working of a systematic whole.

Isn't this what the Atheists have done? They have created their own religion from a system that has been formed and established out of their own ideas and conclusions.

New Atheism has its own belief system, its own doctrine of God, a doctrine of origins, a doctrine of man, a doctrine of sin, a doctrine of salvation, a body of prophetic literature, and an eschatology.

It seems that their holy book is Charles Darwin's *On the Origin of Species by Means of Natural Selection* or the *Preservation of Favored Races in the Struggle for Life*, and they defend Darwin's book with fervency.

There are four men responsible for introducing this new Atheistic belief system through their books and philosophies. They are known as "the four gospels of the New Atheism." Below are their books and some brief biographical information.

Christopher Hitchens' *God Is Not Great: How Religion Poisons Everything,* one of the many books he wrote. He was an author, columnist, essayist, orator, religious and literary critic, social critic and journalist.

Daniel Dennett's *Breaking The Spell: Religion as a Natural Phenomenon* is among the many books he authored.

Dennett is a philosopher, writer, and cognitive scientist whose research centers on the philosophy of science, and biology particularly in the fields that relate to evolutionary biology and cognitive science.

Richard Dawkins, *The God Delusion*, is one of many of his written works. He is an English ethologist and evolutionary biologist.

Sam Harris' *The End of Faith: Religion, Terror, and the Future of Reason* and author of five New York Times bestsellers. He is a philosopher and neuroscientist.

As I review these men and their doctrines, please understand that I am in no way condoning, nor do I agree with their doctrine or the New Atheistic beliefs. I am only providing information to increase awareness about this movement and its teachings.

My heart is truly saddened and grieved because of their blatant mockery of the Bible, and heir belittling of Christians, Christ, God, Sin, Salvation, Atonement, Man, and Creation. The more we know, understand and are informed, the more ammunition we have to work with. In these times we desperately need that advantage.

What Is Their Doctrine Of God?

The Atheist's doctrine of God was quoted by the late Christopher Hitchens, a well-known Atheist, in his book, *God Is Not Great: How Religion Poisons Everything*. He said, "God did not make us, we made God,"

The New Atheists proclaim that a deity of any description, and particularly the God of the Bible, is an invention of the human mind. That the belief in God stems from primitive man's efforts to explain what he could not explain otherwise such as the existence of the universe, man, evil, and so on. Belief in God is a relic of a primitive past, and an impediment to a brighter future for mankind.

Dawkins says this about God, "The God of the Old Testament is arguably the most unpleasant character in all fiction: jealous and proud of it; a petty, unjust, unforgiving control-freak; a vindictive, bloodthirsty ethnic cleanser; a misogynistic, homophobic, genocidal, filicidal, pestilential, megalomaniacal bully and things I can't repeat here… it is unfair to attack such an easy target. The God Hypothesis should not stand or fall with its most unlovely instantiation, Yahweh, nor his insipidly opposite Christian face, "Gentle Jesus meek and mild." Dawkins has been called the Rottweiler of New Atheism and I can understand why.

My spirit is grieved when I read such venomous accusations against God. Righteous indignation rises within me. Yet, at the same time, I pity the men and women who promote such lies and deception. My prayer is that the veil of lies and deception is lifted from their eyes and that their stony hearts are replaced with hearts of flesh.

Another of their beliefs is that "the God of Abraham is not only unworthy of the immensity of creation; he is unworthy even of man." And to make matters worse they put themselves in place of God with statements like this:

We are the final judges of what is good, just as we are the final judges of what is logical…The only angels we need to invoke are those of our better nature: reason, honesty, and love. The only demons we must fear are those that lurk inside every human being: ignorance, hatred, greed, and faith, which is surely the devil's masterpiece…The days of our religious identities are clearly numbered.

And as far as Jesus Christ fulfilling all the Old Testament prophecies in the person, and the work of Jesus Christ, as evidenced of His deity - they say it all constitutes an insurmountable leap of faith.

Atheists Arguments of God's Existence

Atheist's logical assumption and conclusion about God's existence says that:

1. A being capable of creating anything can only come into existence by evolving.

2. Because of the nature of evolution, such a creative intelligence comes late in the evolutional process.

3. Therefore, God could not have existed first.

They are claiming that belief in God is false because evolution is true. They define evolution as molecules becoming a man through billions of years of natural selection and mutation.

The kind of evolution the New Atheists preach as the basis of their entire would view requires additional information to be added to genetic selection and mutation theory. However, science has demonstrated that at every stage of the development of an organism, genetic information is lost, not gained. Organisms do not gain in complexity from one generation to another.

In my opinion, it takes more faith to believe in evolution than to believe in a God that created everything. They put their faith in scientific and philosophical conclusions and doctrines that lack real evidence or truth. They would rather believe a lie and continue to grope in darkness and uncertainty as they continue stumbling over and missing the point. God is not a deity among all the other deities that man has worshipped, He is the one true God that has created all things.

Man did not evolve from an amoeba, he was created as Genesis 1:1 tells us: *"In the beginning God created."*

'Beginning' (the Hebrew word *Re'shiyth*) means the first in place, time, order or rank. 'Created' (Hebrew word *Bara)*, means to form, make, produce, to bring into existence out of nothing.

Colossians 1:15-17 "And He is the image of the invisible God, the first-born of all creation. And He is before all things, and in Him, all things hold together." (Hebrew-Greek Key Study Bible)

Atheists and the Bible

New Atheists emphatically reject the Bible. They reject the Law of God as the eternal life and death standard of righteousness, and Biblical morality as being a beneficial influence on society. In essence, Atheists are at war with God.

They also reject that the Bible gives us God's standard of perfect holiness. They believe that the Bible is a weird, obnoxious, chaotically cobbled-together anthology of disjointed documents that were supposedly composed, revised, translated, distorted and improved by hundreds of anonymous authors, editors, and copyists unknown to us and mostly unknown to each other. In addition to this, they believe the Bible took nine centuries to complete.

The New Atheism's "Holy Book"

New Atheists have embraced a holy book of their own which is Charles Darwin's *"On the Origin of Species by Means of Natural Selection,"* along with the *"Preservation of Favored Races in the Struggle for Life."*

According to Richard Dawkins, a fundamentalist is a person who believes in some holy book and therefore will not change his mind. He also said that an Atheist, on the other hand, is interested in the truth, open to new ideas, willing to change his mind, but are pretty hostile toward any rival doctrine.

Ironically New Atheists fit into their own description of a fundamentalist because they defend Darwin's writings with passion and are unwilling to change their minds. They hold Darwin and his writings with great reverence and unquestionable devotion as if he were God and his theory was the final and unquestionable truth.

They believe that Darwinian processes are the basis of everything, including "Mind, Meaning, Mathematics and Morality" and that cultural diversity is a product of Darwinism. They also make it very clear that religious fundamentalism has no place in diversity.

The New Atheists doctrine of God is this: Belief in God is false because Darwinian evolution – molecules becoming a man through billions of years of natural selection and mutation – is true. They have embraced Darwin as their "savior" from God.

The Doctrine of Creation.

How interesting to know that many New Atheists use the term *creation* to describe the universe and the activities that brought it about. Their doctrine of creation is the Big Bang. The Big Bang theory is generally taught in public schools, colleges, and universities today.

The Big Bang is a scientific theory about how the universe began, and then made the groups of stars called galaxies we see today. The universe began as very hot, small, and dense, with no stars, atoms, form or structure, this is referred to as a singularity. Then, approximately 14 billion years ago, space expanded very quickly, thus the name "Big Bang", resulting in the formation of atoms, which eventually led to the creation of stars and galaxies. They believe that the universe is still expanding today, and growing colder.

New Atheists proclaim this doctrine of creation to be infallible, despite having little evidence that this was how the universe was created. They consider this theory to be self-evident and not in need of proof.

Questions I want to ask Atheists are: where did the original matter of the universe come from? Where did all that power and energy come from? Who or what caused the time to begin? How does anything exist without a creator? Why creation, or what is the purpose for the universe, earth, man and every living creature?

Outside of God and the Bible these questions cannot be answered, not by science, observation, mathematics, experimentation or analysis.

Romans 1:20 "For since the creation of the world His invisible attributes, His eternal power, and divine nature, have been clearly seen, being understood through what has been made, so that they are without excuse." (Hebrew-Greek Key Study Bible)

Christians believe the Genesis account of a literal six-day creation and our starting point for interpreting the scientific evidence is that the Genesis account is accurate and trustworthy. Evolutionists presuppose that the Genesis account is inaccurate and that the scientific evidence of creation must be explained in some other way.

Christians and evolutionists both look at the same evidence, but with a different set of beliefs.

How blinded and deceived we can become when we stand in rebellion, pride, and self-sufficiency apart from God?

Why is it that Atheists spend so much time trying to convince the world and prove that there is no God if they aren't threatened by the thought that maybe there is a God who created all things and they are wrong?

Psalms 14:1 "The fool has said in his heart, there is no God." (Hebrew-Greek Key Study Bible)

Doctrine of Man

New Atheism believes that man is a product of random processes of time and chance and that we are the result of evolution. They believe that human reasoning is merely the product of electrochemical processes taking place in the brain and that human life is bytes and bits of digital information.

They also believe that if our presence here on earth, in our present form is random and contingent, then we can expect the further evolution of our brains to bring stupendous advances in medicine and life extension that will derive from our elementary stem cells and umbilical cord blood cells. All of this will be clarified and understood through nature; no divine plan or angelic intervention is required.

Richard Dawkins states, "We are jumped-up apes and our brains were only designed to understand the mundane details of how to survive in the Stone Age African savannah."

It's absurd and hard for me to wrap my head around this New Atheist thinking of man and how they believe he evolved. As a Scripture driven Christian, I understand that man is God's special creation and we are not as the New Atheists preach. We are not creatures of "lowly" origins – "jumped up apes" with a tenth-rate brain, and we are not mere products of random electrochemically induced "neutral events." Everything within me wants to scream. Scripture declares the very opposite of their beliefs in *Genesis 1:26-31.*

God made man in His own image and likeness. Adam was created as a full-grown man and immediately began to talk, walk and make decisions. He communicated with God in a complex language. Adam had knowledge, understanding, and wisdom and comprehended what God instructed him to do. He was intelligent enough to carry out God's instructions and to have dominion over the earth.

In *Job 38:36* confirms this as God asks Job *"Who has put wisdom in the innermost being, or has given understanding to the mind?"* Answer: "GOD"

In *Job 33:4* we also read the significance of God's breathing life into man: *"There is a spirit in man, and the breath of the Almighty gives him understanding." (Hebrew-Greek Key Study Bible)*

Doctrine of Sin

New Atheists speak of evil, truth, and justice, and view religion as the root of all evil. They say that the ultimate truth is that there is no God, and the ultimate justice is the eradication of faith. The distorted moral of New Atheism's doctrine of sin is *the smartest and strongest will always win.*

Atheists openly argue and scorn the biblical doctrine of sin and misuse the biblical terms of good and evil. To them, religion is the root of all evil and they believe that religion is an insult to human dignity. They also say: "With it or without it, you'd have good people doing good things and evil people doing evil things. But for good people to do evil things, it takes religion."

The New Atheists believe that the story of Adam's fall is ridiculous and that the original instance of someone being created free and then loaded with impossible-to-obey prohibitions is nonsense.

They define evil as anything that stems from violation of two "transcendent values" of truth and justice, and claim that all cultures share the idea of a transcendent value that is like a perfectly straight line – not achievable in practice, but readily accepted as an ideal that can be approximated even if it can't be fully articulated.

Transcendent value is a value placed on a person, place, entity or thing that is above in value than any other person, place, entity or thing. It is the most valuable. That which is of transcendent value can be known from the statement made by Jesus when He was here on earth *Matthew 16:26 "For what is a man profited if he gains the whole world, and loses his own soul? Or what will a man give in exchange for his soul?" (Hebrew-Greek Key Study Bible)*

The problem here is that New Atheists have no genuine transcendent values because these values are relative; the values are based on however men define truth and justice. When a man is lost, he is his own authority, because in the New Atheist mindset is that there is no one higher than man. Truth and justice are whatever man defines them to be. In their view, the ultimate truth is that there is no God, and the ultimate justice is the annihilation of faith.

In the New Atheist view evil, on the other hand, is simply part and parcel of evolution. They say it just comes with the package and what we see in the world merely reflects the age-old Darwinian struggle for survival. They believe that man became a man through billions of years of death and struggle, and the chilling moral of the evolutionary story is that *the smartest and strongest will always win.*

In rebuttal to their belief, as a Christian, I believe the true definition of sin is found in God's Word. Sin is any lack of conformity to, or violation of the law of God according to *1 John 3:4* and *Romans 4:15*. Sin is not merely an offense against God's law, but an offense against

God the lawgiver Himself. It is an offense by the creature (man) against the Creator (God).

Sin originated with Adam and Eve in the garden. Even though God gave them a commandment to obey, they out of their own free will chose to disobey Him. Because all mankind is Adam's descendants, when Adam fell into sin all mankind fell with him. (*Genesis 3; Romans 5:12-21, 1 Corinthians 15:22-45*)

The perfect nature of Adam and Eve were lost and they took on the nature of the one that tempted them to sin. When we are without God, we as human beings are in a state of depravity and commit acts of sin. We sin in word and deed and neglect the good that we ought to do. We are not sinners because we sin – we sin because we are sinners.

For this reason, it's easy for Atheists to deny there is a God because every part of man has been affected by the original sin. Therefore, we are blinded, futile in our thoughts, foolish, our conscience is seared, we are desperately wicked, and the heart of man is deceitful above all things. The natural man does not accept the things of the Spirit of God; they are foolishness to them. (*1 Corinthians 2:1; 1 Timothy 4:2; Jeremiah 17:9*)

Atheists Doctrine of Salvation

Christian's definition of Salvation is deliverance from the power and effect of sin. New Atheists define salvation as liberation from ignorance or illusion.

The New Atheists openly mock Christ and His atonement. They mock the biblical doctrine of salvation from sin through the atonement of Jesus Christ and believe that the central doctrine of Christianity: that of atonement for original sin which lies at the heart of New Testament theology, is almost as morally obnoxious as the story of Abraham setting out to barbecue Isaac.

Quoting Richard Dawkins and his perspective he says: *original sin itself comes straight from the Old Testament of Adam and Eve. Their sin eating the fruit of a forbidden tree – seems mild enough to merit a mere reprimand. But the symbolic nature of the fruit (knowledge of good and evil, which in practice turned out to be the knowledge that they were naked) was enough to turn their (apple-stealing) escapade into the mother and father of all sins. They and all their descendants were banished forever from the Garden of Eden, deprived of the gift of eternal life, and condemned to generations of painful labor, in the field and in childbirth respectively.*

He goes on to say: *So far, so vindictive: par for the Old Testament course. New Testament theology adds a new injustice, topped off by a new sado-masochism whose viciousness even the Old Testament barely exceeds. It is, when you think about it, remarkable that religion should adopt an instrument of torture and execution as its sacred symbol, often worn around the neck (the cross of Christ) and the theology and punishment-theory behind it is even worse. The sin of Adam and Eve is thought to have passed down the male line…What kind of ethical philosophy is it that condemns every child, even before it is born, to inherit the sin of a remote ancestor?*

Atheist Sam Harris says in his Letter to a Christian Nation: *Your principal concern appears to be that the Creator of the universe will take offense at something people do while naked. This prudery of yours contributes daily to the surplus of human misery. God incarnated himself as Jesus, in order that he should be tortured and executed in atonement for the hereditary sin of Adam. Ever since Paul expounded this repellent doctrine, Jesus has been worshipped as the redeemer of all our sins. Not just the past sin of Adam, future sins as whether future people decided to commit them or not.*

This is the distorted thinking of the world of Atheists. Satan has blinded their minds and distorted their thinking to the point of believing the lie. It is the Antichrist spirit in full manifestation.

Here Is the Salvation That the Atheists Offer

Daniel Dennett, who spreads the Atheist doctrine of salvation says:

I, too, want the world to be a better place. This is my reason for wanting people to understand and accept the evolutionary theory; I believe that their salvation may depend on it! How so? By opening their eyes to the dangers of pandemics, degradation of the environment, and loss of biodiversity, and by informing them about some of the foibles (weakness) of human nature. So isn't my belief that belief in evolution is the path to salvation a religion? No; there is a major difference. We who love evolution do not honor those whose love of evolution prevents them from thinking clearly and rationally about it... So I feel a moral imperative to spread the word of evolution, but evolution is not my religion. I don't have a religion.

The New Atheist view man's salvation centers on Darwinian environmentalism: Man's environment must be "saved" so that the struggle of the fittest to survive, climbing upon the carcass of those who are not fit to survive, can continue from generation to generation. But don't you dare accuse those who love evolution and believe that it is "the path to salvation" of having a religion. Don't you dare say that the death of the allegedly unfit among humanity – through abortion, euthanasia, holocausts, wars, disasters or any other means – is their religion's sacrament?

As a Bible-believing Christian, I know that God has not, nor will he ever leave man in the state of despair or hopelessness as the Atheists would describe or want man to believe. God's word assures us that "*He will never leave us, nor forsake us*" *Hebrews 13:5b*

The End Times View of the New Atheism

In 2006 Stephen Hawking, a British scientist and know Atheist, wrote an article for the London Daily Mail stating "mankind will need to leave planet Earth to ensure the long-term survival of the species."

Hawking is certain that some man-made environmental disaster, or some external force such as an asteroid collision, will make earth uninhabitable. "There isn't anywhere like earth in the solar system, so we would have to go to another star." Therefore, he says, industrialized nations should focus on developing vehicles capable of traveling just below the speed of light, so that human beings could reach some other inhabitable (yet to be discovered) planet in about six years of space travel.

In April of 2008, Hawking spoke at George Washington University in honor of NASA's 50th anniversary, repeating his call for man to prepare to leave earth. He concluded by saying, "The human race has existed as a separate species for about two million years. If the human race is to continue for another million years, we will have to boldly go where no one has gone before." Does this quote sound familiar?

Hawking is among the growing number of Darwinists who are willing to admit that their desire to see increased funding for space exploration is not rooted primarily in a desire to expand scientific knowledge but in their belief that intergalactic travel is the key to the salvation of the human species.

Several prominent New Atheists speculate that this is exactly how Earth was populated in the first place – by a race of intelligent beings who seeded life here from another part of the universe. New Atheists believe that man will solve every problem that ever confronts him and go on, and will evolve onward and upward.

In Daniel Dennett's book *Breaking the Spell*, he says, *looking ahead, anticipating the future, is the crowning achievement of our species. We have managed in a few short millennia of human culture to multiply the planet's supply of look-ahead by many orders of magnitude. We know when eclipses will occur centuries in advance; we can predict the effects on the atmosphere of adjustments in how we generate electricity; we can anticipate in broad outline what will happen as our petroleum reserves dwindle in the next decades. We do this not with miraculous prophecy but with basic perception. We gather information from the environment, using our senses, and then we use science to cobble together anticipations based on that information. In every area of human concern, we have learned how to anticipate and then avoid catastrophes that used to blindside us. We have avoided economic collapses in recent years because our economic models have shown us impending problems.*

They feel that man has the capability to work through any problem or challenge and avoid future problems. In other words, they don't need God to rescue them. Their naturalistic worldview is man's only hope for a bright future.

The New Atheists are quite open about their eschatological hopes for religion in general, and Biblical Christianity in particular – they would like religion to become extinct. Their goal is to bring this part of their view of the future to fulfillment sooner rather than later.

Atheists view various religions as institutions that sell self-help enabling moral teamwork, using ceremony and tradition to cement relationships and build long-term fan loyalties. They see religious organizations and their members become more like being part of a fan club.

The New Atheists' hopes are that religion diminishes in prestige and visibility, rather like smoking they say that is tolerated since there are those who say they can't live without it, yet it is discouraged. They believe it is a crime to teach religion to impressionable young children and look forward to the day that it is frowned upon, and outlawed in a majority of societies.

You can plainly see why Atheists wanted to abolish prayer and bible reading from the classroom. The statement that children are impressionable is accurate, and this is exactly why scripture instructs us to *"Train up a child in the way they should go and when he is old, he will not depart from it." Proverbs 22:6*

Another of the New Atheists' hope for the future of religion in general, and for Biblical Christianity is:

"Religion is in its death throes; and that today's outburst of fervor and fanaticism are but a brief and awkward transition to a truly modern society in which religion plays at most a ceremonial role. Their hope is that the major religions of the word soon go just as extinct as the hundreds of minor religions that are vanishing faster than Anthropologist can record them, and that the Vatican City becomes the

*European Museum of Roman Catholicism, and Mecca is turned into
Disney's Magic Kingdom of Allah, and the local Bible-believing
Protestant church building is put to some better use, such as a local
headquarters for the new thought police."*
-Daniel Dennett

How Do We Approach an Atheist or Evolutionist?

We must realize that we cannot break the inseparable connection
between the New Atheists and the belief in Darwinian evolutionary
theory. We must know that the evidence for the Genesis Biblical creation
account abounds. See www.answersingenesis.org

If you were to ask an Atheist to give even one single genetic example
to support their case for molecules-to-man evolution via mutation and
natural selection, they couldn't, because there aren't any.

Scientists, creationists or evolutionists understand that such evolution
requires the addition of information to DNA and that natural selection
and mutations always mean the loss of DNA information, never an
increase. This is a fatal flaw in the theory of evolution.

How do we approach the New Atheism as a belief system? One area
you can agree with them in is religion.

If we look at the history of the world in light of scripture, we clearly
see that religion has been used as a tool for evil in the world. A great
example of this would be found in *Matthew 23: 39.* The Pharisees added
layers of man-made commentaries and regulations to the point where the
people of Israel were perishing under the mountain of legalism. Jesus
condemned the religious rulers of the Jews for their evils. Freedom in
Christ from legalistic religion was a major focus of the ministry of the
Apostle Paul as we see in *Acts 17; Colossians 2:8-10, and 1 Corinthians
1:18-31.*

Even though we can agree concerning the evils of religion, and that it
is at the heart of the world's evils when used to promote legalism, it is at
this juncture that we part ways. The New Atheists' definition of religion

is a belief in the supernatural, which they also equate with mysticism. To the naturalistic mind, belief in the supernatural is the root of all evil. At this point, because we stand on the authority of the Bible, we must disagree with the New Atheists. It's not that man needs to deny the supernatural, but that man needs to stop denying the supernatural true and living God, His eternal power and Godhead, and understand and submit to Him.

The supernatural is not mystical – it is the real world. It is all that we see, hear, feel, touch, taste and smell that God has created and we have that authority based on scripture that tells about a supernatural Creator and Redeemer. How this all came into existence supernaturally and how the natural order is held together supernaturally by Christ is found in *Genesis 1* and *Colossians 1*.

Our third step is to point the New Atheists to Jesus Christ, God incarnates (John 1:1-18). We need to present Jesus Christ to them with good apologetics (a defense of the divine origin of) and present the Bible as the only supernatural Book. Further explaining that the Bible is the only book that provides an explanation of man's origin, and present condition, with which the data that we find in the universe agrees. Example: Biblical Archeology, Christian Physicist, and Astronomers.

Remember that the New Atheist is the natural man as *1 Corinthians 2* talks about, who does not receive the things of the Spirit of God and he does not accept them as true – nor can he because they are spiritually discerned.

All of the points I have made must be combined with much prayer, because all the evidence in the world, and all the arguing in the world, will not bring an Atheist or any person to believe unless the Spirit of God draws him and regenerates him *(John 6:44)*. One of the most powerful things you can do for an Atheist is to tell them you are praying for his salvation.

What Are Some Reasons People Become Atheists?

As I searched for information one of the reoccurring reasons I found was in those raised in a religious household. They had become very critical of their own religion and its traditions and eventually began to reject their religion and their belief in the existence of God or any other gods.

Another reason was that they had a bad experience with religious leaders that had become oppressive, hypocritical, evil, or unworthy of following.

The mission and message of their church was vague. They seldom saw any connection between the message of social justice, community involvement, or being good, to Jesus Christ and the Bible.

They felt their churches offered superficial answers to life's difficult questions such as evolution vs. creation, sexuality, and the reliability of the biblical text, questioning Jesus as the only way. Some attended church hoping to find answers to these questions. Others hoped to find answers to questions of personal significance, purpose, and ethics. They often concluded that church services were largely shallow, harmless, boring and ultimately irrelevant.

Others became Atheists through studying science, anthropology, and through reasoning during their college years.

Many Atheists indicate that they became convinced that either an all-powerful, all-knowing, all-present, creator God does not exist, or the probability of the existence of such a God is unlikely.

Another reason was unanswered prayer during childhood that led them to believe that God was not real.

Others gave reasons due to the people in their lives, books, seminars, YouTube videos, and website forums.

Quoting from an article entitled *Listening to Young Atheists – Lessons for a Stronger Christianity,* an Atheist college student stated, "Christianity is something that if you really believed it, it would change your life and you would want to change (the lives) of others. I haven't seen too much of that."

The youth of today are idealists who long for authenticity and having failed to find it in their churches, or religion, have settled for a non-belief that, while hopeless in its promises, feels more genuine and attainable to them.

What are the Demonic Influences Behind Atheism?

Note: Some of these were mentioned in prior chapters, but should be restated and reemphasized.

1. Spirit of Antichrist – *1 John 4:3 "And every spirit that does not confess Jesus is not from God; and this is the spirit of the antichrist, of which you have heard that it is coming, and now it is already in the world." (Hebrew-Greek Key Study Bible)*

Anti is a Greek word that has two meanings which apply. 1. Against or opposition to, and 2. In place of, or a substitution. This spirit works to bring a substitute, or fallacy, into your life with the intent of replacing the true. It also works to come against the truth by using great opposition. Antichrist means anti-Messiah.

This is a very powerful spirit that intensifies and gets stronger as we come closer to the end of the age. The antichrist spirit is at the root of all that comes against, opposes and denies God, the deity of Jesus Christ, His virgin birth, His atoning death, His physical resurrection, and His return. It has the power to deceive even the elect if given the chance and to break through and penetrate the church to spread deception. Satan's intention is to replace the true Messiah with a false messiah.

2. Spirit of Deception – *Revelations 12:9 "And the great dragon was cast down and out - that age-old serpent, who is called the Devil, and*

Satan, he who is the seducer (deceiver) of all humanity the world over." *(Amplified Bible)*

This leads to Self-deception, delusion, lying, pride, arrogance, criticism, mockery, and steers its victims into blasphemy, doctrinal & religious error, confusion, binding and blinding of the mind that resists biblical truth.

3. Spirit of Unbelief – *Hebrews 3:12 "Take care, brethren, lest there should be in any of you an evil unbelieving heart in falling away from the living God." (Hebrew-Greek Key Study Bible)*

Unbelief leads to apostasy, faithlessness, and refusal to hear God. The hardness of heart through refusal to hear and obey God develops. Unbelief is a consequence of hardening the heart against God. Open rebellion against God and all faith in God and His redemptive work are abandoned because of unbelief. It is a deliberate rejection of revealed truth.

4. Spirit of Rebellion – *1 Samuel 15:23a "For rebellion is as the sin of witchcraft, and stubbornness is as iniquity and teraphim (household good luck images, idolatry." (Amplified Bible)*

Rebellion leads to disobedience and disrespect for authority, and ultimately God. It asserts self-will, pride, haughtiness, stubbornness, selfishness, arrogance, ego and intellectualism, and is behind the spirit of antichrist.

A great example and manifestation of the spirit of antichrist is Islam, working through the false prophet Muhammed.

Derek Prince, a well know teacher and author has this to say about the spirit of antichrist:

"Mohammed arose in the 7th century in the Arabian Peninsula, claimed to be a prophet, and claimed to receive from an archangel the revelation of the religion, which became Islam. He also claimed that Islam was the true fulfillment of the old and the New Testament. He claimed that the Christians and the Gospels had perverted the real truth, but he was resisting it. That is the basic claim of Mohammed. He first believed that because he rejected idolatry and because he rejected the claims of Christianity, the Jewish people would follow him. And when they did not follow him, he turned against them and became a persecutor of them."

Christians and Jews have been given the title Dhimmi, which means a second-class citizen almost slave who is subject to deprivation of any legal and human rights because he is a non-Muslim. While it is true that Islam has not been guilty of anything as terrible as the Holocaust, it has a long record of 13 centuries of suppression and contempt for Christianity and Judaism.

Islam bears most of the marks of the spirit of antichrist. It started in association with the Old and New Testament. It claimed to be the outworking of the revelation of God. But it denies certain basic fundamentals of the Christian faith, like the atoning death of Jesus on the cross.

Mohammed taught that Jesus did not die, but that an angel came and spirited Him away before. Because there is no death, there is no atonement, and because there is no atonement, there is no forgiveness. And no Muslim has the assurance of sins forgiven at any time.

Derek Prince goes on to say that Islam absolutely denies that Jesus is the Son of God. You can talk to the Muslims about Jesus as a prophet, and they will give you careful attention. In fact, the Qur'an acknowledges Jesus as a prophet – even as a savior, even as a messiah. But when you say He is the Son of God, you bring out the most intense, bitter opposition.

In the famous mosque in Jerusalem that is called the Dome of the Rock – built on the site of what was the Temple of Solomon – the Arabic inscriptions around it twice says, *"God has no need of a son."*

The New Age Movement

New Age Explained

New Age is a term that applies to a range of spiritual or religious beliefs and practices that developed in the western nations around the 1970s. It has many subdivisions, but it is generally a collection of Eastern-influenced metaphysical thought systems, a hodge-podge of theologies, hopes and expectations held together with varied teaching of salvation, and other ways of thinking. New Age beliefs encourage one to do whatever feels good and to have universal tolerance and morality.

In the New Age Movement, man is central and viewed as divine. There is also a strong emphasis on the spiritual authority of self. This is accompanied by a common belief in a wide variety of semi-divine non-human entities such as angels and masters, with whom humans can communicate through channeling. Man is considered a co-creator and the hope for the world's future, peace, and harmony. The movement typically adopts a belief in a holistic form of divinity, which fills the entire universe, including human beings themselves.

The New Age Movement is said to be tolerant of almost any theological position, yet opposed to the so-called narrow-mindedness of Christianity that teaches that Jesus is the only way and that there are moral absolutes.

The term *New Age* refers to the "the Aquarian Age" which, according to New Age followers, is dawning near. This Aquarian Age is supposed to bring in peace and enlightenment and reunite man with God. They believe that man is presently considered separated from God not because of sin, but because of lack of understanding and knowledge concerning the true nature of God and reality.

New Agers believe that "the Christ" (also known as 'Lord Maitreya"), will come to teach them to live at peace with each other. Some goals of the movement are to establish a World Food Authority, World Water Authority, World Economic Order, and an entirely New World Order. One of the requirements for a person to enter this so-called New Age is that he or she will have to take what is known as a "Luciferic Initiation," a kind of pledge of allegiance to the Christ (Anti-

Christ) of the New Age and to the New World Order. The primary goal of the movement then is to prepare the world to receive "the Christ" and to enter the Age of Aquarius, thus establishing the New World Order

What is the Age of Aquarius?

Astrologers believe that evolution goes through cycles corresponding to the signs of the zodiac, each lasting 2,000 to 2,400 years. New Age advocates say we are now moving from the cycle associated with Pisces into the one associated with Aquarius. The Aquarius Age will supposedly be characterized by a heightened degree of spiritual or cosmic consciousness.

They have two basic beliefs: Evolutionary Godhood and Global Unity.

1. What is Evolutionary Godhood?

It is their belief that the next step in evolution will not be physical but spiritual. They believe in the evolution of both body and spirit, and that man developing will soon leap forward into spiritual horizons. Some of the ways they believe they will do this is through astral projection, which is training the soul to leave the body and travel contacting spirits, so they may speak through you or guide you, using crystals to purify the body's and mind's energy systems, and visualization using mental imagery to imagine yourself as an animal in the presence of a divine being, or being healed of sickness.

It also teaches that mankind will soon see itself as a god, as the "Christ principle," and that man's basic nature is good and divine. Since man believed to be divine by nature, he has divine qualities. This is an important part of the New Age Movements thinking. Because the average New Ager believes himself to be divine, he can then create his own reality and follow his own path. Most New Agers believe in reincarnation, many of which also believe the Bible was changed to remove verses that might have taught this.

2. The second major element is Global Unity and consists of three major divisions.

The first division teaches that they will all learn their proper divine relationship with one another achieving harmony, mutual love, and acceptance through realization and acceptance of this divine proper knowledge. The average New Ager is looking for a single world leader who with New Age principles will guide the world into a single harmonious economic whole, and also unite the world into spiritual unity; a one-world religion. (Does this sound like the antichrist?)

The second division's belief is that since God is all, and all is God, then nature is also part of God. Man must get in tune with nature and learn to nurture it and be nurtured by it. In this, all people can unite. New Agers are drawn to American Indian philosophies because they focus on the earth, on nature and man's relationship to them. They believe man and nature are on equal levels and are not more or less important, or different from animals, birds or fish. Their general philosophy is that all of us must learn to live in harmony with them and understand them. The New Agers call earth, Gaia, and believe that it is to be revered and respected. Some New Agers worship the earth and nature.

The third division of New Agers teach that man is divine by nature and once they see themselves as such they will be helped in their unity of purpose, love, and development. They say their goal is to fully realize their own goodness and to show others also. Their belief is that god (it) is impersonal, omnipresent and benevolent and he (it) does not condemn anyone. The New Age god is impersonal and because he is impersonal he will not reveal himself, nor will he have specific requirements as to morality, belief, and behavior. This is why reincarnation is appealing to them because there is no judgment and continual change until you accomplish full realization.

Because New Agers seek to elevate themselves to godhead, they must lower the majesty and personhood of the true God. Thus, the universe isn't big enough for one true God, but it is big enough for a bunch of little ones.

In the New Age Movement, there are no moral absolutes and they claim to have a spiritual tolerance for all "truth systems." This is what they call harmonization. The one and only good thing I can say about the New Age Movement is that they do believe in honesty, integrity, love, and peace. The problem is that they want to live without God. That way they don't have to answer to anyone but themselves.

The History of New Age

One of the earliest influences on the New Age was the Swedish Christian mystic Emanuel Swedenborg (1688-1772) who professed the ability to communicate with angels, demons and spirits from Jupiter, Mars, Saturn, Venus, and the Moon. He attempted to unite science and religion. His spiritual interpretation of the Seven Days of Genesis (understood as meaning successive stages in human regeneration) for example, corresponds to the development of the seven centers of consciousness in the Eastern teaching on the chakras according to author Ursula Groll. (See center for studies on new religions; Swedenborg, A Herald of the New Age for further study; article by Jean-Francois Mayer, University of Fribourg).

Another early influence in the late 17th and early 18th century was a German physician and hypnotist Franz Mesmer, who claimed the existence of a force known as "animal magnetism" running through the human body. The ideas of Spiritualism, New Thought, and esotericism traditions were prominent influences on the New Age development.

The establishment of Spiritualism, an occult religion influenced by these men in the U.S., was established during the 1840s and was a precursor to the New Age Movement, through its rejection of Christianity, claims to represent a scientific approach to religion, and its emphasis on channeling spirit entities.

Another major influence on the New Age Movement was the Theosophical Society, an occult group co-founded by the Russian Helena Blavatsky in the late 19th century. Her books *Isis Unveiled,* and *The Secret Doctrine* claimed that her society was the essence of all world religions, and they emphasized a focus on comparative religion.

Another stepping stone that paved the way to the New Age Movement was New Thought, which developed in the late 19th century

New England. It was a so-called Christian-oriented healing movement before spreading throughout the United States. Around the same time, Hinduism also found its way to the U.S. through the Hindu philosophy of Vedanta.

In the early to mid-1900s, an American mystic, theologian, and founder of the Association for Research and Enlightenment, Edgar Cayce would contribute to and greatly influence what would be known as the New Age Movement. Cayce was known for channeling. Another prominent influence was psychologist Carl Jung, who advocated the Age of Aquarius.

In the 1950s, within the New Age Movement, an element of the UFO religions could be found. This belief focused heavily on the coming of a new age that would be brought about by and through contact with extra-terrestrials.

By the start of the 1970s, the counterculture of the 1960s was rapidly declining in large part due to the collapse of the commune movement. However, it would be many of the former members of the counter-culture and hippy subculture who would become the early devotees of the New Age Movement and help in its full development in the 1980s.

The early form of the movement was based in Britain and made its way into America bringing a strong influence from Theosophy (teaching about God and the world based on mystical insight) and Anthroposophy (a 20th Century religious system growing out of theosophy and centering on human development). It expanded to cover a wide variety of alternative spiritual and religious beliefs and practices.

In 1971 a transformational training course called EST- Erhard Seminars Training was founded by Werner Erhard and became a prominent part of the early movement along with the use of Dr. Helen Schucman's *A Course in Miracles*, who claims to have channeled Jesus Christ and the one who supposedly relayed the information to her for the book on miracles.

Several key events raised public awareness of the New Age subculture: 1. The best-selling astrology book called *"Sun Sign's"* by Linda Goodman. 2. The release of Shirley MacLaine's book entitled *"Out on a Limb,"* which deals with reincarnation, meditation, mediumship (trance-channeling and unidentified flying objects). And 3. James Redfield's 1993 work *"The Celestine Prophet,"* which is based on psychological and spiritual ideas that are rooted in many ancient Eastern Traditions and New Age spirituality.

The New Age Plan of Deception

The word deception means the act of making someone believe something that is not true; can also be statements, thoughts, and teachings intended to make people believe something that has not been proven to be the truth, and are, in reality, fraudulent and misleading.

Satan has managed to pull off the grandest subterfuge ever conceived in the history of the world.

Satan packages and disguises himself to look like light and truth. He tricks the world into thinking that he can reveal and guide them to the true pathway of understanding, to know the mysteries of the universe, and have the ultimate mystical spiritual experience of oneness with the divine energy, its life force, and the earth.

In reality, New Age is mostly a repackaged form of Theosophy (mystical insight) as presented in the writings of Helen Blavatsky and Alice Bailey – two high-level practitioners of witchcraft. Their writings, in turn, are new marketing for and form of Hinduism, interwoven with elements of Buddhism, Kabbalah, and traditional witchcraft. Both women have stated quite candidly on several occasions that their writings were dictated to them by their spirit guides and that they were a comprehensive account of the Luciferian doctrines taught in Babylon and ancient Egypt. Their only purpose is to lure the individual in with lies that ultimately lead to destruction.

Despite its seemingly goodwill and non-threatening exterior, New Age is extremely dangerous. It exerts a strong appeal to our fallen nature. Some New Age authors even boasted openly that their god is Lucifer.

Helen Blavatsky gave the title *Lucifer* to a magazine she founded in 1888. However, most New Agers are unaware of the profoundly Luciferian nature of their belief, or the sinister agenda behind the well-planned New Age program.

Part of the deceptive plan of Satan is to ensure that the use of drugs is part of the so-called deeper spiritual experience designed to help achieve a greater out of body experience. They are devised to entice the unexpected with the falsehood of ancient Eastern religious philosophies, which ultimately entangle them and draw them deeper into darkness and evil, with the promise of access to the innermost secrets of the universe.

Lies, lies, and more lies are spoken from the dark side so the unsuspecting victim eventually opens himself to demon possession and control. Another part of the plan is to present to the New Age believer the biggest counterfeit of them all, the opportunity to host their very own spirit guide. This is a counterfeit of God's Holy Spirit.

What Draws People to The New Age Movement?

The New Age Movement is not seen as a religion, but as a new way to think and understand reality. It is attractive to the natural man who has become disillusioned with organized religion and Western rationalism. He desires spiritual reality but doesn't want to give up materialism, address his moral problems or come under authority.

To some the New Age Movement offers an answer to their deep needs and desires for meaning, fulfillment, and hope, peace among people, spiritual experiences, guidance, and personal worth. Unknowingly, people are being brought under the spell of a seducing spirit that leads them away from God and undermines Christianity with false promises of a New Age and a New World to come.

Others become disillusioned with the church and its traditions, rituals, laws, and sterile lifeless services. They are hoping to find answers to their questions about God, the Bible, life and death, heaven and hell, purpose and meaning, and truth. Sadly, many are not finding their answers in the church.

Behind the New Age Movement is an enemy that wears many masks to disguise its deception and the true face of Satan. Even though many are drawn into this movement, there are also many that Jesus rescued and delivered out of the controlling deception of Satan, whose doctrine promises to take you to the light, but in truth takes you into greater darkness.

The Ultimate Testimony

There is a book titled *Inside the New Age Nightmare* written by a former New Ager, Randall Baer, who came to Christ in a most dramatic way. This is a small portion of his testimony:

One night… my spirit was roaming some of the farthest reaches of "heavenly light" that I had ever perceived. That night I had an experience that would change my life forever.

During this experience I was surrounded by a virtually overwhelming luminosity – it was as if I was looking straight into the sun. Waves of bliss radiated through my spirit. I was totally captivated by the power.

Suddenly, another force stepped in. It took me by complete surprise. In the twinkling of an eye, it was like a supernatural hand had taken me behind the scenes of the experience that I was having.

I was taken behind the outer covering of the dazzling luminosity and there saw something that left me literally shaking for a full week.

What I saw was the face of devouring darkness! Behind the glittering outer facade of beauty lay a massively powerful, wildly churning face of absolute hatred and unspeakable abominations – the face of demons filled with the power of Satan.

For a moment that seemed like an eternity, I realized that I was in major-league trouble, for this devouring force was now closing in on me. In absolute, stark terror I felt powerless to stop what appeared to be inevitable doom. Horror filled me like a consuming flame.

Then, miraculously, the same supernatural hand as before delivered me from the jaws of this consuming darkness, and hours later, I found myself waking up the next morning...the horror of the last night's experience had left me terribly shaken. My mind was racing uncontrollably in all directions at what felt like the speed of light. My body was shaking involuntarily, sometimes rather violently. This nightmare continued without respite for a full week. I thought I was going stark raving mad.

What I didn't know at the time was that it was Jesus who had intervened by His greater grace into my life. At that point, though, I only knew that some force greater than that of the devouring darkness had done two things: 1) It had shown me the real face of the New Age "heavens" and "angels" that I was so deeply involved with, and 2) It had delivered me from certain doom.

It took Baer awhile to adjust to all of this and come to a full acceptance of the fact that Christ had intervened personally to save him from certain death at the hands of Satan. Along the way, he says, *"I also had to sort out the shocking realization that the light that appeared so heavenly was really a counterfeit front for devouring darkness."*

He goes on to say, *The more of the Bible I read, especially the Gospels, the more I saw that the teachings of Jesus plainly were at variance with New Age philosophy on many key points. A few of these issues included:*

- *The sinful nature of man (the New Age says that man is inherently perfect and a "god")*
- *Man's need for redemption through Jesus Christ (the New Age says there is no need for redemption)*
- *The final judgment (the New Age holds that each person is ultimately his own judge and that the "lake of fire" is a myth)*

- *The personal and visible Second Coming of Jesus Christ (the New Age maintains that another "Christ" (not Jesus Christ) and/or "Christ consciousness" will lead the world into the New Age).*

After this experience, he went through a huge internal struggle for many weeks as Satan and his demons worked hard to retain their control over him. When he finally repented and accepted Jesus Christ as his Lord and personal Savior, he said *"The Lord had cut through my horrific satanic bondage and set me free as He received me into His Body as He washed my scarlet sins as white as snow. I was captive, but now I was free."*

Looking back on my 15 long, intensive years in the New Age, it is clear how Satan tempted a naïve, searching teenager, seduced a well-meaning, but blinded truth-seeker, and bound a man in chains with each step of a meteoric New Age career. The tragic poignancy of this entire scenario is that I truly believed through all this that the New Age did indeed hold ultimate truth and spiritual supremacy.

Not until I had a dramatic encounter with the devouring face of darkness behind all of the beautiful counterfeits did I begin to suspect that Satan is the author of the New Age. The saddest part of all is that millions and millions of New Agers today haven't a clue to the fact that they are caught up in a masterful, powerful delusion that leads only to the lake of fire. Today, my heart still breaks when I think of all the people, young and old, who are flocking toward the false light of the New Age like moths to a flame.

New Age Terminology

Most people have heard (and used) many of the buzzwords used by New Agers. Yet, do they really understand the concepts and ideas of the New Age and these terms?

New Agers often play semantic word games, using the same words Christians do, yet the definitions used bear no resemblance to the

Christian definitions. I have listed some of the major words to help you to understand their thinking and beliefs.

Agent: A person sending a telepathic message.

Alpha: The Physical body.

Animism: The belief that inanimate things such as plants possess a soul or spirit. New Age advocates see animism as a way of rededicating the earth.

Anthroposophy: An esoteric cult founded by German mystic Rudolf Steiner. The term literally means "wisdom of man." It teaches that we possess the truth within ourselves and that the human intellect has the ability to contact spiritual worlds.

Ascended Masters: Refers to those who have reached the highest level of spiritual consciousness and have become guides of the spiritual evolution of mankind.

Ascension of Christ: This is reinterpreted in a mystical way to refer to the rise of the "Christ-consciousness" in mankind. It describes the awareness that man is divine.

Astral: Astral refers to an "after-death", or "out of the body" experience. In Humanism, demonism, Satanism, and Theosophy, the extended umbilical cord holds the "astral" and the "physical" together. The experience is an "astral flight."

Astral Body: A spiritual body capable of projection from the physical body. The astral body survives death according to those of the New Age following.

Astral Flight: Soul travel occurring particularly during sleep or deep meditation.

Attunement: A New Age counterpart to prayer with the idea that complete oneness with God can be experienced by human beings by and through hypnotic consciousness through meditation, Nirvana, guided imagery, yoga, hypnosis, chanting of mantra, ecstatic dancing, channeling of spirit guides, New Age music, positive thinking or Alpha Mind techniques.

Aura: Radiated glow or halo surrounding living beings.

Automatic Writing: Writing produced without conscious thought of a living person, the written message given through a spirit guide.

Avatar: A person who "descends" into human form from above as a manifestation of divinity and who reveals divine truth to people.

Blood of Christ: This is understood by some New Agers to refer to the "life-energy" of the Cosmic Christ. This "blood" flowed from the cross into the etheric (or spiritual) realms of the earth. From these realms, Christ seeks to guide the spiritual evolution of mankind.

Channeling: A New Age form of mediumship or Spiritism. The channeled yields control of his perceptual and cognitive capacities to a spiritual entity (demonic spirit) with the intent of receiving paranormal information.

Cosmic Consciousness: A spiritual and mystical perception that all in the universe is "one." To attain cosmic consciousness is to see the universe as God and God as the universe.

Crystals: New Age advocates believe that crystals contain incredible healing and energizing powers, and are used to restore the "how to energy" in the human body.

Esoteric: A word used to describe knowledge that is possessed or understood only by a few.

Globalism: A modern-day term referring to the need for a transformation from the present nation-state divisions into a one-world community.

God: A being who has many faces. He (it) is considered a radically immanent being that is often referred to as universal consciousness, universal life, or universal energy. The New Age god is an impersonal force that pervades the universe.

Harmonic Convergence: The assembly of New Age meditators gathered at the same propitious astrological time in different locations to usher in peace on earth and one-world government.

Jesus: They believe that he is an avatar who attained a high level of attunement to the Cosmic Christ. This enabled him to become a bodily vehicle for Christ for a period of three years.

Karma: Refers to the debt accumulated against a soul as a result of good or bad actions committed during one's life (or lives). They believe that if one accumulates good karma, he will be reincarnated in a desirable state. If one accumulates bad karma, he will be reincarnated in a less desirable state.

Kundalini: The elemental energy of the human body which, like a serpent, rests coiled at the base of the spine. In yogic theory, is a primal energy, or Shakti, located at the base of the spine. Different spiritual traditions teach methods of awakening Kundalini for the purpose of reaching spiritual enlightenment. Kundalini is described as lying coiled at the base of the spine, represented as either a goddess or sleeping serpent waiting to be awakened. Kundalini awakening is said to result in deep meditation, enlightenment, and bliss. This awakening involves the Kundalini physically moving up the central channel to reach within the top of the head. Many systems of yoga focus on the awakening of Kundalini through meditation, pranayama breathing, and the practice of asana and chanting of mantras.

Mantra: A word or phrase that is to be chanted repetitively in an effort to empty the mind and attain "cosmic consciousness, i.e. oneness with God and the universe.

The Plan: A phrase that occurs often in the writing of Alice Baily. It refers to specific preparations in the world for a New Age and New Age

Christ. These preparations are carried out by the "Masters of the Hierarchy," a group of exalted beings who supposedly guide the spiritual evolution of people on earth.

Reincarnation: Refers to the cyclical evolution of a person's soul as it repeatedly passes from one body to another at death. This process continues until the soul reaches a state of perfection.

Second Coming of Christ: Understood by some as the coming of the Cosmic Christ in all of humanity, related to the New Age concept of the "mass incarnation." The Second Coming is supposedly now occurring in the hearts and minds of people all over the earth. Others associate it specifically with the appearance of Maitreya as the avatar of the coming age.

Spirit Control: A disembodied spirit who relays messages from dead people to the living through a trance medium.

Spirit Guide: A spiritual entity who provides information on guidance, often through a medium or channeled. The spirit provides guidance only after the channeled relinquishes his perceptual and cognitive capacities into its control.

Spiritual Hierarchy of Masters: New Agers believe these spiritual masters are highly evolved men who, having already perfected themselves, and are now guiding the rest of humanity to this same end.

Third Eye: An imaginary eye in the forehead believed to be the center of psychic vision.

Transformation: New Age advocates promote both personal and planetary transformation. Personal transformation involves the changes wrought in one's life by increasing Self-realization. They believe that as more and more people are personally transformed, the planet too will be transformed into a global brotherhood.

Yoga: A means of becoming united with the Supreme Being, or with the universal soul.

Yoga is from the Sanskrit word Yug, meaning union with the Divine; your higher SELF. Yoga is a path for transcending the ordinary mind (who you think you are) in order to merge with your higher SELF or God SELF. Yoga means to yoke – to yoke with Brahman (i.e., the "Infinite," the "Universal Spirit," the impersonal force that the Hindus call "God") via the realization of an altered state of consciousness, thereby theoretically releasing oneself from the bondage of endless reincarnation.

Yoga comes out of the Hindu Vedas. It can be traced back to Patanjali, a religious leader. Shiva, one of the Hinduism's three most powerful gods known as The Destroyer is called Yogi Swara or the Lord of Yoga.

Chapter 13
The Deep Longing

"For He satisfies the longing soul,
and fills the hungry soul with goodness."
Psalms 107:9

You may be thinking, what in the world does all that I have read concerning idols have to do with me and what I face in the world today as a believer? How is this going to help me to know and face the forces of darkness? How does this relate to my everyday life?

All of us have a deep longing, a void we feel in our heart and soul that can only be satisfied by and through the one and only true God, the Creator, made known through Jesus Christ.

No idol or worldly pleasure can satisfy and truly fill the void that you feel. That void will eventually become a large vacuum in the heart and soul, eventually demanding attention.

St. Augustine stated, "You have made us for yourself, O God, and our hearts are restless until they find their rest in you."

Whether we realize it or not, we all hunt desperately for something to satisfy and fill the empty places. Our craving to be filled is so strong that the moment something or someone seems to meet our need we feel an overwhelming temptation to worship it. This is exactly what man has been facing since the fall.

People are curious about the supernatural and are longing to experience, see and understand the supernatural realm. Many are longing to know what truth is and what is false, searching for purpose, fulfillment, and identity.

We long for a place where we fit in and are comfortable and where we feel free to express ourselves and are emotionally moved by an encounter with our Creator, God.

A. W. Tozer, a Christian writer said, "True religion confronts earth with heaven and brings eternity to bear on time."

As Christians: "To gain knowledge and have insight are tools and weapons that can be used against the forces of deception, lies and the demonic darkness."

The more we understand deception and recognize truth verses fallacy, is when a true encounter with our Creator the Lord God almighty begins to unfold.

What Is Religion?

Unger's Bible Dictionary defines religion as outward religious service, the feelings of absolute dependence, and the observance of the moral law as a divine institution. In general, it refers to any system of faith and worship, such as the religion of the Jews, of pagan nations or of Christians.

Every person has faith in something whether you believe in God, many gods, or you claim to be an atheist and believe in evaluation, you still have faith. There are people, sources, views, and ideas that you put your faith in and that you trust.

Everyone worships something or someone. Worship is adoration, love, reverence, respect, whom or what you are devoted to, deify and pray to.

The worship of demons is just as prevalent today as it was in ancient times. Idols names may have changed along with their outward appearance, but it's the same demons that inhabit idols.

Satan and his demonic kingdom will continue to work tirelessly to keep those steeped in idol worship deceived and blinded to who and what they really are.

Our knowledge and understanding of Satan, demons, demonic spirits, principalities, and powers allow us, to know *who* we are dealing with, *what* we will have to face and experience, and *where* we need to fight daily. As we face these last days and perilous times, a greater deception will manifest upon the earth.

2 Timothy 3:1-13 "But understand this, that in the last days will come (set in) perilous times of great stress and trouble [hard to deal with and hard to bear.]. But wicked men and imposters will go on from bad to worse, deceiving and leading astray others and being deceived and led astray themselves." (Amplified Bible)

The enemy has always used deception to come against man; yet the escalation and the myriad of ways demons work to deceive the world and believers is astounding.

Demons have had thousands of years to perfect the techniques needed to mislead, trick, trap and fool mankind. They literally hate us because we were made in God's image and were created to worship Him and Him alone. If they can mislead us into believing there are many gods and many ways or paths to God, or there is no God, then they have accomplished their goal.

Man's ignorance and weaknesses become the enemy's playground when we are not informed educated or aware that there is an enemy to contend with and demons to identify. They will push you and test you to your limits of understanding, and will take advantage of every opportunity to catch you off guard and unprepared.

We must be aware of and remember that the enemy operates in the invisible realm whether we want to believe it or not. There is the visible realm and an invisible realm that God created according to *Colossians 1:16 "For by Him all things were created, both in the heavens and on earth, visible and invisible, whether thrones or dominions or rulers or authorities all things have been created by Him and for Him." (Hebrew-Greek Key Study Bible)*

Satan and demonic spirits work in the invisible realm and have the power to be stealth and work undetected. Therefore, we need to understand and be aware that there is an invisible enemy always operating behind the scenes.

In *2 Corinthians 11:3, 14b* - Paul states how Satan deceives and disguises himself and works through men and he says: *"But I am afraid lest as the serpent (Satan) deceived Eve by his **craftiness**, your mind should be led astray from the simplicity and purity of devotion to Christ." "For even Satan **disguises** himself as an angel of light." (Hebrew-Greek Key Study Bible)*

This word craftiness in this scripture means cunning, unscrupulousness, sly, fraudulent, and deceitful. Satan masquerades himself to us and orchestrates events in the invisible realm to work collectively against us with his dark skilled powers and abilities.

In knowing all of this, I want to encourage you that God has given us the ability to overcome the enemy.

Your victory is never dependent on seeing the enemy in the visible realm. Your battles are not fought in the natural realm but in the spiritual realm.

Remember: *"You are from God, little children and have overcome them; because greater is He (Jesus and the power of the Holy Spirit) that is in you than he (Satan and his demonic spirits) that is in the world." 1 John 4:4 (Hebrew-Greek Key Study Bible)*

Let's reflect for a moment on *Genesis 1-3*. The God I am talking about is the God that created the heavens. He is not a God that has been created by man. He is the God that spoke forth the universe and placed every star, planet and the constellations we can see and study with wonderment.

He is the God who said, "Let there be light," and it was so. He is the God that called the waters to come together that created the vastness of the seas and then gathered the remainder of the firmament; the drylands and called it Earth. He is the creator of every living thing that lives and moves upon the Earth, whether plant, animal, bird or creeping thing; He created.

The greatest of His creations was Adam, the man, and Eve, the woman. One of the most awesome things to think about is that He created us in His likeness and in His image. Scripture says that He then blessed them and looked upon all that He had made, and He said it was very good!

And God gave them dominion and authority over the Garden of Eden and all that He had made and they were covered and protected by God, yet they had an enemy that they did not know. This enemy, Satan was another of God's creations, but had rebelled against God, his creator and was cast out of heaven along with one-third of the angels and became the ruler of the world we call Earth.

Satan did not want to share his world with another, especially beings that had been formed and created in Gods own image and ones that God loved so much. Scripture describes Satan as *"the ruler of the world"* in *John 12:31*, the prince of the power of the air, in *Ephesians 2:2* and he is the ruler over a powerful kingdom of evil, darkness and demonic spirits.

Satan wanted to be worshiped and exalted like God and wanted to carry out his own will as opposed to the divine will and plan of God for mankind. So, Satan devised a diabolical plan of deception, evil and lies by tempting Adam and Eve to doubt God's words. The snares were laid; they fell into his trap and became his captive. Then that, which was conceived in the darkness of Satan's invisible realm was brought forth into the visible realm. Satan took his claim, established his territory and began his reign to rule and dominate mankind and the world.

Even though Satan's plan was for man to fall and to be forever cursed, it was in the plan and work of the incarnate Christ that Satan's power was forever broken, and the curse was reversed (*Hebrews 2:14, 15*). The battle was won, and the enemy was defeated at the cross and the resurrection.

This same victorious Christ, who single-handedly defeated the devil, lives in us. Therefore we declare that *"greater is He that is in you than he that is in the world." 1 John 4:4*

Chapter 14
Forbidden Realms

"Even Satan disguises himself as an angel of light."
2 Corinthians 11:14

Spiritual Dimension – Spiritual Realm

It is vitally important that every person knows and understands that there can be an interaction between a spiritual dimension of existence, and an unknown spiritual realm that is extremely dangerous if you try and communicate or interact with them through outside spiritual forces other than through God and the power of the Holy Spirit.

In the natural world, we know that there are four proven dimensions that we know and relate to every day that are height, length, width and time dimensions that can be proven through the science of physics.

The spiritual world, on the other hand, is not another world in another place, it is additional dimensions to the physical world we observe, but can't see with our natural eyes.

Think of the physical world as four additional dimensions tacked on to a multi-dimensional spiritual world.

The heavens God created just isn't the sky that we see. The heavens are the biblical name for the spiritual world that exists in parallel to the physical world. God created a multi-dimensional universe and just because we can only see three dimensions of physical space plus time, doesn't mean that there aren't many more dimensions of reality beyond what we know and
experience.

First, let me explain what I mean by spiritual dimension. A spiritual dimension is a parallel realm that exists and operates along with our physical world. We may not see it with our natural eyes, that doesn't mean that it doesn't exist.

Secondly, let me establish that a realm is a kingdom, domain, territory, jurisdiction, area or sphere in which one holds a permanent and dominant position.

Demonic spirits are able to move between the spiritual and physical dimensions; they operate from the unseen spiritual realm and they can cross over into the physical realm to accomplish their evil.

Participation in spiritual experiences forbidden by God such as witchcraft, satanic rituals, and séances, mystical and other world experiences using drugs and alcohol opens this forbidden realm.

The Bible teaches that Satan can appear as an angel of light *(2 Corinthians 11:14)*. Satan and demonic spirits are very skilled and willingly participate at granting false supernatural experiences that appear to be of the True Light. Satan and his demonic spirits are more than happy to provide counterfeit experiences.

All of us have within us a hunger for the supernatural and an inbred curiosity to know and see into these unknown dimensions and what exists within these realms. Too often people succumb to the temptation to seek out someone or something that promises they can help them to enter or experience realms they have not known, but these ways and practices are demonically influenced.

The transference of demon spirits from the forbidden realm comes when a person knowingly or unknowingly opens either a door, portal or a gate that gives them a legal right and access to enter into your life. Those who open their hearts and minds to the realm of the supernatural, apart from God, invariably come under the deceptive influence of Satan. Our spiritual eyes are then opened to see into a dimension of the spirit realm that God did not intend for us to see or experience outside of Him.

Here are some of the practices and ways that open up doors and expose us to the forbidden realm.

Astral Projection

Within the New Age movement along with many of the eastern mysticisms and religions is found a practice called astral projection or astral travel. It is supposedly an out of body experience that assumes the existence of an astral body separate from the physical body, and capable of traveling outside it. This occult phenomenon consists of the spiritual traveler leaving the physical body and travels in his astral body (or dream body) into higher realms through forms of meditation.

Some say in order for astral projection to occur, something must be generated so that a combination of brain waves together will cause this separation or altered state of consciousness.

It is said that when one participates in this supernatural phenomenon, the person remains attached to their physical body by a silver umbilical type like a cord. When one travels on an astral plane (the spiritual realm) there are testimonies of those who have seen unknown beings, spirits that appear as light, ascended masters and higher being. These are disguised demonic spirits that can appear in many ways and forms to deceive and lead you deeper into deception and darkness.

There is also a growing practice that goes beyond the so-called normal astral projection experiences called astral sex. They claim they have sex with other entities and beings within the realm of altered consciousness.

Those who practice astral projection are opening their mind and body to demonic spirits. We must realize the dangers and pure evil that wait on the other side of our physical dimension for opportunities to come in contact with us. The truth is, any dimension in which we currently live, without question, are dimensions where spiritual entities and beings exist.

When a person participates in soul travel they leave their body unprotected. It is the mind (part of the soul nature), that knows to ward off evil.

It is our responsibility to resist the devil and his demons. If you permit your soul to leave your body, you are leaving a door open for demons to enter and influence your life that could ultimately end in demonic possession and control.

Nowhere are we told in scripture to seek an out-of-body experience or to astral project and why? Because it centers on occult practices that are rooted in Satan and demonic control.

The Third Eye

Another way people can open themselves up to the forbidden realm is through a practice called the third or inner eye – a metaphysical opening which refers to the 7 chakras (serpent power) that leads to higher consciousness. Each of these chakras (that are in reality doorways to the soul) also has its own deity or demigod.

It is a mystical and esoteric concept referring to a speculative invisible eye that provides perception beyond ordinary sight- religious visions, clairvoyance, the ability to observe chakras and auras, precognition and also out-of-body experiences.

The third eye refers to the gate that leads to inner realms and spaces of higher consciousness and is supposedly located around the middle of the forehead just above the eyebrows. Those who practice this believe they are passing into a spiritual portal for enlightenment by opening their third eye that opens the gate between two realms.

This chakra is described as one of the main exits out of the body into the astral realm a spiritual dimension said to be directly above this natural plane.

Within the New Age movement, the third eye is a technique they use to connect to psychic abilities they use for psychic readings. But it is not an ability nor the power of a third eye they connect to, it is a demonic familiar spirit that leads to deeper deception.

Through deep meditation (not as meditating on the word of God or opening to the Holy Spirit) they open themselves up to the spirit realm and demonic spirits. It is through this process that they achieve an altered state of consciousness. By emptying their mind, they open a doorway that eventually becomes a demonic doorway that enables demons to come and go as they please.

There are many deceived people who believe that opening the third eye or pineal gland is a harmless spiritual practice that is necessary for spiritual maturity. In truth, they are openly inviting demons to enter their lives, deceive them, and draw them into greater satanic bondage.

Kundalini Yoga

Yoga opens a door to the forbidden realm. The word yoga is connected to religion according to The Encarta World English Dictionary and gives this meaning:

Yoga: Hindu discipline; any of a group of related Hindu disciplines that promote the unity of the individual with a supreme being through a system of postures and rituals. It also means to yoke. Yoga is the act of yoking the practitioner to a Hindu god. This god is called Brahman the Divine or the Universal World Soul, who is said to enlighten the human soul by uniting with the human body. This union is accomplished through intense concentration, controlled breathing techniques, and prescribed yoga postures. Brahman and yoga practitioners are united as one.

Can you see the counterfeit of Satan here? The scriptures tell us that we are to be united with Christ and that we are united with Christ as a believer just as God and Christ are one as *John 17:21a* states:

"That they all may be one [just] as You, Father, are in Me, and I in You." (Amplified Bible)

Whatever and whoever you open your soul to you become joined to, bonded to, fused to and yoked with; you become one.

It's the same idea as being united in marriage and you become one with your spouse. You are two separate people, but as you come together to consummate the union your souls are united and become one.

The practice of Kundalini yoga (meaning coiled one), in yoga theory, is a primal energy, or Shakti meaning power, or empowerment that is located at the base of the spine. It is a method of awakening Kundalini for the purpose of reaching supernatural enlightenment. The truth is Kundalini is a demonic spirit and a counterfeit for the Holy Spirit.

Kundalini is described as lying coiled at the base of the spine, represented as either a goddess or sleeping serpent waiting to be awakened. It is said to result in deep meditation, enlightenment, and bliss. This awakening involves the Kundalini physically moving up the central channel to reach within the Sahasrara that is said to be located at the top of the head and is awakened through meditation, pranayama breathing and the chanting of mantras.

Wakening Kundalini is practice by Hinduism, Buddhism, Jainism, Sikhism, Taoism, Shinto, Confucianism, New Agers, and some Satanist and Wiccan's. Some yoga teachers explain it to be the dormant power of infinity, coiled energy at the base of the spine that must be aroused. Kundalini has been called an unconscious, instinctive or libidinal force, or mother energy or intelligence of complete maturation according to the modern commentaries.

Kundalini is demonic and there is no way to explain it physically – it is a non-physical force. Medically speaking, there is nothing coiled at the base of the spine that is three and one-half times coiled, like a serpent that's going to spring up when you get in the proper state of consciousness. This is the same occult power that all the occultists are in touch with, or try to be in touch with, and it is demonic, deceptive and controlled by Satan.

Why are Satan and his demonic spirits trying to advance this and encourage this practice? Remember in the Garden of Eden when the serpent lied to Eve when he said to her in *Genesis 3:5 "For God knows that in the day you eat from it your eyes will be opened, and you will be like God."*

If you believe the lie of Satan (the serpent), then who needs God, if you are a god? Who needs the God of the Bible who claims to be the Creator and says that I am a sinner? You see, yoga doesn't tell those who practice it that they are a sinner. In fact, Hinduism says there's no such thing as a sinner and the only sin is to call yourself a sinner. If you are a god, then you are not accountable to anyone, and all you need to do is become one with the universe.

Can you see how this undermines the truth and the Bible? Satan continues to deceive man and use every tactic and strategy he has to promote the lie that he told in the Garden of Eden. It's the same lie and the same demons just promoted and presented with a new name.

While searching for information on the Kundalini spirit, I came across an article written by a researcher in 1995 and this is what the writer had to say:

Meetings which mystic Hindu gurus hold are called Darshan. At these meetings, devotees go forward to receive spiritual experiences from a touch by the open palm of the hand, often to the forehead, by the guru in what is known as the Shakti Pat or divine touch.

The raising of the spiritual experience is called raising Kundalini. After a period when the devotee has reached a certain spiritual elevation they begin to shake, jerk or hop or squirm uncontrollably, sometimes breaking into uncontrolled animal noises or laughter as they reach an ecstatic high.

These manifestations are called Kriyas. Devotees sometimes roar like lions and show all kinds of physical signs during this period. Often devotees move on to higher states of spiritual consciousness and become still physically and appear to slip into an unconsciousness.

This is another example of the counterfeit ministry of Satan and how he uses false prophets and so-called holy men whom he has deceived to impart demonic spirits into naïve people who are seeking a true spiritual connection and experience.

Satan is the great imitator of God and his intention is always to deceive man. Satan always tries to create what God has created, but the truth is that he can't create anything. All he can do is counterfeit and imitate God, Jesus, the gifts of the Spirit and the power of the Holy Spirit to try and keep man believing his lies.

The article continued by quoting from the writings of a well-known guru and this is what he had to say concerning the effects of activation:

When your body begins trembling, the hair stands on roots, you laugh or begin to weep without your wishing, your tongue begins to utter deformed sounds, you are filled with fear or see frightening visions, and the Kundalini Shakti has become active.

I have purposely included this to illustrate that there are all kinds of counterfeit manifestations and impartations that are not from the Holy Spirit. I urge you, please *test the spirits (1 John 4:1)* as we are commanded to do in Scripture and be aware that in the last days we will see and experience *seducing spirits, (1 Timothy 4:1) false prophets (Matthew 7:15)* working in the world and within the church.

To further clarify just how deceptive the enemy is; these yoga masters claim that Kundalini serpent power makes them born again and baptizes them into a new life. Credit is given to the Kundalini serpent for connecting them to the all-pervading power of Divine love. What a lie that is directly from the pit of hell!

There is only one way to receive Divine love and that is through Jesus Christ. There is only one way to be born again and baptized into a new life and that is through Jesus Christ and in the power of the Holy Spirit.

John 3:3, 5, 6 & 16

"Truly, truly, I say to you, unless one is born again, he cannot see the kingdom of God. Except a man be born of water and of the Spirit he

cannot enter into the kingdom of God. That which is born of the flesh is flesh, and that which is born of the Spirit is spirit. For God so loved the world, that He gave His only begotten Son, (Jesus Christ) that whosoever believeth in Him (Jesus) should not perish, but have everlasting life." (Hebrew-Greek Key Study Bible)

Chapter 15
Heavens ~ Portals ~ Gates ~

"Be exalted above the Heavens, oh God;
Let Thy glory be above all the earth."
Psalms 57:11

The Heavens

In the beginning, God created the heavens and the earth. Genesis 1:1

The Hebrew word for heavens is the word *shamayim,* and is used herein a plural form that means heights, and or elevations. Did you know that Scripture speaks of three heavens and when the term heaven is not used symbolically in Scripture, it usually refers to one of three realms?

In *Hebrews 4:14* scripture tells us that Jesus, Himself passed through the heavens.

"Since then we have a great high priest who has passed through the heavens, Jesus the Son of God, let us hold fast our confession." (Hebrew-Greek Key Study Bible)

The First Heaven

The first heaven apparently refers to the atmospheric heaven that includes the air that we breathe, (*Matthew 6:26*) where birds fly, (*Genesis 6:7*) the clouds rest, (*Daniel 7:13*) and the space that immediately surrounds the earth.

The scientific term is called troposphere and extends about twenty miles above the earth. The space above this is called the stratosphere.

Genesis 1:6 – 8 declares: *"And God said, Let there be a firmament [the expanse of the sky] in the midst of the waters, and let it separate the waters [below] from the waters above."*

"And God made the firmament [the expanse] and separated the waters which were under the expanse (firmament) from the waters which were above the expanse. And it was so."

"And God called the firmament Heaven. And the evening and the morning were the second day." (Hebrew-Greek Key Study Bible)

The word firmament in this scripture is the Hebrew word *raqiya* and means an expanse, i.e. the firmament or visible arch of the sky. The sky is sometimes referred to as a dome or a covering; however, scripture nowhere supports the pagan mythology that the sky is a type of solid covering.

God put an expanse between the upper waters and the lower waters and made heaven, what we know as the sky. It seems that these waters were a vaporous blanket that covered the original creative mass. When separated from the landmass, the lower waters eventually became the ocean and the seas. Some scholars believe that these upper waters played a part in the flood during Noah's day.

The Second Heaven

This is what we refer to as the Celestial heavens, better known as outer space. The second heaven contains the sun, moon and the stars.

Genesis 1:14-18 confirms

"Then God said, Let there be lights in the firmament of the heavens to divide the day from the night; and let them be for signs, and seasons, and for days and years; and let them be for lights in the firmament of the heavens to give light on the earth, and it was so."

"Then God made the two great lights: the greater light to rule the day, (sun) and the lesser light to rule the night. (Moon) He made the stars also."

"God set them in the firmament of the heavens to give light on the earth, and to rule over the day and over the night, and to divide the light

from the darkness. And God saw that it was good." (New King James Version)

Unger's Bible dictionary says that it is the stellar spaces and the abode of all supernatural angelic beings.

The second heaven is what *Ephesians 6:12* refers to as the heavenly places and where the higher-ranking demons are positioned in Satan's kingdom and control much of the evil activity that occurs on earth. They are the principalities, powers, the world's spiritual forces of wickedness and darkness, rulers and the authorities in the heavenly places. (*Ephesians 3:10*)

Ephesians 2:1-2 tells us that Satan and many of his demons work from the position of the second heaven – the air.

"And you He made alive, who were dead in trespasses and sins, in which you once walked according to the course of this world, according to the prince of the power of the air, the spirit who now works in the sons of disobedience." (New King James Version)

Satan is the prince or the ruler of the air because in this realm Satan's high-ranking demon spirits dwell, all of whom are under his dominion in the heavenly places or the second heaven. The second heaven is where some of the battles will occur between God's angels and some of Satan's fallen angels.

We need to understand that Satan has an organized structured demonic army in place in the second heaven, however, he also has demons/demonic evil spirits who are working on earth and are directed and controlled by these higher-ranking demons positioned in the second heaven. These second heaven demons also control the action over certain geographical areas on earth as confirmed in scripture.

Daniel 10:13 "But the prince of the kingdom of Persia withstood me for twenty-one days; And behold, Michael, one of the chiefs of the celestial princes, came to help me, for I remained there with the kings of Persia." (New King James Version)

The word *withstood* means: to stand up against, oppose with firm determination and to resist.

The prince of the kingdom of Persia, according to scripture was the ruling principality (higher-ranking demon) that controlled this certain geographical area over Persia. This principality opposed and stood against the angel that God sent to answer Daniel's prayer. In other words, initially, the angel from God could not pass through from the second heaven into the first heaven and get to Daniel.

This principality was so powerful that God had to send Michael the archangel (who was more powerful than the ruling demonic principality over Persia) to oppose him, so the angel could get through and deliver the message and revelation from God.

To further confirm, the angel continues to tell *Daniel* in verse *20b* and *21b* who and what he will face once he leaves Daniel.

"And now I will return to fight with the (hostile) prince of Persia; and when I have gone, behold the (hostile) prince of Greece will come."

"There is no one who holds with me and strengthens himself against these (hostile spirit forces) except Michael, your prince (national guardian angel)." (Amplified Bible, Classic Edition)

Even though we cannot see with our natural eyes into the second heaven doesn't mean these principalities, powers, and angels are not engaged in heavenly combat. Scripture is clear that earth was affected by the battles fought and won in the heavens.

The Third Heaven

In *2 Corinthians 12:2,3 & 4* Paul reveals that there are *three heavens* as he describes his experience when he was taken up to the third heaven where God the Father, the holy angels, and Jesus is seated.

"I know a man in Christ who fourteen years ago – whether in the body I do not know, or whether out of body I do not know, (only) God knows – such a man was caught up to the third heaven."

"And I know how such a man – whether in the body or apart from the body I do not know, God knows."

"Was caught up into Paradise, and heard inexpressible words, which a man is not permitted to speak." (Words too sacred to tell) (Amplified Bible)

If Paul was taken up to the third heaven, then there must be a first and a second heaven. The third heaven is where we have been created to spend eternity and what scripture describes as paradise. *(Luke 23:43)*

Ephesians 4:10 says that *"He (Jesus) ascended far above all the heavens, that He (His presence) might fill all things (the whole universe from the lowest to the highest)*, implying there is more than one heaven.

In *Revelations 4:1-2* the Apostle John was called into the third heaven.

"After these things, I looked, and behold a door standing open in heaven, and the first voice which I had heard, like the sound of a trumpet speaking with me, said, "come up here, and I will show you what must take place after things."

"Immediately I was in the Spirit; and behold, a throne was standing in heaven, and One sitting on the throne." (Hebrew-Greek Key Study Bible)

Deuteronomy 10:14 also refers to the third heaven as *the heaven of heavens,* and *I Kings 8:27* declares *the heavens, even the highest heaven, cannot contain you.*

From Genesis to Revelations God's word is clear that there are heavens – plural and that each heaven has a purpose and a function.

By knowing this truth we have a greater awareness of the invisible realm (the second heaven) and the dark forces that are battling God's forces of light.

My intention to explain each of the three heavens is to help you to understand another aspect of the invisible and the visible heavens that we can and cannot see, and how they greatly influence and affect our lives every day.

Portals

God constantly reveals the truth to us in scripture and by making known to us His marvelous mysteries when we study and understand His Word.

According to scripture, there are heavenly portals, doors, and passageways that lead to and from the heavenly realm. *(Revelations 4:1-2a, Psalms 78:23* and *Psalms 24:7* among others.)*

In *John 1:51* this truth is confirmed: *"Most assuredly, I say to you, hereafter you shall see heaven open, and the angels of God ascending and descending upon the Son of man."(New King James Version)*

A heavenly portal is an opening that allows angels and heavenly beings to come and go without demonic interference.

Jacob's Dream

Genesis 28:10-18 is the account of a dream that was given to Jacob by the Lord. In the dream, it describes a portal that had been opened in the precise location Jacob was resting in. In the dream, Jacob saw a ladder that was set on the earth with its top reaching to heaven, and the angels of God were ascending and descending on it.

Once Jacob awoke from sleep, he said, *"Surely the Lord is in the place, and I did not know it…. How awesome is this place! This is none other than the house of God, and this is the gate of heaven."*

We know from scripture that afterward, Jacob erected a monument and named the place, *Bethel* or the "dwelling place of God." Jacob would return to Bethel several times after his first encounter, and it was there that God would speak to him.

A Portal in Sin City

Many years ago, I had a similar dream. I was living in Las Vegas, Nevada at the time and had been in prayer and intercession for the city. If ever there was a city that needs grace, Las Vegas has to be at the top of God's list.

The Fremont street dream:

It was night time in Las Vegas and I found myself walking on the backstreets of the east side of the city. Most of the streets I walked down were faintly lit and void of people. As I continued to walk the scene suddenly changed and I found myself walking towards an area that was full of light and action. As I turned to my right I found myself facing a street that was lit up so bright with lights that it looked like it was daytime. I then realized that I was standing at the south side of a well know street in Las Vegas called Fremont Street.

Fremont Street is in the heart of the old downtown casino corridor, and it was the original area in Las Vegas with a license to gamble. Along with gambling came prostitution, organized crime, and mobsters who owned and operated many of the well-known casinos in Las Vegas. All contributed to not only its growth but its moral degeneration as well.

Las Vegas has been called Sin City and the saying associated with this city is *whatever happens in Vegas, stays in Vegas*, need I say more?

In the dream, I could see thousands and thousands of people dashing from hotel to hotel as they lined the busy sidewalks. The street seemed never-ending although in reality is only a two-block area. The street began growing more narrow while at the same time expanding as the people came they seemed to be oblivious to one another and what was taking place all around them, it was as if they had been hypnotized and under some kind of a spell.

Suddenly it was as if a veil had been lifted from my eyes and I could see what was taking place in the spiritual realm that very moment. Here is what I saw:

Genesis 28:12 "And he dreamed, and behold a ladder set up on the earth, and the top of it reached to heaven: And behold the angels of God ascending and descending on it." (Darby Translation)

God had placed right in the middle of Freemont Street a very large ladder. At the top of the ladder, you could see a very large circular portal that had been opened from heaven to earth allowing the ladder to extend directly onto the street below. On this ladder, I could see angels ascending and descending all at the same time carrying messages of truth and salvation to those below.

It was *Hebrews 1:14* in action. *"Are they not all ministering spirits sent forth to minister for them who shall be heirs of salvation?" (King James Version)*

I knew what was taking place was the direct result of the prayers of faithful Christians God had brought into Las Vegas at the very conception of the town in 1905. Their prayers spiritually dug up the dry and fallow ground while others watered and prepared the way for those who would follow. Others came with the sound of warfare on their lips and a sword in their hand. Then there were those who planted the seeds of faith and truth with the power of prophetic prayers.

All along God was building a militant praying army that would stand against the works of Satan, pull down the strongholds and pierce the darkness that laid heavily over that city. The more God's people prayed the more of God's light and glory would be poured out and over the city and its people.

From a book *Quiet Talks On prayer* written by S. D. Gordon is a chapter called *The Earth, the Battle-Field in Prayer:*

The greatest agency put into man's hands is prayer. And to define prayer one must use the language of war. Peace language is not equal to the situation. The earth is in a state of war and is being hotly besieged. This one must use war talk to grasp the facts with which prayer is concerned.

Prayer from God's side is communication between Himself and His allies in enemy country. True prayer moves in a circle. It begins with the heart of God and sweeps down into the human heart, so intersecting the circle of the earth, which is the battlefield of prayer, and then goes back again to its starting point, having accomplished its purpose on the downward swing.

Revival Fires

In the late '80s throughout the '90s, Las Vegas began to grow by leaps and bounds. Builders began to buy large pieces of land that were once only sand, cactus and desert waste places. Tract after tract of homes began to spring up seemingly overnight and life was brought to the desert. People began to move to Las Vegas in droves from all over the United States, and from all walks of life.

Some people were drawn to Las Vegas because of the nightlife and others were looking for a new start. Others thought they could make a fortune gambling or by hitting a million-dollar jackpot with a couple of spins.

I was moved to Las Vegas kicking and screaming all the way, not realizing that God was in it. Weeks after moving God's plan and the reason for me being there began to unfold right before my very eyes.

Soon God began to show me that He had strategically drawn people and ministries, birthed new churches and placed them into key areas and positions to preach, pray and war spiritually for the city and its people. He revealed that the timing for me (and many others) to be positioned in prayer, in Vegas, was of the utmost importance, and the effects of our obedience to pray would far exceed the sacrifices we had made.

I knew God's plan was to bring the fires of revival to Las Vegas and that it would sweep over that valley like wildfire. He also showed me tracts of homes that had flames of fire hanging directly over their roofs. This represented the fire of the Holy Spirit and that they would be places of ministry and safety for those hungry for God.

All who had come before us and all who were faithful to pray were to be a part of an awesome move of God and were vital in helping to openi this portal over Las Vegas.

Never underestimate the power of prayer or the power that you possess as a believer. *James 5:16b "The heartfelt and persistent prayer of a righteous man (believer) can accomplish much. (When put into action and made effective by God – it is dynamic and can be tremendous power). (Amplified Bible)*

Speculation or Truth?

Question: Are There Extra Dimensional Portals?

There is a theory within the scientific world called the string theory; string theory is a theoretical framework in which the point-like particles of particle physics are replaced by one-dimensional objects called strings. It describes how these strings propagate through space and interact with each other. In string theory, one of the many vibrational states of the string corresponds to the graviton, a quantum mechanical particle that carries gravitational force. Thus, string theory is a theory of quantum gravity.

Within the past decades, great advances in the research of the string theory indicate the existence of dimensions beyond the four dimensions we experience.

The European Organization for Nuclear Research, (also known as CERN), built a Large Hadron Collider that is 17 miles in circumference and goes as deep as 575 feet beneath the ground. This is the largest most complex experimental facility ever built in the world and is located between the Switzerland and France border near Geneva, Switzerland.

The Hadron Collider is the world's largest and most powerful particle collider that races protons to just beneath the speed of light and then crushes them down into the size of a human hair width. These particles racing collide together and break off into different directions.

One of the experiments they are working on is to open miniature black holes. Some Physicists believe that we are surrounded by multi-universes and are seeking to understand dark matter and the nature of the dark matter in the universe. They are also experimenting to find out if there are extra dimensions, as predicted by various models based on the string theory.

The former Director of Research & Scientific Computing at CERN, Physicists Sergio Bertolucci made a statement himself that the Large Hadron Collider could open a doorway (portal) to an extra dimension and out of this door might come something, or we might send something through it.

In an interview given to the British Press by CERN's Director-General Rolf Heuer and its Director of Research, he admitted that one of the key overall aims of CERN's Large Hadron Collider is to open a portal to another dimension. General Heuer stated to the press, "When we open the door, something might come through into our reality! Or, we might send something through it into their reality!"

The experiments conducted at CERN are the most powerful experiments ever done in the history of mankind and they are trying to access parallel universes. They are particle physicists that believe in what they call multi-universe and that we are surrounded by other realities, dark matter, and invisible matter. They don't realize that we are surrounded by a dark world, an invisible world.

CERN is also using its massive rings to study and create anti-matter, anti-gravity, and perhaps even torsion fields, which have been theorized as a means to travel through time and space (and perhaps dimensions).

Torsion fields – if they exist – are like wormholes into another dimension.

They are also looking for "gluon" which is essentially the overlaying of sound waves...it's what holds everything together. The "gluon" they are searching for is the God in *Genesis 1 "And God spoke and God said Let there be."* God emits sound waves and He calls forth something out of nothing, and He creates. They are looking for the voice of God. Ironically, in physics the subatomic particle that gives mass to matter is called the God Particle.

Some theorize that CERN is trying to recreate the Big Bang Theory to prove to the world that this is how earth was created. They want to model the elementary particles that existed at the moment that the big bang supposedly took place. This is where the "Higgs boson" or "Higgs particle" theory comes in and is said to have been discovered to be the first particles that were produced at the moment of The Big Bang. It is part of the standard model in physics, which means that it is found everywhere and thought to be a key building block of the universe.

You may be asking the question, why are they doing all this? Because particle physicists want to know about the nature of creation and what is holding the universe together.

If physicists and scientists don't believe in God and that He created all things, then they must try and explain creation, the universe and what holds everything together by searching for answers through other sources, i.e. science.

Ecclesiastes 8:17 "And I saw all the work of God, I concluded that man cannot discover the work that is done under the sun. Even though man may labor in seeking he will not discover; and (more than that), though a wise man thinks and claims he knows, he will not be able to find it out." (Amplified Bible)

Invisible Boundary Lines

There are invisible boundary lines God created that not only separate the three heavens but were designed to keep man from crossing over into other dimensions through natural means. See *Psalms74:17, Job 38:9-11, Proverbs 8:29, Job 26:10, and Jeremiah 5:22.*

Psalms104:9 declares *"You set a boundary (for the waters) which they may not pass over, that they turn not again to deluge the earth.." (Amplified Bible)*

There are good reasons why God created the known and the unknown universe that He kept certain aspects separated from man. One very important reason was for our protection *(Ephesians 6:12).*

CERN has no idea what and who they are dealing with. Scripture is very specific concerning the spiritual realm and that it is a place where battles are being raged between the forces of darkness and the forces of light, and that it is a dangerous place for a man to be.

Many scientists do not acknowledge or believe that a spiritual realm even exists. To them, it is a fantasy.

Is it possible that these scientists inadvertently could end up opening a portal or a door not to another dimension, but into the spiritual realm?

The Cosmic Dancer

Another interesting known fact concerning CERN is the statue they proudly display. Positioned in front of CERN's building headquarters stands a statue of Shiva Nataraja, the Lord of Dance. He is the Hindu god that symbolizes Shiva's cosmic dance of creation and destruction.

This statue was given to CERN as a gift from the Indian government and represents a very powerful god they worship. The Shiva statue depicts the Hindu god in his Nataraja position, performing the Tandave, a dance believed to be the source of the cycle of creation preservation and destruction. This cosmic dance supposedly destroys the old universe in favor of a new creation. This ritual is performed on the back of a dwarf, a demon named Apasmara who is said to represent ignorance.

Shiva is one of the main gods in Hinduism, also known as Mahadeva (Great god). He is regarded as the destroyer, transformer, and transcendent, unchanging and formless god.

Shiva is also known as the patron god of yoga and the arts. The main statues and artwork depicting Shiva show him having a third eye on his forehead. This eye represents the passing into a spiritual world, or the eye of clairvoyance and wisdom, and is said to be the source of his untamed energy.

The snake that is coiled around Shiva is known as Vasuki who is one of the king serpents of Hindu, and Buddhist mythology and is one that they worship as a god. You will also notice the adorning of the crescent moon symbolizing the time cycle through which creation evolves from the beginning to the end. The holy river or goddess Ganga flows from his matted hair, representing the nectar of immortality.

The trishula is his weapon and is believed to destroy the three worlds: the physical world, the worlds of the forefathers, and the world of the mind. The three worlds are supposed to be destroyed by Shiva into a single non-dual plane of existence that is bliss alone.

And the damaru is his musical instrument that is said to have been created by Shiva to produce spiritual sounds by which this whole universe has been created and regulated.

Here is a picture of the statue Shiva the Lord of Dance that was given to CERN by the India government.

Shiva

Questions

Why would CERN, the world's premier research institute, allow a statue of Shiva, (a well-known god, i.e. idol) of India to be placed at their headquarters? Do they understand the spiritual implications and the statement they are making to the world and those who understand spiritual matters?

Whether they do or don't doesn't discount the ramifications that are and will continue to be manifested in the first and second heavens. (The spiritual realm)

Whenever you give honor or place to an idol god, you are recognizing them for who they say they are and giving them authority to manifest and rule where they have been placed. The principalities, powers, rulers, and authorities in the spiritual realm readily manifest themselves and take advantage of those who open up doors to them. (*Ephesians 3:10; 6:12*)

Gates

"For His Divine Power reinforces your gates." Psalms 147:13a (The Voice)

In ancient times a majority of cultures built high walls around their cities. Within these walls were gates to allow the people of the city to come in and go out.

The most important reason for building walls and gates was to prevent their enemies from entering the city, destroying their homes, ravaging their land and from capturing its people. A gate represents power because it controls access. He that controls his gates (the soul, spirit) determines the fate of the treasures within.

Proverbs 25:28 "Like a city that is broken down and without walls (leaving it unprotected) is a man who has no self-control over his spirit (and sets himself up for trouble)." (Amplified Bible)

The word spirit in this scripture means the rational mind as the seat of the senses, affections, and emotions of various kinds, according to the Lexical Aid to the Old Testament.

Please note: there are times in the Old Testament where Ruach (spirit), and nephesh (soul) are parallel.

Let's picture ourselves as a city that has walls and gates. Our outer walls are our bodies and our outer gates and entranceways are our eyes, ears, nose, tongue and our sexual organs. The soul and spirit are our inner gates that can be breached through the five senses. Our five senses are what we see, hear, taste, touch and even smell.

Proverbs 1:21 says "She crieth in the chief place of concourse, in the opening of the gates; in the city, she uttereth her words." (Dake's Bible)

Our mind is the chief concourse – concourse being where great commotion or tumult occurs. It is also described as an open space where roads or paths meet (as in a railroad terminal) and where crowds gather.

The mind is a gate, door, or entrance where the enemy will assemble for one purpose and that is to attack and try to build his roads into our mind and carve out paths into our thoughts. If the gate of your mind is left open and unprotected the enemy will work to infiltrate your thought life, because your mind is where thoughts are birthed, and actions are planned.

It is your responsibility to destroy and cast down every contrary, evil and impure thought. *2 Corinthians 10:5: "(Inasmuch as we) refute arguments and theories and reasoning's and every proud and lofty thing that sets itself up against the (true) knowledge of God, and we lead every thought and purpose away captive into the obedience of Christ." (The Messiah, the Anointed One) (Amplified Bible, Classic Edition)*

Your mind is either an open pathway where the enemy can meet or a gateway that is closed, reinforced and protected by the blood of Jesus and the word of God. You alone are responsible for what you allow your mind to think, your eyes to see, what you allow your ears to hear and what you permit your mouth to speak.

Taking Charge of our Gates

We are responsible for taking charge of the gates of our city, the soul, the mind, will, and emotions. No one else can do that for you. We are to be watchful, alert, armed and ready to defend our gates.

Stationed above the gates of a city was always an armed sentinel. His job was to stand in the position of a watchman and protect the gates. He was to be alert, constantly on guard and watching for any approaching enemy. If an invasion threatened the city, he would call for reinforcements and together they would defend and defeat the enemy at the gates.

The Bible has a lot to say concerning gates and explains what some of these gates were made of. Usually, they were made of wood, or wood overlaid with metal.

Psalms 107:16 speaks of gates of brass and gates of iron; often there were two leveled gates *(Isaiah 45:1)* and others that were equipped with heavy locks and bars. *(1 Samuel 23:7)*

A vital part of the strength of a gate was not only what it was made of, but also what it was reinforced with.

Part of reinforcing the gates of a city would be to bolster them with bars of iron. They would also overlay them with bronze or iron to provide greater strength. Gates not reinforced with iron were liable to be set on fire by an enemy and destroyed.

When a gate is attacked by its enemies, it is always attacked at its weakest point. And what is the weakest point of a gate? It's center.

In order to reinforce your gates, you need to fortify them by adding additional support and strength for endurance.

Psalms 147:13a "For His divine power reinforces your city gates." *(The Voice Bible)*

What is this divine power? The power of the Holy Spirit, His *dunamis power*, His inherent power; power to reproduce itself, like a dynamo.

There is another Greek word scripture uses for the word power and that is the word *kratos,* which is God's demonstrated power. In other words, *kratos* power is not a power that you merely adhere to and believe in intellectually. *Kratos power* is a power that is demonstrative, eruptive, and tangible and it almost always comes with some type of external, outward manifestation that one can see with his/her eyes. This is the power God used to raise Jesus from the dead that we read of *Ephesians 1:19, 20.*

If you had been present at the resurrection you would have seen *"kratos power"* in action. You would have felt the ground trembling as this electrifying force entered the tomb where Jesus's body lay. It was an eruptive power; it was the strongest kind of power that is known to God or man.

When the empowering presence of the Holy Spirit operates in our lives, it releases in us the very same power that physically raised Jesus Christ from the dead.

This *"kratos power"* is an outwardly manifested type of power – a power that you see, and a power that you will experience. It is a power that reinforces, fortifies and builds our gates, which are the entrances into our soul.

The Spirit Builds Our Gates

Psalms 127:1a "Unless the Lord builds the house, they labor in vain who build; unless the Lord guards the city, The Watchman keeps awake in vain." (Amplified Bible)

In the Greek the words "builds the house" are the words *Oikos* a house and *domeo,* which means to build. Combined they can imply to build a house, tower, town, walls, gates, etc. They are also used in scripture with the meaning to build in a spiritual sense, for edification, spiritual profit or advancement.

Galatians 5:25 teaches us "If we live in the Spirit, let us also walk in the Spirit." (Darby Translation)

Gates are built when we reside and abide under the constant guidance and influence of the Spirit. When we are in Him, He supplies the tools and sources needed to construct an impenetrable gate that the enemy cannot enter.

As the Spirit builds, He also gives us the power beyond our own capabilities to maintain, guard and keep our gates intact and protected. He is the force that surrounds and envelops our gates totally and completely.

Without the Spirit in your life, your labor is in vain.

The Spirit Strengthens Our Gates

Ephesians 3:16 "Father, out of Your honorable and glorious riches, strengthen Your people. Fill their souls with the power of Your Spirit." (The Voice Bible)

Let's revisit *Ephesians 6:10* where Paul provides subsequent evidence of the Spirit's empowering work in our lives: *"Finally, be strong in the Lord, and in the strength of His might."*

This verse is about the supernatural power that God gives us through His Spirit to fight with unseen demonic powers, and how we are infused with an abundant dose of inward strength. This *"endunammo power"* is so strong, it can withstand any attack and it can successfully oppose any kind of force that would try and tear down your gates.

The word strong used in *Ephesians 6:10* is the word *"endunammo."* To historically prove the supernatural nature of this word, it was used by early writers from the Greek classical periods to denote special individuals, like Hercules, who had been handpicked by the gods and were supernaturally invested with superhuman strength to accomplish a superhuman task.

With this *"kratos power"* at our disposal, the devil is no match for us, and we are well-able to fight with the armor God has provided. This is the kind of strength God makes available to us by and through the power of the Holy Spirit.

Paul continues to reinforce with the word might *be* taken from the Greek word *"ischuos,"* that gives us a picture of a very, very strong man; a strong man like a body-builder, a man who is able, a man who is mighty, or a man with great muscular capabilities.

This picture is not of himself or us, it is a picture of God! God is the one who is able, mighty and muscular. There is no one more powerful than God. And this same mighty arm of God is still working today. In you and in me.

One expositor translation of *Ephesians 6:10* accurately states *"be strong in the Lord and in the powerful, outwardly demonstrated ability that works in you as a result of God's great muscular ability."*

All the power that God possesses and all the energy of His muscular and mighty ability is the *"kratos power,"* that is now at work in believers who have been empowered by the Spirit. There is no greater power we can tap into than the power of the Spirit and the power of God's Word. Together they work to build, strengthen, reinforce and fortify our gates.

With these powers in your arsenal, there is no attack your gates can't withstand or confrontation you can't win, as you guard your gates.

The Spirit Equips to Pursue

We are to be fearless as we pursue and attack the gates of the enemy. We are to raid the dark places where the enemy hides and works evil upon our land. To pursue our enemy means to follow, to overtake, capture, kill or defeat.

And the Word of God equips us giving us the power to be fearless to pursue the enemy, rather than be pursued, overtaken, captured or defeated by our enemy.

It is the *"dunamis power"* of the Spirit that gives us the power to pursue. We become the aggressors and can engage our enemy with the power to stand, defend, and fight at the entrances to our gates. Also, we can attack the gates of the enemy.

Ephesians 6:11 tells us to *"Put on the full armor of God (for His precepts are like the splendid armor of a heavily-armed soldier), so that you may be able to (successfully) stand up against all the schemes and the strategies and the deceit of the devil."* *(Amplified Bible)*

Being equipped to pursue means that we have "put on" which is taken from the Greek word *"enduo"* and is frequently used throughout the New Testament. It is the exact word used in *Luke 24:49 "And behold, I send the promise of my Father upon you: but tarry ye in the city of Jerusalem until ye be endued with power from on high."* *(King James Version)*

This word *"enduo"* refers to the act of putting on a new set of clothes. The Amplified Bible translates it as *"until you are clothed (fully equipped) with power from on high."*

This is not putting a new set of clothes on outwardly. It is putting on the new man and producing the fruit of our new life. "*Enduo*" is also the word used in connection with the putting on of our spiritual armor, to be dressed in full battle array; the whole armor of God

The whole armor of God is the supernatural set of weaponry that comes directly from God Himself. God is the source for this armor; it's His very Spirit.

Just as we draw our life, our nature, and our spiritual power from God, so does our spiritual armor also come from Him. The armor of God is ours by virtue of our relationship with God and is freely bestowed upon those who continually draw their life and existence from God.

Our unbroken, ongoing relationship with God is your absolute guarantee that we are constantly and habitually dressed in the whole armor of God, we are fully dressed in His armor from head to toe.

The Holy Spirit has given us everything we need to successfully combat and pursue opposing spiritual forces and protect and defend our gates. *(Ephesians 6:1-18)*

Closing Comment

As I prayed, searched the scriptures and sought out the truth, my intention was to help you to grasp a fuller understanding of who and what we are battling against- the spiritual realm, our spiritual weaponry, warfare, the battles we will face and the victorious position we have over Satan and demonic spirits.

I want to encourage you to stand in your position of power and in the authority that Christ has given to you as a believer and soldier of Jesus Christ. To discern the attacks of the enemy, apply the Word of God to your circumstances, and know who and what you are facing daily.

When one's intention is to encourage another, it means that you inspire, cheer, reassure, boost, embolden, raise spirits, give confidence to, urge, assist, and aid and help others. This has been my prayer and my heart from the very beginning of this book unto the end.

And so, I conclude with the words and instructions Paul stated in *Ephesians 6:10-19*

> *"In conclusion, be strong —not in yourselves but in the Lord, in the power of his boundless resources. Put on God's complete armor so that you can successfully resist all the devil's methods of attack. For our fight is not against any physical enemy: It is against organizations and powers that are spiritual. We are up against the unseen power that controls this dark world, and spiritual agents from the very headquarters of evil. Therefore, you must wear the whole armor of God that you may be able to resist evil in its day of power and that even when you have fought to a standstill you may still stand your ground. Take your stand then with truth as your belt, righteousness your breastplate, the Gospel of peace firmly on your feet, salvation as your helmet and in your hand the sword of the Spirit, the Word of God. Above all be sure you take faith as your shield, for it can quench every burning missile the enemy hurls at you. Pray at all times, with every kind of spiritual prayer, keeping alert and persistent as you pray for all Christ's men and women."*
> *(Phillips New Testament)*

References

Afifi, Mohamed, "Surah Al-Maidoh; 5:18, 5:42", (accessed August 25, 2017), http://www.quran.com.

Angelo, Michael, Sistine Chapel painting, "The Temptation and Fall", Gallery of Sistine Chapel ceiling, (accessed August 21, 2016) http://www.en.wikipedia.org_sistinechapel.

Author unknown, "Steven Hawkins", (Survival of Man,) 2006, (accessed May 24, 2016), www.dailymail.com.

Baer, Randall (deceased) "Inside the New Age Nightmare", (youtube.com testimony) November 8, 2011, accessed August 26, 2017, http://www.youtube.com_user_bleibrandpolsky.

Benton Septuagint Translation, 1884, "Numbers 13:33, 34, Giants, Nephilim", (accessed May 8, 2016), Used by permission, http://biblestudytools.com_bibleversions/septuagint_bible_w_apocrypha _numbers.

Brown-Driver-Briggs, Hebrew and English Lexicon, (unabridged electronic database), Biblesoft, Inc., 2002, 2003, 2006, (accessed October 28, 2017), Used by permission, http://www.studylight.org.

Chappell, Mike, "The British Army in WWI, the Western front 1916-18: vol. 2, Osprey Publishing, Elms Court, Chapel Way, Bottey, Oxford ox29lp,UK, 2005.

Charles, R.H., "The Apocrypha and Pseudephigrapha of the Old Testament in English," 1895, The Clarendon Press, (accessed August 8, 2016), http://www.ccel.org_c_charles_otpseudepig_enoch_Enoch1.htm.

Charles, R.H., "The Fall of the Angels and their Punishment the Deluge Foretold," (Geneses V.1-20, Genesis VI. 1-12,) "The Book of Jubilees," Society for Promoting Christian Knowledge, London, 1917, (accessed August 2, 2017), http://www.sacred-texts.com_bib_jub.

Charles, R.H., "Journey through the Earth and Sheol" (chp. XIX), "The Book of Enoch," 1917, (accessed August 5, 2017), http://www.sacred-texts.com_bib_boe.

Coon, Charles S., "Southern Arabia, A problem for the Future", papers of the Peabody Museum of American Archology and Ethnology – 1993, vol. 20, pg. 195.

De Guaita, Stanislas, "Goat pentagram, La Clef de la Magie Noire 1897, synonymous with Baphomet, Sabbatic Goat", (accessed August 21, 2017), http://www.en.wikipedia.org_stanislasdeguaita_goatpentagram.

Easton, Matthew George, "Nephilim," Easton's Bible Dictionary on line, Thomas Nelson, 1897, Genesis 6:4; Numbers 12:33, (accessed November 7, 2016), http://biblestudytools.com_dictionaries_nephilim.

Fleming, John, "The Fallen Angels and the Heroes of Mythology, Genesis 6, The Nephilim", part III fallen angels, chapter 14, pg96-110 (accessed August 29, 2017), http://www.joelness101.jimdo.com_on-line_books_fallen_angels_part_3_1879_john_fleming.pdf.

Fuss, Michael, "New Age and Europe – Theology and Word Christianity," 1991, Mission studies volume 8, issue 1, pages 190-220

Gaines, Janet Howe, "Lilith" (Bible History Daily), (accessed August 14, 2017), www.biblicalarchaeology.org_lilith.

Gills, John, "Acts 16:16 Spirit of Python", Gills Exposition of the New Testament, (3 vols. 1746-08), internet sacred texts archive, (accessed August 21, 2017) www.biblehub.com.

Gills, John, "Exposition of the Entire Bible," 1746-63, (accessed August 4, 2017), http://www.biblehub.com.

Got Question Ministries, "What is the New Age Movement", (accessed August 5, 2017), www.gotquestions.org_newagemovement. Used by permission

Got Questions, "What is Atheism", (accessed August 5, 2017) http://www.gotquestions.org_whatisatheism.

Groll, Ursula, "Swedenborg: A Herald of the New Age," article quote taken from Center for studies on New Religions, (accessed October 31, 2017), http://www.cesnur.org.

Hensley, George W., "Snake handling, Pentecostal Holiness Church", (accessed August 21, 2017), http://www.en.wikipedia.org_georgewhensley_pentecostalholinesschurch.

Hilali, PHD, Muhammad Muhsin Khan, "The Noble Quran in Modern English", "Al-Qasas 28:77; Al-Hadis volume 3, pg. 803; Bukhari 4.52.280, 288; Al-Nisa 4:4, 34; Al-Baguarah 2.193, 216, 244, 282; Al-Saff 61:4; Al-An'am 6:141; An-Nahl 96:23, (accessed August 22, 2017), http://NobleQuran.com_translation_surah.

Houtsma, M. Th., T.W. Arnold, R. Basset and R. Hartman, "First Encyclopedia of Islam Online, First Edition, 1913-1936", pg. I:302, I:406, Brill Online Reference Works (accessed August 22, 2017), http://www.brill.com_products_reference-works.

Ibojie, Joe PHD, "Illustrated Dictionary of Dream Symbols", Destiny Image Europe, December 12, 2005, p67, 70, 72, 85, 86.

Ishaq, Muhammad Ibn, "Biography of the Islamic prophet Muhammad", (accessed August 7, 2017), http://en.wikipedia.org_ibnishaq.

Jackson, John Paul, "Dreams and Visions Seminar", February 9, 2005, PDF on line manual p37, 46, (accessed August 12, 2017) http://www.scribd.com.

Johnson, Michael Paul, "World English Bible at Wikisource, 2000, The American Standard Version 1901, (accessed August 22, 2017), http://www.ebible.org

Josephus, Flavius, "Antiquities of the Jews", translated by William Whiston, A.M., William P. Nimmo, Edinburgh, Scotland, 1867, reprinted by Kregel Publications, Grand Rapids, Michigan 1963, 1964, and 1966, Antiquity Book I, chapter III –Antiquity Book V, chapter II.

Laurie, Greg, "Mosab Hassan Yousef testimony", Islam and End Time Prophecy conference 2010 interview, youtube.com testimony, (accessed August 26, 2017) www.youtube.com_mosabhassanyousef.

Levi, Eliphas, "Dogma and Ritual of High Magic," "published in two volume's 1854-1856; translated into English by Aruther Edward Waite, 1896", (accessed April 21, 2016) http://www.en.wikipedia.org_eliphaslevi.

Mahdi, Muhsin S., Fazlur Rahman, Annemarie Schimmel, "Allah", pg. I-643, Encyclopedia Britannica, (accessed August 5, 2017), http://www.britannica.com_allah.

Mayer, Jean-Francios, (University of Fribourg), "Swedenborg: A Herald of the New Age," Center for studies on new religions, April, 1998, pp 186-199, (accessed October 29, 2017), http://www.cesnur.org.

Merriam-Webster Online, s.v. "Cult, Occult, Occultism, Witchcraft, Satanism, Islam", (accessed August 15, 2017) http://www.merriam-webster.com.

Merriam-Webster Online, s.v. "seduction", http://merriam-webster.com/dictionary/seduction, (accessed April 1, 2015)

Merriam-Webster's Collegiate Dictionary, 11th Edition (Springfield, MA: Merriam-Webster Incorporated, 2003) s.v. "oppression", (accessed August 2, 2016).

Merriam-Webster's Collegiate Dictionary, 11th Edition (Springfield, MA: Merriam-Webster Incorporated, 2003) s.v. "doorway",(accessed November 2, 1016).

Morgan, Games, "Decoding the symbols on Satan's statue", BBC News, Washington DC, (accessed August 1, 2017), http://BBC.com/news/magazine-33682878.

New Testament Greek Lexicon, "Anthistemi," Thayer and Smith, 1999, (accessed August 4, 2017), http://biblestudytools.com_lexicons_greek_kjv.

Pember, G.H. M.A., "Earths Earliest Ages-Nephilim", 1876, Hodder and Stoughton, London, England, Digitized by the Internet archive in 2010 University of Toronto iBook's, (accessed August 29, 2017) http://www.archive_details.

Prince, Derek, "The Spirit of Antichrist", Foundational Teaching from Derek Prince Ministries, April, 2002, (accessed February 1, 2016), www.derekprince.org_teachingletters_spiritofantichrist,the.

Prince, Derek, "They Shall Expel Demons", Chosen Books, a division of Baker Book House Company, Grand Rapids, MI, 1998, pg89, 99.

Simeon, Rabbi, "The 12th-century Rashi, "Jewish Rabbinic Commentary on Jeremiah 7:31", (accessed August 24, 2017), http://www.pinterest.com_pin.

Simkin, John, "Frontline Trenches", September 1997, free educational materials, (accessed October 27, 2017), http://www.spartacus-educational.com.

Sproul, R.C., PHD, "Nephilim Genesis 4, The Reformation Study Bible", Ligonier Ministries, 2015, (accessed August 28, 2017), http://biblegateway.com_resources_toc.

Sykes, Egerton, "Allah, the moon god of the Kaba", (accessed August 30, 2017), www.bible.ca_ca_islam_os;am-moon-god_a.

The Oxford University Press, "Golden calf – Apis," "The Oxford Dictionaries" (accessed August 14, 2017) http://www.en.oxforddictionaries.com_goldenchal_apis.

Thompson, G. Caton, "Allah, the Moon God", "The Tombs and Moon Temple of Hureidah, 1944, (accessed August 23, 2017), http://www.biblebelievers.org.ai_moon.

Unger, Merrell F., "Define religion as", Unger's Bible Dictionary, Moody Press; 1957, p1072.

Unger, Merrell F., "Desert," Unger's Bible Dictionary, Moody Press, 1957, p299, 300.

Wikipedia.org, (Surah", (accessed August 13, 2017), http://en.wikipedia.org_surah.

Wikipedia.org, "Anat", (accessed August 23, 2017), http://en.wikipedia.org_wiki_anat.

Wikipedia.org, "Anton LaVey", (accessed August 22, 2017), http://en.wikipedia.org_LaVeyan_Satanism.

Wikipedia.org, "Apis", (accessed August 2, 2017), http://www.en.wikipedia.org_apis_(diety).

Wikipedia.org, "Asherah", (accessed August 23, 2017), http://en.wikipedia.org_wiki_asherah.

Wikipedia.org, "Astral projection", (accessed February 6, 2016), http://en.wikipedia.org_wiki_astralprojection.

Wikipedia.org, "Baal", (accessed August 23, 2017), http://en.wikipedia.org_wiki_baal.

Wikipedia.org, "Battle of the Hornburg", (accessed August 2, 2017), http://en.m.wikipedia.org_battleofthehornburg.

Wikipedia.org, "CERN", (accessed May 9, 2016), http://www.en.wikipedia.org_cern.

Wikipedia.org, "Five Pillars of Islam", "Jihad", "Islamic schools and branches", "glossary of Islam", "Black Stone", (accessed July 10, 2016), http://www.en.wikipedia.org_fivepillarsofislam_Jihad_islamicschoolsan dbranches_glossaryofislam_blackstone.

Wikipedia.org, "Freemasons", (accessed August 4, 2017), http://www.en.wikipedia.org_freemasons.

Wikipedia.org, "Glossary of spirituality terms", (accessed August 29, 2017), http://en.wikipedia.org_wiki_Glossary_of_spiritual.

Wikipedia.org, "Greek Mythology-Apollo-oracle of Delphi", (accessed August 14, 2017), http://en.wikipedia.org/simple/wiki/greek_myth.

Wikipedia.org, "History of Las Vegas", (accessed August 29, 2017), http://en.wikipedia.org_wiki_history_of_las_vegas.

Wikipedia.org, "Hudud," (accessed August 7, 2016) http://www.en.wikipedia.org_hudud.

Wikipedia.org, "Kaaba (kaba)", (accessed August 4, 2017), http://www.en.wikipedia.org_kaaba.

Wikipedia.org, "Kundalini Yoga", (accessed February 8, 2016), http://en.wikipedia.org_kundalini_yoga.

Wikipedia.org, "Lilith," The Babylonian Talmud, (3rd and 5th. Century), (accessed August 14, 2017), http://www.en.wikipedia.org_lilith_talmud.

Wikipedia.org, "Luciferianism", (accessed August 15, 2017), http://en.wikipedia.org_luciferianism.

Wikipedia.org, "Mosab Hassan Yousef Biography, career, conversion, autobiography", (accessed August 26, 2017), http://en.wikipedia.org_mosabhassanyousef.

Wikipedia.org, "Muhammad", (accessed August 12, 2017), http://en.wikipedia.org_wiki_muhammad.

Wikipedia.org, "Nehushtan", (accessed January 4, 2016), http://en.wikipedia.org_nehushtan.

Wikipedia.org, "New Atheism", "The God Delusion" (accessed August 5, 2016), http://en.wikipedia.org_thegoddelusion_richarddarkins.

Wikipedia.org, "Pan", (accessed July, 18, 2017), http://www.en.wikipedia.org_pan.

Wikipedia.org, "Quran", (accessed August 13, 2017), http://en.wikipedia.org_wiki_quran.

Wikipedia.org, "Shiva", (accessed February 9, 2016), http://en.wikipedia.org_shiva.

Wikipedia.org, "Stanislas de Guaita, Goat pentagram", (accessed August 4, 2017), http://www.en.wikipedia.org_stanislasdeguaita_goatpentagram.

Wikipedia.org, "The Big Bang theory", (accessed August 5, 2016), http://en.wikipedia.org_thebigbangtheory.

Wikipedia.org, "The Four Horsemen", (accessed February 6, 2016), http://en.wikipedia.org/thefourhorsemen_richarddawkins_samharris_christopherhitchens_danieldennett.

Wikipedia.org, "Third eye", (accessed February 7, 2016), http://en.wikipedia.org_thirdeye.

Wikipedia.org, "Trench Warfare," http://en.wikipedia.org_trenchwarfare. (accessed August 9, 2017)

Wikipedia.org, "Witchcraft", (accessed August 7, 2017), http://en.wikipedia.org/witchcraft.

Wikipedia.org, Eliphas Levi, 1854, "Dogme et Rituel de la Haute Magie-Digma, Translated by Arthur Edward Waite as "Transandental Magic, its Doctrine and Ritual (1896), (accessed August 1, 2017), http://en.wikipedia.org_elipaslevi.

Wilipedia.org, "Moloch", (accessed August 23, 2017), http://en.wikipedia.org_wiki_moloch.

Wise, Michael, Abegg Jr., Martin and Cook, Edward, "The Dead Sea Scrolls: A New Translation, Harper San Francisco, 1996, p246-250, (accessed August 25, 2017), http://www.gnosis.org_library.

Elma Garlock

Wrenn, Chase B, "Naturalistic Epistemology," The Internet
Encyclopedia of Philosophy, ISSN 2161-0002, http://www.iep.utm.edu/,
(accessed August 24, 2017), Used by permission.

About the Author

Elma Garlock is a respected teacher, intercessor and minister of the gospel. Author of "Behind the Lines of the Enemy, The Dream." Ordained in 1988, through the International Ministers Forum in Dayton, Ohio and licensed in 2002 to preach, teach and minister the gospel through Regency Christian Center International, Inc., in Whittier, California where she has led the Altar Ministry and serves on the prophetic and deliverance team and Instructor/Coach in Prophetic teaching.

Elma has had the honor of serving as President and Vice President of Huntington Beach Women's Aglow and ministered for many Women's Aglow groups in California, Minnesota, Nevada and Utah. She also served as prayer advisor for Huntington Beach Christian Woman's Club and is Co-founder of Love Reaching Out Ministries that has enabled her to minister to thousands of men and women in the local church, fellowships and through her blog that goes all over the world.

She is a retreat and conference speaker and helped to support Victory Outreach Women's Recovery Home in Long Beach, California, taught at Regency Christian International Bible College and helped train and equip women for ministry sponsored by Love Reaching Out Ministries. Co-lead a recovery group on Life after Divorce, and helped facilitate in classes for Hope for My Marriage Seminars at Rose Drive Friends Church in Brea, California.

Elma's passion is to teach, train, equip and to minister truth. Her expertise in spiritual warfare, intercessory prayer, the spiritual realm, spiritual weaponry and the victorious position we have over Satan and demonic spirits is evident in life and ministry today.

Elma resides in Norwalk, California along with her husband Dan. She can be reached by email at elmagarlock@gmail.com or through her website at www.elmagarlock.com